WILD
FATHERS

WILD FATHERS

WILD
FATHERS

What Wild Animal Dads Teach Us About Fatherhood

ERNA WALRAVEN

What Wild Animal Dads Teach Us About Fatherhood

*In memory of Kibabu, the most magnificent
silverback gorilla dad,
and to all the other dedicated animal fathers
I've been privileged to know.*

CONTENTS

6. Monogamy – Just You and Me, Babe 122

7. Tools for the Job 142

INTRODUCTION

As a zookeeper in my early career and later a zoo curator I talked a lot about sex. I also watched a lot of it in real time or on a screen, all in aid of my rather unusual job which involved managing global and regional breeding programs for endangered species. I regularly spent time looking at animals courting and mating either in real life or from footage of hidden cameras that taped any overnight action.

Commonly I'd be there with other zoo colleagues dissecting what we could see. 'Did he get it in?' was not a smutty comment but a real question, particularly in the case of a male Sumatran Tiger's mating attempts. We brought him from a German zoo to mate with a female tiger born in Sydney. Both animals were virgins at the time but seemed keen enough to have a go. The problem with the male was that his aim was not particularly good. He kept missing the all-important target. Putting tigers together for mating is a scary undertaking. In the wild, tigers select their own mates, whereas in human care we do this for them. And like any arranged marriage, they may get on well or really hate each other at first sight.

Sumatran Tigers are critically endangered: less than 400 remain in Indonesia, which means there are more of them in the global breeding program than in their wild habitat. These tigers in zoos around the world are carefully selected for breeding through a managed studbook. The aim is to retain 90 per cent of the genetic diversity found in the wild over a planned breeding program spanning 100 years. Every baby tiger born is designed to have the best possible gene diversity. Right now, we could breed many, many tigers for release in Sumatra but that would only put more pressure on the remaining tigers still there. The problem for Sumatran Tigers is not a lack of tigers but a lack of suitable habitat in which tigers can live and procreate.

Zoos aim to keep genetically priceless tigers reproducing in human care until such time that the release of tigers in Sumatra is possible – either when human population growth slows, or habitat destruction is a thing of the past. These breeding programs exist for numerous endangered species and are known as Insurance Breeding Programs – insurance against extinction in the wild.

The purpose of explaining this upfront is to point out why it is so important to produce the next generation of endangered species from the *right* individual animals. In the case of the Sumatran Tiger, Satu's aimless appendage had us worried. The female, Jumilah, would present her rear end to him and do all the right tiger-seduction things but he would fail time and time again to insert his penis. Jumilah would get cranky – very cranky, even threatening to kill him, and we'd be there with fire extinguishers ready to distract and separate them if things got really nasty. We could quickly open corridors and entice one or the other to the enclosure next door. Luckily, it never got that scary with this pair. Every time they failed to mate, we'd try again the next time Jumilah came into oestrus.

To get a pair of tigers to have sex without killing each other you need to know certain stuff about tigers. This includes:

- how to detect ovulation in the female so you can introduce them to each other at the best time;
- how to read the behaviour of both tigers before you open any doors to put them together in the safest possible way;
- how to best set up the circumstances and environment for a successful mating;
- and knowing that a tiger with a full belly is less likely to get bad-tempered.

At the third attempt, Jumilah fell pregnant and had four cubs who all went on to have their own offspring in other zoos. Satu and Jamilah's story was a common one across many of the species I cared for. I had to research their reproductive behaviour thoroughly. I had to understand how courtship worked, who built the nest, what nesting materials they needed, who sat on the eggs or cared for the young. Breeding bowerbirds, for example, won't work unless the male has all the right gear to build his bower so he can impress a female bowerbird enough so she will allow him to mate with her. I learnt that insects, fish, frogs, reptiles, birds and mammals across thousands and thousands of species all have their own unique and intricate strategies to reproduce. These strategies involve issues like who does what at what time. What is the role of the male and what is the role of the female? And the variations between the species are an endless source of interest.

In a career spanning more than three decades, my research into reproductive strategies of a multitude of species revealed that while the role of the mother is usually well documented, that of the father is often ignored. Animal fathers of the same species have a basic fatherhood blueprint to which they adhere but in practise some are more dedicated or experienced than others.

In writing this book, I have found my thoughts wandering to my own father. I had two fathers in a way. A Dutch one and an Australian one. The Dutch one was a tall, handsome, rather macho man who ruled the roost during my childhood; a man who felt entitled to whatever he wanted in life without much regard, it seemed, for his wife and offspring. Yet, I always knew he would give his life for me or my sister if the need ever arose. He was a man of his time, expecting and demanding the privileges of being male in the latter half of the last century, when women were meant to know their place. Yet he was also a damaged human being. Emotionally scarred by the Second World War, spending time in the Dutch underground and later in a German concentration camp. How much of his detachment was biology or culture and how much of it brought on by his truly harrowing experiences as a young man, I will never know.

I was fortunate to have another chance at a dad. My husband's father cared for me from the day I arrived in Australia as the new girlfriend of his only son. He was a kind and soft man who was far removed from any displays of machismo. Indeed, he was proud of the fact he did not know how to change a car tyre. In that man I found a loving, involved father who had nurturing qualities I had never experienced in my own dad. He showed a genuine interest in my welfare, gave advice without personal interest, and was supportive and kind. My Aussie dad was a man of his time too: he had been in the war in New Guinea, although his experiences were not as traumatic as those of my Dutch dad.

Numerous aspects of life influence the way both human and animal fathers parent their progeny, from culture, to the shaping of life experiences and the role model of their own father. Animals of the same species can show their fathering skills in a variety of ways, influenced by their own experiences.

This book is about the role of fathers in the animal world and what we humans can learn from fatherhood in nature. Caring for and raising young is still often seen as a job for mum. The role of the father is frequently stereotyped as little more than an 'egg-fertiliser', or at best a protector and hunter, providing food for his family and not much else. But on the other side of the ledger, there are wild fathers who dedicate a huge part of their life to raise their progeny. Some dads go even further and actually give birth to their young.

The stories in this book draw on natural history, evolutionary biology, philosophy, economics, psychology, anecdotes, observations and the lives of the most extraordinary animal dads with whom we share this planet. By the time you finish reading I hope you will see that there are many awesome, loving and caring animal fathers who deserve much more than their 'sperm-donor' reputation.

I believe that human dads can be inspired by the many and varied ways fatherhood can be achieved and by the diversity of wild fathers in the natural world.

CHAPTER 1

BECOMING A DAD: PASSING ON YOUR GENES

'If you watch animals objectively for any length of time, you're driven to the conclusion that their main aim in life is to pass on their genes to the next generation.'

DAVID ATTENBOROUGH

Becoming a father usually involves sex. We have sex for fun as well as making babies. Humans and Bonobos – another great ape related to us and Chimpanzees – are amongst the few species that are known to have sex for pleasure as well as reproduction. Most animals mate when the female is 'in season', that is she is ovulating and ready to be fertilised. Only then are either gender interested in sex. By contrast, sex among humans is not specifically to make babies but for a multitude of other reasons: it feels good, it creates and maintains bonds between people and it's better than watching television.

The males and females of our species both spend a lot of time thinking and talking about sex. Sex is a biological necessity and our keen interest in sex is matched in the wild world. In nature, the primary purpose of sex is to make babies, even if the participants don't know this may be the outcome. The reproductive aspect of sex is a significant feature in every species on the planet. We know that all species are driven by a desire to have sex and it is a huge motivator in human societies. Unless a species has a strong sex drive it would become extinct very quickly.

It is surprising then that Western civilisation has made such a big deal about sex being sinful. Lust has been listed as one of the seven deadly sins, along with pride, envy, anger, covetousness, gluttony and sloth. Lust is defined as uncontrolled sexual desire or appetite. Yet without it, humans would cease to exist.

SOME RECORD-HOLDER DADS

Despite our apprehension about sex and the morality of intercourse, some people just get on with it. Historically, some people have done more than their fair share to make sure our human line does not go the way other hominids did before us. The record for the most children produced by one man is reportedly held by Genghis Khan who was born in 1162 on the border between modern-day Siberia and Mongolia. It is claimed Genghis fathered somewhere between 1,000 to 2,000 children. He must have had an extremely vigorous libido to produce this number of offspring before his death at the age of 65. He also had many sons to carry his genetic lineage to the next generation. A study on the genetic legacy of the Mongols published in 2003 found that one in 200 men in the entire world are direct descendants of Genghis Khan. With the advances of DNA, it

Many other animals take to parenthood with commitment and passion as humans do, but in our species this solicitude continues unabated for a couple of decades. We are no different from our wilder cousins in our desire to pass on our genes, to bring up baby safely and to set up a new generation for success.

is now believed that 0.5 per cent of the current world population is a descendent of Genghis Khan himself.

In more recent times, another fatherhood record is supposedly held by King Saud, son of Ibn Saud of Saudi Arabia, who lived from 1902 to 1969. According to one source, Saud had 52 sons and about 54 daughters from 'a wider range of women' than his father who had 22 wives. Yet an alternative source credits him with 115 offspring. It seems that polygamy is a useful strategy for a man who wishes to add an impressive number of mini-me offspring to the next generation. Polygamy was once a common practise in some human cultures and religions and still is in some places.

Rulon Jeffs, the leader of the Fundamentalist Church of Jesus Christ of Latter-day Saints, at his death in 2002, was reportedly survived by 19 or 20 wives and approximately 80 children. Interesting, but hardly surprising, is that a position of power either in religion, business or inherited status can usually lead to increased access to women for sex. Many cult leaders in modern times have claimed a 'divine' obligation to sleep with all or most of their female congregation, at least the young and good-looking ones. Although less popular in the Western world these days, polygamy continues to find its fans in the sects, cults and some religions around the world.

The urge to reproduce drives all species but some men do take this urge to pass on their genes to extremes. The old-fashioned way to make babies will always be popular but some modern technologies have made it possible to speed up the process without having to provide care beyond conception. Several fertility clinic doctors in the UK, Netherlands and the USA were discovered to have been using their own sperm to impregnate clients. The numerous children of these doctors now have dozens of half siblings and this raises poignant questions about the gene pool. It does show that if the opportunity is there, it is hard for some men to pass up the chance to create an impressive number of progeny.

The strategy of these fertility doctors is reminiscent of members of the cuckoo family (family Cuculidae) in birds. There are more than a hundred species of cuckoos around the world and a great number of these are parasitic breeders. They have all the fun of courtship and mating and then sneakily lay their eggs in other birds' nests to be looked after by unsuspecting foster parents. The cuckoo chicks will kick out the eggs or hatchlings already there to make room for their superior body-size. The poor foster parents of the changeling are often run ragged trying to raise this huge baby. Birds do seem to suspect there is something dodgy about these adult cuckoos, though, as they are always being chased by other birds.

Apart from fertility doctors using their own sperm, the services provided by fertility clinics are a welcome addition to our modern world. Formal donations to a sperm bank can enhance a man's overall genetic legacy, if so desired. While sperm donation laws vary by country, most have some rules around how many children can result from one donor's contribution, whether the sperm can be used after the donor dies and issues of payment for the donation.

WAYS TO PASS ON SPERM

Sex can broadly be divided into two classes: external fertilisation and internal fertilisation. Animals that live in water do not have the same limitations as those of us who live on land. In water, eggs and sperm don't dry out and sex can be non-penetrative. There are many animals who practice external fertilisation, such as most frogs and fish. Males and females each deposit their reproductive cells into the water and it's up to those cells to find each other. The chances of egg finding sperm are obviously much enhanced when males and females deposit their cells at the same time.

Fishes stimulate each other with mating rituals and when they are in the right mood, she will discharge her roe and he his milt. This egg and sperm release is called spawning. When fish are spawning, huge congregations of the species gather in an orgy of egg and sperm release. This orgy is designed to increase the chances of fertilisation and the crowd helps to protect the embryos from predation. The offspring produced during these orgies are left to their own devices to survive.

Land mammals have penetrative sex like we do and internal fertilisation occurs. If you are reading this, I assume you're old enough to know how this works. The sperm cells of the male have to enter the body of the female to fertilise the eggs. How this is achieved occurs in many different ways, which we'll discuss in more detail in the next chapters.

When it comes to fertilisation, most bird species fall somewhere in the middle of penetrative and external fertilisation. Male birds tend not to have a penis and they pass on sperm via a 'genital kiss' at the cloaca. The cloaca is a body cavity in birds, reptiles, amphibians, most fish, marsupials and monotremes, into which the intestinal, urinary and genital tracts come together in one external opening. In females it also serves as a depository for sperm. The sperm is internalised by the female bird via this 'cloacal kiss'. Despite this being the more customary avian practice, there is a duck with an amazing penis. The South American Lake Duck (*Oxyura vittata*) has a corkscrew penis measuring nearly 43 centimetres (17 inches) in length which perfectly fits the female's corkscrew vagina. I'm always surprised this duck species is not more widely known for its special 'attributes', but more about it in Chapter 7.

While the way living things reproduce is enormously varied, the creation of new life mostly involves the fertilisation of an egg by a

A good animal father passes on more than his genes to the next generation – he brings up his sons and daughters by example. Human progeny also rely on their special adults to teach them the things they need to know in order to live independently and successfully.

sperm. The fertilised egg produces a new individual, an individual with a mother *and* a father.

QUALITY OR QUANTITY

There are two evolutionary reproductive strategies that trade off quality over quantity of offspring. The 'quantity' approach is used by species which produce a huge number of offspring that did not cost them much in terms of energy or time. They gamble that at least some will survive and go on to breed themselves. This 'cheap' approach is used by animals and plants that live in unstable environments where things can change quickly. For example, field mice whose homes can transform from flood to drought, or from plenty of food to no food at all, utilise this strategy. At the other end of the spectrum, animals which use the 'quality' approach produce a few 'expensive' offspring with a long gestation and rearing period, in which they have invested a lot of time and effort. These animals tend to live in stable environments. Any reproductive strategy a species evolves has to do with quantity versus quality of offspring. All species are somewhere on the quality over quantity spectrum.

But how much parental care is needed to make sure some offspring will survive to reproduce themselves, thus carrying forward the family genes? Caring for a brood of hundreds or even thousands is usually not an option. Animals who produce vast numbers of young in one go, such as many species of fish, lobsters and butterflies, don't offer much parental care. Those who produce a huge number of offspring don't spend energy in providing for them or defending them against predators. Only a few may survive but that's enough to supply the next generation. At the other extreme are the parents who dote on their offspring for many years. These include humans, elephants, apes and bears. Devoted parents produce few or a single young, often after a long gestation. There's usually a fairly long rearing period, so all in all a significant parental investment in the hope that this next generation will survive to carry their genes forward into the future.

Humans have a substantial gestation time but the longest pregnancy in a mammal is found in African Elephants. They carry their young for nearly two years (up to 680 days) before giving birth to them. The young are born weighing close to 100 kilograms (220 pounds).

SEXUAL STRATEGIES IN WILD ANIMALS

Our species, like all others on the planet, strives to produce offspring. The urge to reproduce may not be a conscious thought process, but our biology makes us want to have sex and if that sex is unprotected, a baby could be the unintended result.

Getting our genes to survive to the next generation is what we are programmed to do. Evolution has resulted in many variations on that theme and species have adapted ways to achieve this successfully given their unique circumstances and environment. Some of the more common strategies for males to pass on their genetic material are:

- The *wham bam, thank you, ma'am* strategy, whereby the male impregnates a female but that's it. Tigers are a good example of this strategy in mammals. At most, male tigers allow the female to live in their territory, which they then defend against other would-be dads.
- The male impregnates the female and manages the environment but does not help to rear the offspring. This is the strategy employed by zebras.
- The male impregnates his special female and looks after the young. This strategy is exemplified by the tamarins and marmosets.

- The male impregnates the female and together they share all the chores from nest building to incubating eggs and feeding the young. Ninety per cent of birds follow this strategy.
- The male fertilises the eggs, takes care of them and 'gives birth' to the offspring. This is how seahorses and Darwin's frogs go about spreading their genes.
- Finally, there is the strategy employed by some megapodes and ratites, such as the Emu, in which the male looks after the fertilised eggs in exchange for the right to mate. Some birds get the raw end of the deal with this arrangement. Despite his dedication to looking after the nest and eggs, the male Australian Brush-turkey, for example, can't be really sure that the eggs he's looking after are his progeny as the female is not monogamous.

SEX AND UNDERSTANDING THE CONSEQUENCES

The urge to reproduce is so strong that some male birds, like the Australian Brush-turkey, spend a significant proportion of their lives tending a mound that may or may not contain eggs fertilised by him. This begs the question: Do animals understand fatherhood? Or even that sex can make babies? What evidence is there for that? The way some animal fathers care for their progeny with commitment and dedication would make one believe that they feel quite sure the offspring is theirs, suggesting that these fathers know they are investing their time, effort and energy in the survival of their genes. Why would they otherwise spend time caring for youngsters, often to their own detriment? Robert Sapolsky, a noted primatologist, studied baboons for many years. In his book *Behave: The Biology of Humans at Our Best and Worst,* he states: 'And there are species that figure out relatedness by reasoning; my guess is that male baboons make statistical inferences when identifying their likely offspring: 'How much of his mom's peak oestrus swelling was spent with me? All. Okay, this is my kid; act accordingly.''

Jason Buchan and colleagues in an article in *Nature* agree with the premise that male baboons know which offspring they fathered. The Buchan team paternity-tested 75 juveniles in a population of Savanna Baboons and observed who supported whom in disputes. These observations demonstrated that males were significantly more likely to intervene in disputes if they were the dad of the youngster involved.

On the other hand, given that humans did not link sex to making babies for a long time, there could be other explanations about fathers in multi-male/multi-female animal groups. Charles Darwin, the father of evolution, wrote in 1862: '*We do not even in the least know the final cause of sexuality; why new beings should be produced by the union of the two sexual elements. The whole subject is as yet hidden in darkness*'. Humans may not always have known that babies resulted from having sex with the opposite gender. After all, in humans, not all sex leads to pregnancy and there is a long time between the sex act and the birth of a baby. Although there is not a lot of information about what people were thinking hundreds of thousands of years ago, there's some evidence that there may have been an understanding of the link between sex and babies in the Neolithic era. During an archaeological dig in the ancient town of Çatalhöyük in Turkey, a wall decoration depicting a couple embracing on the left and showing a woman with a child on the right was found. Although humans may have understood the relationship between copulation and childbirth well before, there is little material evidence to support that theory. The Çatalhöyük find however seems to confirm that some 6,000 years ago there was the idea amongst humans that one thing leads to another.

In the late 1960s, indigenous people in Maningrida, northern Australia, interviewed by Annette Hamilton, an anthropology student, linked the sex act to the birth of a baby in a roundabout way. The role of the prospective father was initially described as 'helping the girl get menstruation' through intercourse. Clearing the way so to speak! Menstruation now means the girl is capable of falling pregnant. Most conception stories however involved the presence of spirit children in different locations, such as freshwater pools. Only a woman who wants a child or is already pregnant would go near such a place. The spirit child selects the girl or woman they want for a mother. They enter her directly through her vagina when she is menstruating. The role of the father in this is to dream the spirit child so it can enter the mother. Alternatively, the spirit child can be in a fish or other animal to be eaten by her, often caught by the father. Sex as a reason for pregnancy was alluded to by some of the people Hamilton interviewed. However, there may have been significant cultural reasons her subjects did not talk about copulation specifically to a young female student. The spirit-children stories abound in different parts of Australia as do stories about the stork bringing babies in Europe where I grew up.

In the Basque region of France, shepherds understood conception from their specific knowledge base. In their folklore, the semen curdles the woman's menstrual blood to form a baby, in a similar way to rennet curdling milk to make cheese. The use of semen to get pregnant is a recurring theme in many cultures far and wide. The Hua of New Guinea also believed that the mix of semen and blood are the building blocks for a foetus and newly pregnant woman ought to have sex a lot so that there is enough material to make a whole baby.

In various ancient cultures the role of the father in conception varies. It is expanded or minimised according to the kind of society and existing gender norms. The people of the Trobriand Islands, an archipelago of coral atolls off the east coast of New Guinea, believe conception occurs when a spirit child enters a woman's womb where it mixes with, you guessed it, menstrual blood. These spirit children were formerly alive but now deceased Trobriand islanders. The lack of involvement by any male in these conception beliefs may reflect that Trobriand society is matrilineal. Descent is from mother to daughter and the social structure is based on matrilineal clans that control land and resources.

In other more male-dominated societies, the role of the mother is diminished. In Malay tradition there was a belief that a baby forms in its father's brain. It then drops to his chest where it is imbued with human emotion. The father then thrusts the tiny baby into its mother's womb. This belief gives a lot of agency to the future dad whilst the mother's role is minimised as a nurturer of the father's creative efforts.

Given the many and varied cultural beliefs around the world about conception, it is not surprising that we do not really know how much our closest relatives, the primates, understand about making babies. Holly Dunsworth and Anne Buchanan in an article for *Aeon* magazine also write about the concept that primate fathers may recognise the offspring they have sired. They propose that it may be more likely that: 'male baboons, gorillas and chimps might kill infants, but they're less likely to kill ones clinging to females with whom they've mated because sexual relations between primates builds affiliation.' Friendships and relationships are of utmost importance in primates. 'Don't kill your friend's baby' would be a fairly reasonable code of conduct in any social group.

Individuals living in committed, monogamous relationships are most likely the ones to take an active fathering role. An example of this kind is seen in Siamang, a multitasking lesser ape which can swing through the rainforest and care for a baby with great devotion. Siamang dads, which are monogamous, have a lot of certainty about paternity and are therefore perhaps more likely to take a dynamic fathering role. Right now, there may not be solid evidence to suggest that even higher-order animals like primates living in large promiscuous groups would intellectually link sex and baby making. Sex drive is not about making babies. It's more likely to be simply about having sex. Ultimately, the extent of what animals understand about the sex act and it's resulting offspring is not clear. What is clear, though, is that all species go to enormous lengths to find a sexual partner and mate. The urge to have sex is an all-important driver of behaviour in both animals and humans. What is also clear is that some animal fathers will risk their lives to care for and protect their offspring, whereas others never meet the progeny they produce.

HUMAN DADS

No other species has the huge burden of long-term childcare that humans have and yet many line up voluntarily to take on the enormous task. Nearly two decades are dedicated to raising our human progeny, whilst we have the shortest birth interval between babies compared with our related primate species. Our red-haired cousins, the orangutans, have a break between babies that averages some seven years. Gorillas in the wild may give birth every four years, whereas Chimpanzees (*Pan troglodytes*) and Bonobos (*Pan paniscus*) have an interval of some five years. Human babies are born less well developed than those of our hairy relatives and yet we can take as little as 18 months between births. No wonder we need

Like many animal species, human fathers evolved to look after their children, to feed and protect the family unit. How much human fathers do is not as prescribed as it is in other species. Human fathers seem to be the only species that can decide what level of involvement they have with their kids.

fathers for our little humans more than most other creatures, even if fatherhood is more flexible in humans than in any other species.

Paternal involvement in humans ranges from being completely absent to being the primary carer. Some fathers care for their children all day every day for years. Other fathers see their children briefly when they come home at the end of a long day and just before the kids go to bed. Still others have access to their children only on occasional visits once a month or even once a year. Only in humans do we see this huge range of options for fatherly involvement.

The workload for a human raising a kid is greater than for any other species. Mothers evidently go through a lot of trouble with pregnancy, birthing and breastfeeding for a couple of years, but fathers, too, are there for the long-haul, nurturing, protecting, teaching and loving. Many other animals take to parenthood with commitment and passion as humans do, but in our species this solicitude continues unabated for a couple of decades. Despite that, we are not so different from our wilder cousins in our desire to pass on our genes, to bring up baby safely and to set up a new generation for success. Just as in the natural world, a male must consider a range of factors before becoming a father, starting with finding a suitable mate and making sure he is her chosen one.

THE LARGEST SPERM BANK IN THE WORLD

The new Viking invasion! Payment for sperm donations is permitted in Denmark and the Copenhagen sperm bank is close to the city's university, making it easy for male students to earn a little extra pocket-money. This sperm bank is the largest in the world and exports hundreds of litres of sperm to fertility clinics in more than 70 countries, winning Copenhagen the title of sperm capital of the world. So far, this one sperm bank has produced some 30,000 babies at a rate of 2,000 each year. Screening for genetic disorders is commonplace and the donor's health and family history is evaluated.

Chapter 2

SEXUAL RIVALRY AND OUR WILDER COUSINS

'In love there are no friends, everywhere where there is a pretty woman, hostility is open.'

VICTOR HUGO

Sexual rivalry between animals is rampant. There's rivalry between males for females, between females for males, and between males and females because they have different interests. Generally speaking, males want to mate with a large number of particularly faithful females. Thus, spreading their genes far and wide. Female animals have different interests. They want choice and to potentially mate with a large number of males to produce varied and healthy progeny. If males and females do not have the same reproductive interests, sexual conflict and rivalry arises.

Male-to-male competition is exceptionally noticeable in the animal world. In his 1871 book *The Descent of Man, and Selection in Relation to Sex* the great Charles Darwin wrote: 'it is certain that amongst all animals there is a struggle between the males for the possession of the female. This fact is so notorious that it would be superfluous to give instances.' Even the establishment of a territory is a way of marking mating rights. Sex and reproduction are areas of perpetual conflict. Males compete with each other for the opportunity to mate and females may compete with each other to choose the best mate from the available population.

Myriad animals have evolved novel, intriguing and some plain astounding ways to deal with rivalry. Our closely related great apes each have evolved a different way to handle rivals. The development of sexual weaponry is an extreme example of this prolific conflict.

SEXUAL 'WEAPONRY'

The rivalry between males drives the development of one-upmanship. This in turn can lead to males displaying a vast arsenal of weaponry. Elaborate antlers and tusks haven't evolved to fight scary predators but to impress the females. If they were for defence then it would make sense for both genders to have them. Deer stags, for example, shed their antlers after the breeding season. If the antlers were intended for combat, this would surely signal to predators, 'come and get me now, I have no defence.' Instead, these elaborate physical enhancements are thought to be driven by a desire for sex.

These sexually selected adornments, made bigger and better through evolution, are a feature throughout the animal kingdom from rhinoceroses to insects (of which, by the way, the rhinoceros beetles are an apt example). Rivalry to impress the opposite gender is thought to have influenced the evolution of the dinosaurs and is responsible for how an awful lot of creatures look today. Evolution has devised a wide selection of sexual weaponry: horns, pincers, tusks, antlers, saws, spears and spikes are just some of the ammunition

Elaborate antlers and tusks haven't evolved to fight scary predators but to impress females. These sexually selected adornments, of which the rhinoceros beetles are a striking example, are a feature throughout the animal kingdom.

animals show off. Males with a big horn 'get lucky' more often than ones with a puny little one. These 'big horn' genes are then passed on to the progeny, who may be born with even bigger horns and on it goes.

A male with huge antlers almost never has to fight. Rivals size him up and if he looks significantly bigger, they won't challenge. Only similarly matched specimens will take the conflict to a physical level. The one-on-one duels almost never lead to death but are rather a showy performance in which the winner is most likely to get the girl. This male-to-male competitiveness undoubtedly drives the development of more and more weaponry, but females also take a great interest in seeing who's winning. A big horn or a good rack

Walrus tusks are an illustration of 'sexual weaponry' – enlarged canine teeth that are used in threat displays and actual fighting. These ivory adornments can reach 1 metre (3 feet) in length and weigh 5 kilograms (11 pounds).

of antler can mean older and perhaps better genes, as the male has survived thus far with his big headgear. The male with the bigger antlers get the mating which perpetuates the weaponry to bigger and bigger proportions. Unlike rhinos with horns or walruses with tusks, chimps and humans have no impressive sexual weaponry. Males are a bit bigger and more muscular than females, but that's it. Not all animals have therefore opted for weapons to challenge the competition. Alternative strategies can be just as effective.

STINKY RIVALS

Ring-tailed Lemurs (*Lemur catta*), a little primate from Madagascar, have stink fights to establish who is boss – an unusual weapon to defeat rivals. They live in large social groups of 20 to 30 lemurs and it's important to avoid fierce fighting amongst the troop. All's well until the breeding season comes along and males compete for females. To avoid violence, these lemurs aim to out-stink each other to overwhelm other contestants. Using scent glands on their wrists and shoulders male lemurs secrete a substance which they wipe onto the tip of their tail. Both males lift their tails high and wave them around aggressively spreading their stink in the direction of the opposition until one of them backs off. This usually resolves the situation quickly but if neither backs down they can keep going for an hour or more. Apparently, the most stinky one wins the attention of the female. This is a brilliant way to resolve conflict without anybody getting injured. Odour being used as a weapon in the dating game is a novel idea, although in human courtship the use of perfumes may be a similar technique.

GREAT APES AND SEX

Our closest ancient relatives, the great ape species with whom we share a common ancestor, each have a different approach to procreation. The forebear we share with these magnificent apes lived between 8 million and 6 million years ago, which in evolutionary times is a mere blink of the eye. As a result, nearly 99 per cent of our genetic make-up is the same as Chimpanzees and Bonobos and only slightly less is shared with gorillas and orangutans. These last two split from our common predecessor a few million years earlier than humans, chimps and Bonobos. We are in fact more closely related to Chimpanzees than chimps and gorillas are to each other.

Jared Diamond, the science writer, proposes in his book *The Rise and Fall of the Third Chimpanzee* that both the Bonobo and chimps belong with humans in the genus *Homo*, rather than in the genus *Pan*, where they are currently classified. Other animals with far less genetic similarity have been put in the same genus. In addition to our many resemblances, our human sex lives show both similarities and differences with our ape cousins.

CHIMPANZEES

Chimps make up for their lack of sexual weaponry with impressive dominance displays. They live in large multi-male, multi-female troops with an alpha male in charge, supported by a coalition of other high-ranking males. This dominant male has lots of sexual rivals as he gets to do most of the mating. Sexual rivalry is an ongoing challenge for this alpha male and he has to work hard to keep his top job.

To make sure the other males in the group know he's still got it, he performs grandiose bluff displays. These start with rocking back and forth more and more vigorously, hair-on-end, hooting and incorporating banging on something, often just the ground. The chimps I looked after frequently used the metal doors to their night quarters as percussive props to enhance their dominance displays. They'd take a fast run up towards the doors and at the last moment turn in the air to give the door an almighty thump with both feet. This made a dramatic reverberating noise which the chimps found very satisfying. Males in the Taronga Zoo colony employ different techniques to individualise their dominance displays, almost like a signature. In the wild, they thump trees with their feet or wave branches about to make themselves look bigger and scarier.

The alpha is frequently challenged as the other males attempt to get a slice of the action. The lower-ranking males do get to sire some offspring, often on the sly, by mating willing females when the alpha is not looking. Some alpha males turn a blind eye to these covert unions but only on the days the females are less fertile. The female chimps are regularly willing to cooperate with these sneaky couplings. In zoos, we do paternity checks on newly born chimp babies just to be sure we know who daddy is. A surprising proportion of these babies turn out not to have been sired by the dominant male but by another male in the troop the female quite fancied.

The same thing occurs in the human world. You may have heard the oft-repeated statistic that some 9 to 30 per cent of paternities are misattributed, suggesting that often daddy is not the biological daddy. Biologists call these 'extra-pair matings'. The problem with these figures is that paternity tests are only done when there's already doubt about who the father may be. The quoted figures for misattributed paternities were traced by Swinburne University sociologist, Michael Gilding, who found the source of the transcript to be of a symposium held in 1972 where a British gynaecologist, a Dr Elliot Phillips, mentioned this estimate from a small sample of parents. This statement at the symposium took off and 'went viral' as we would call it now.

It is difficult to sample paternity randomly as women who volunteer for random testing are likely to be very sure of the paternity of their child and women who aren't may be unwilling to participate. Although the quoted 30 per cent figure refuses to die, the number of children whose social father is not their biological father is suggested to be more accurately between 1 and 3 per cent.

A lot of strife in chimp society is due to sexual tension. To appease his potential rivals, a dominant male may let other males mate with receptive females just to keep his loyal lieutenants happy. Not so Snowy, a male chimp I knew in Taronga Zoo, who was very much the jealous type. As the alpha male he felt entitled to sex with any of the females. Snowy considered all other males a rival and stopped all other couplings. If he ever caught any of the males 'in the act' with a female, he would run the length of the enclosure to beat up his new enemy. As a result, he was continually challenged for leadership by up-and-coming males. They all wanted some action and knew they could only do so under the leadership of a different, more tolerant male. The new alpha male, Lubutu, who gained the top position after Snowy, was not overly bothered if he saw or heard other males have some special time with one of the females. Because of this sexual leniency, Lubutu was not challenged by other males for a slice of power as they already had what they wanted.

Great apes usually have sex out in the open. The chimps I knew during Snowy's reign hid their amorous encounters only because the dominant male did not approve. Interesting to think that we are the only ones in the primate family to have sex privately and often in the dark? Although chimps do sometimes entice a female away from the group for a few days, so they can have sex without any competition. Perhaps humans hide from others also to avoid rivalry from a more powerful male?

BONOBOS

Not all sexual activity amongst animals and humans is designed for or results in reproduction. Sex between two members of the same gender is as popular in nature as it is in humans. The most frequent sexual encounter between giraffes is reportedly between males. Bonobos too have sex with either gender, for fun, to bond and for other social motives, not just for reproduction. The Bonobo is an equally close relative to us, sharing the same amount of DNA with us as we do with the chimps. They too live in similar multi-male and multi-female troops, but their society is female-led and there is little or no sexual rivalry. It is most likely that we and our Bonobo cousins are not the only animals to enjoy sex for the sake of sex. However, when we talk about 'sex for fun', Bonobos do deserve a special mention as their enthusiasm for sexual activity surpasses that of most species. They will have sex under any circumstances, anywhere and with anybody, which cuts out sexual rivalry nicely. Sex in Bonobo society is used to diffuse tension, resolve conflict, to celebrate the finding of a tree laden with a favourite fruit, or just as a friendly greeting. Bonobos will go out of their way to help strangers and share food with unfamiliar visitors so they may become friends. It is not uncommon to discover them having sex with new Bonobos they meet shortly after 'hello, how are you?'

Researchers Brian Hare and Jingzhi Tan ran some experiments in Lola ya Bonobo Sanctuary in the Democratic Republic of Congo, the results of which illustrate just how magnanimous Bonobos are. The experiment involved placing desirable food in a central enclosure, with a Bonobo who knew how to open the doors on one side and a Bonobo they'd never met and who didn't know how to open the doors on the other. The individual Bonobos 'in the know' nearly all entered the room with the food to let the stranger in to share before they sat down to eat themselves. They probably had sex shortly after that! They do not seem to consider other Bonobos rivals as much as male chimps see most other males.

However, I've also heard it said that: Chimps use power to gain sex. Bonobos use sex to gain power.

GORILLAS

Another great ape relative, the gorilla, lives in a harem with one dominant male – the so-called silverback – his two, three, four or even more 'wives' and their offspring. Gorillas are gentle creatures, despite their fierce reputation, and the silverback rarely makes use of his super strength. The gorilla harem-keeper is enormous compared with the females in his care. He has what's called secondary male characteristics in adulthood. The hair on his back and thighs goes silver and he develops a big domed head, called a sagittal crest. Research suggests that female gorillas favour a male with a big sagittal crest.

A young male may wait until he's around 20 years old and fully grown before he has the urge or the ability to take over an established harem. The silverback is the only one to mate the females and sire their offspring, providing plenty of motivation for challengers to have a go. The harem system means that there are a lot of males without any females, whereas the harem-keeper monopolises quite a few females. A silverback looks ferocious and beats his chest to show any challenger he means business. Young males testing their

A gorilla silverback is enormous compared with the females in his harem. He has what's called secondary male characteristics in adulthood. The hair on his back and thighs turns silver and he develops a big domed head, called a sagittal crest.

mettle can be intimidated by an intense display of super silverback bluff. His bulk, sagittal crest and canine teeth are usually impressive enough to scare competing males away instead of having to fight them. If needed, the harem-keeper will fight to the death to defend his troop.

ORANGUTANS

Our Asian, red-haired cousins are more solitary than the other great apes. They have secondary male characteristics too and are highly sexually dimorphic. I was fascinated watching the physical changes in Jantan, a young male at Taronga Zoo I knew from birth, whom I observed grow into adulthood. I particularly liked his 'flanges' – large cheek pads made up of muscle and fat which made him look manly and handsome. In addition, he developed a large muscle-covered throat pouch, a musty aroma and luscious long flaming red hair.

As orangs tend to mostly live a solitary existence high up in the rainforest canopy, calls are the best way to communicate with both rivals and future mates. Males are territorial and protect their territory against other grown males. His territory can provide food and shelter for a few females though. A fully-grown male has a well-developed throat pouch that can produce an impressive growl which can be heard from a long way away through the forest. His 'long call', this throaty growl, not only repels the competition but attracts sexually receptive females. Males and females get together when she's in oestrus and ready to make whoopy. The female may initiate sexual activity and is an active facilitator in this get-together.

The larger the cheek-flanges the more dominant the male. Sexual dimorphism – a distinct difference in size or appearance between the sexes in addition to the sexual organs themselves – is clearly evident in orangutans.

The couple may hang out for 20 days or so with many copulations during this time to enhance the possibility of conception. They live separate lives at all other times. They don't stay together after mating and the female eventually raises her single offspring all on her own. The only long-term relationships that happen in the orang world are between mum and her offspring, who stay together until the youngster reaches around eight years of age. In the ape family, only humans raise their children for an even longer period.

Male-to-male rivalry for mating opportunities with sexually receptive females can be a major reason for a good scuffle. Although the male's call is intended to deter other males from approaching it doesn't always work out that way. Males are intolerant of other fully-flanged males and when they do encounter each other they tend to be aggressive, particularly when there's a sexually receptive female to fight over. Many adult orangs show the results of such fights in missing fingers or toes, or scars on their head or face. Injuries from fighting with other males is a significant cause of death for adult male orangs.

HUMANS AND OTHER APES: WHAT WE HAVE IN COMMON

Each of our cousin species has come up with a different way of managing their love life and passing on their genes. Interestingly, humans do not replicate any one of these strategies precisely but do incorporate components of each.

With chimps we have the following similarities:

- powerful males have more sex
- females may have sneaky matings
- paternity tests can reveal surprising results
- males rival each other for sexually receptive females

With Bonobos we have the following similarities:

- sex is enjoyed for bonding and recreation as well as reproduction
- sexual rivalry is minimised if everybody is having sex
- sex can lead to power
- sex can be between any gender and with anyone (except mother and son unions are taboo and females leave home at puberty, thus avoiding incest)

With gorillas we have the following similarities:

- a strong powerful male can have a harem (still common in some human cultures and religions)
- a strong powerful male may not be having as much sex as you'd think
- the male does not help raise the young per se but manages the environment, makes it safe and provides resources
- males without any females are potential rivals

With orangutans we have the following similarities:

- single motherhood is common
- (some) fathers do not acknowledge their offspring or help raise them
- they partake in face-to-face copulation, which is only known in humans and some other great apes
- they will fight other males in acts of sexual rivalry

IMPORTANT DIFFERENCES BETWEEN THE OTHER APES AND US

In most other primates, except for Bonobos and importantly us, the female is sexually active *only* when she ovulates. In many species, including those closely related to us, such as chimps, the ovulating primate females are easy to spot as they develop a genital swelling. This swelling happens at the midpoint between menstrual periods when the females are courted insistently by the males. She's only interested in sex when she has this protuberance and he's is instinctively only interested in her when she sports a good bottom engorgement. Males actively compete for the female with the largest swollen bottom. A mating the height of ovulation increases paternal certainty.

A female chimp's power is at its strongest when she's at her most attractive to the males, namely when she's in season. High-ranking males will do her favours and seek her company. Her genital swelling will rise and fall over the course of ten days, shrinking back to normal size after this period. The swellings vary considerably in size. Some females have bumps as big as a football and sitting down requires a side-slanted posture, while others have smaller, more manageable bulges.

Jane Goodall, the noted primatologist, comments in her book *In the Shadow of Man*: 'Many times, as I have watched a huge swollen female Chimpanzee adjusting her position time and time again, trying to get comfortable on some branch or hard rock, I have thanked evolution for sparing human females a similar periodic disfigurement, though designers and manufacturers of bustles would, I suppose, have been in clover.' I too have always thought how lucky we are, given how much genetic similarity we have with chimps, that this is one feature we do not have in common.

Because sexual activity mostly takes place when the female has this genital swelling at ovulation time, the chance of fertilisation is high. This coincides with the greatest rivalry between males. The alpha male may (reluctantly) allow high-ranking subordinates to mate with a female until she ovulates some six days after maximum tumesces. Then all bets are off and he is the only one. This way he is still likely to sire her next infant and keep his rivals happy.

RIVALRY IN HUMANS

There's rivalry between men, between women, and between men and women. Males tend to be interested in faithful females and are driven to keep other males away so there is more chance they alone can sire young with a specific female. Meanwhile, the females of the species compete to find the best, strongest and fittest males. She does not necessarily want the other males kept away but she knows it is also in her interests to maintain exclusivity with a male if she wants him to stick around and help with the time-consuming task of nurturing young. All of this adds up to plenty of sexual conflict and rivalry.

What's fascinating about human reproduction and rivalry is that we live in multi-male, multi-female societies but maintain monogamous pairs within that social system. This is not replicated by any of our great ape cousins who are promiscuous by nature, not monogamous. This could suggest that we, as a species, are a little sexually promiscuous too, but deny that part of our nature. We keep small territories, our home is our castle and the family unit is often referred to as 'the cornerstone of our society'. The nuclear family can be considered a reproductive unit although 'extra-pair matings' as they are called in biology, do frequently occur. A primate who displays some similarities to human social structure is the Hamadryas Baboon (*Papio hamadryas*). The males have a strict pecking order and high-ranking males keep a harem of a few females. Several families live together in large social groups called 'clans'. Studies show that the male baboons generally respect the 'possession' of females by other males.

Perhaps humans have evolved in similar ways to baboons? We

Hamadryas Baboons have a social structure with some similarities to ours. Studies show that the male baboons generally respect the other male's 'possession' of females.

are highly social and work together to protect our communities and support each other when needed. As a species, when we evolved to be hunters on the plains of Africa, we could not afford to fight each other over mating rights. We needed to work together to do more important things like hunt big animals for food. Our sexual rivalry may therefore have evolved to be less overt to assist in our survival.

The fact that human females show no outward signs of ovulation and are often not even aware of it may help to avoid this conflict. Human females don't have swollen bottoms, but they do often have protruding breasts. Our species is unique among the great apes in this regard. Although large mammary glands are usually thought of as a maternal attribute, there's little evidence that this is the case. Humans, along with the other female great apes, are perfectly capable of suckling young without huge breasts and milk supply can be just as plentiful from a small chest as from the larger variety. Mammary glands are therefore more likely to signal sexual appeal. Desmond Morris in his classic book *The Naked Ape* speculates that the evolution of breasts as we know them may be a way of signalling sexual availability. Breast enhancement surgery is popular in some cultures, perhaps as a way for females to rival other females for the best available males. Protruding breasts are more visible on our species as we're not covered in shaggy hair like our fellow primates.

Humans are sexually attracted to each other at all times, whether ovulating or not. As a result, most human sexual acts do not end in conception. Only those sex acts that coincide with a woman's days of ovulation can result in an embryo. Humans have mostly decoupled sex from reproduction and, like the Bonobos, have sex for bonding and fun more often than not. Unlike many other mammals, in particular the great ape families, humans form pair bonds. We have social monogamy, serial monogamy and even pure monogamy in some cases.

Women wanting the best sire for their kids habitually select a male not only for their physical prowess but also for the resources they can provide. Anecdotally we all know of rich old men with gorgeous young wives. There are very few poor old men with a beautiful young wife. Resource possession and displays (think flash car, buying expensive presents and bragging about possessions) clearly work well in making fellas look alluring and beating the competition. Another common tactic is the derogation of rivals. The advantage of speech is that we can 'groom' our love-interest with words. Words can complement our beloved, but they can also be used to make a competitor look bad by pointing out their least desirable traits, therefore enhancing the attributes of the suitor.

WEAPONS OF SEXUAL RIVALRY

For millennia, competition between males has been driving an arms race in the animal kingdom. Female preferences add additional pressure to develop a vast arsenal of animal weaponry seen in nature. The most exaggerated and elaborate weapons such as horns, claws, tusks and antlers are not shaped to defend against scary predators. Instead, they are driven by a desire to have sex.

Weaponry like antlers does more than discourage the competition, it flags reproductive fitness. A study of 200 Iberian Red Deer stags measuring their antlers for size and complexity found that those with the bigger racks also had the bigger testes and fastest-swimming sperm. Female Red Deer may be right to choose a male with the greatest and most elaborate antlers. He's likely to produce fit and healthy offspring.

Aggression between males is often driven by a desire to achieve and maintain status, resources and mating opportunity – not all that different from our animal cousins. These traits for rivalry and competition arose in our ancestors millions of years ago and are in our DNA. However, our superior reasoning means we have awareness of our behaviours and can keep the nastier side of rivalry under control. Perhaps that's why we invented sport! Instead of evolving antlers or big horns, blokes can show superiority by winning at sport or doing remarkable things like climbing the highest mountain or driving the fastest car. As the development of physical weaponry, like a good set of tusks, is not in our biological capabilities, chaps may rival the competition by curating a strong and muscly body.

On a cautionary note, testosterone-driven displays in humans can often be reckless and court danger. Not all human females are motivated by the same things and some prefer a gentler guy who is kind and caring. They recognise these as essential attributes for a great dad.

The fact that rivals exist drives the need for elaborate courtship displays to persuade females to partner with a particular male. The animal world is resplendent with rituals for attracting a mate. In the next chapter, the natural world once again provides us with a plethora of examples of how to go about courting the other sex and out-competing rivals.

PANDA PISSING CONTEST

It's a behaviour known in humans after a night on the town but now it seems that Giant Pandas too enter into pissing contests. *New Scientist* reports on some intriguing research by Angela White who studied Giant Pandas in the wild in the Wolong Nature Reserve in Sichuan, China. She found that, as they mark their territory with urine, they get more respect the higher they pee. So male Giant Pandas are seen to do handstands for a higher pee. Other pandas think 'this is a mighty big panda' and stay away from spots of urine placed higher up on trees. Only adult males can do these handstands to reach such height. Human males may struggle to emulate this technique.

RATE OF HUMAN REPRODUCTION

In humans there's rivalry between men, between women, and between men and women. As males are interested in faithful females, they keep other males away so there is more chance they alone get to sire young. Meanwhile, the female of the species has an interest in finding the best, strongest and fittest males. She does not necessarily want the other males kept away. There are many compromises to be made for these competing aspects of reproduction. For females with young that take a lot of their time and energy growing up, it is important to have a male around to help raise the young. Sexual conflict and rivalry both create stress on all parties.

Despite that, whether it causes stress or not, humans are born at the rate of knots. UNICEF (United Nations International Children's Emergency Fund) estimates that an average of 353,000 babies are born each day around the world. It is projected that there will be 11 billion people on this planet by 2100.

Chapter 3

WILD COURTSHIP

'No case interested and perplexed me so much as the brightly coloured hinder ends and adjoining parts of certain monkeys.'

CHARLES DARWIN

COURTSHIP ESSENTIALS

The monkeys Darwin refers to in this quote are Mandrills (*Mandrillus sphinx*). The male Mandrill has spectacular genitals shaded in bright red, pink, blue, scarlet and purple. This confident advertising is matched at the other end by a hairless face sporting an elongated muzzle of red and blue, red nostrils and lips and a yellow beard with white tufts. Darwin further wrote in *The Descent of Man*: *'no other member in the whole class of mammals is coloured in so extraordinary a manner as the adult male mandrill.'* All that colour, all that brightness to attract the opposite sex. In addition, Mandrills like to show off their canine teeth, which can be up to 5 centimetres (2 inches) long. They look so striking that they almost seem unreal. Dominant males are more colourful than their subordinates. To court successfully it seems you've got to be noticed and stand out from the crowd in one way or the other.

Darwin introduced the theory of *sexual selection* as an element of his greater ideas on *natural selection*. Sexual selection is central to how animals choose their mates, with courtship being an expression of sexual selection that results in favourable traits being enhanced over time. In the case of the Mandrills, who live in small social units in a larger horde of males and females, the guys have to impress in order to be chosen by a girl. Over an evolutionary timeframe, the features that made them attractive become exaggerated in subsequent generations.

Different species find different ways to impress. Some go for colour, others for sound. Although already winning points for looking extremely good, the Palm Cockatoo (*Probosciger aterrimus*) of Australia and New Guinea has rhythm as well as looks. To make sure he's seen, the male attracts the attention of nearby females by drumming. The only bird known to use a tool for such a purpose, Palm Cockatoo males have been seen to fashion a stick to the right shape to belt out a regular beat. Each cockatoo is thought to have a signature rhythm.

For humans, courtship has changed more rapidly in the last few decades than it has at any other time in human existence. In our species we traditionally see three stages: pair formation (also called courtship), pre-copulation and actual copulation. The courtship stage in humans is often much longer than in other animals, sometimes lasting days, weeks or months. This phase can be extremely exciting, with feelings of yearning, melancholy, nervousness and butterflies in the stomach being reported.

The digital age has, however, had a profound effect on this most enjoyable aspects of finding a mate: courting. Online dating, dating

Apps, texting, sexting and the 'swipe left or right' culture has been around for an extremely short time in evolutionary terms. Whereas before, we used a combination of visual, auditory and olfactory signals, just like other animals, we now typically advertise our availability by enhancing our online dating profile. We take our most flattering photo to show the world our best face in the dating game. Now that fewer people meet through real life situations, electronic courting is a serious strategy that has to be incorporated into courtship protocols. In most cases, though, after this initial introductory online courtship, a physical courtship continues to be an essential prerequisite to the mating game and to becoming a dad. We still have a lot in common with other species when it comes to wooing a potential mate. Some examples from the animal world may have parallels in human courtship.

Bright plumage, posturing displays, pheromones and a beautiful song are some ways male animals try to prove their superior fitness to become a dad. These courtship rituals follow similar patterns in humans. First there is the initial attraction, pursuit and a period of wooing before mating takes place. Courtship patterns can be elaborate and often energetically expensive (think dinners, flowers, chocolates!). Yet intricate courtship rituals are favoured by many species, suggesting this has a significant function in persuading a potential partner to mate.

The quality of offspring a mother produces depends on who she gets to fertilise her egg. Picking the right one is important and that's why the males compete to be the best choice. If a male has what the females like, he's in business. But how a female decides that a particular male is the best she can do varies a lot. Blue-footed Booby

(*Sula nebouxii*) females prefer males with the most gorgeous blue feet. The blueness of the feet can change quickly if a male is not in top condition or is poorly nourished. Just by looking at his feet, the female can tell whether a potential dad is healthy and in excellent form. To help her selection process, Blue-footed Booby males will dance for the females, showing not only their slick moves but their stunning bright blue feet. Perhaps in human society this equates to women who believe you can judge a man by his shoes!

Female humans are evolutionarily hard-wired and, whether consciously or not, seek the fittest male to sire their offspring. Significant advances in equality for women have been achieved in many parts of the world today, but these changes are recent and cultural, not biological. What 'fittest' may now look like has probably changed over the last few hundred thousand years, but even in our modern world there are still a number of criteria that need to be satisfied. Sexual attraction means that looking good still counts. Physical attractiveness is a potential indicator of good health and good genes, which make first-class babies. Being a good provider still regularly counts once a healthy baby is born, since rich resources will nourish and raise it to be strong. Our evolution, biology and culture work together to make a wealthy and successful man more appealing to many women.

How does any male animal attract a female? Good looks, song, dance, smell and gifts. Animals use all possible ways of showing their best potential. Signalling your wares in a visual way is used by a variety of creatures that live in fairly open country so they can be seen easily. Brightly coloured birds, such as ducks and grebes, are often found in wide open water bodies, tropical fish in clear shallow waters, while forest dwellers, such as birds-of-paradise, use high perches to perform elaborate aerobatics showing off their striking colours and shapely feathers. Antelope and other ground dwellers use open elevated spaces where their strutting and posturing can be shown at full advantage.

The natural world has many ways of signalling interest in finding a mate: visual, acoustic, chemical and tactile and humans use all of these too.

LOOKING GOOD

Visual displays have the advantage of being fairly long lasting. Male kangaroos literally flex their forearms to show off their attractiveness. Natalie Warburton and colleagues found that Western Grey Kangaroo males benefit from a well-developed musculature. Their forelimbs act as a sexual signal that this boy is superior.

Once you have the muscles, the bright feathers or large antlers, for example, you can use them over and over again, at least for a whole breeding season. Birds have the most obvious male show-offs. Female choice in birds favours the brightest-coloured male, the best dancer or the best singer and sometimes even a combination of all three. This favouritism has led to these preferred features becoming more and more exaggerated over time through sexual dimorphism between the sexes (a distinct difference in size or appearance between the sexes of an animal, in addition to differences in the sexual organs themselves).

Colour, shape and movement can all combine into an irresistible seduction. Birds-of-paradise, although they are already stunningly

Male Western Grey Kangaroos literally flex their forearms to show off their attractiveness to females. Their forelimbs act as a sexual signal that this male makes good babies. Human males too may benefit from a well-developed musculature in the mating game.

beautiful, perform the most intricate rituals of movement, even hanging upside down from a high branch and shaking it all about. In many species it is the male that has the spectacular attire and the female is the more modestly dressed. There's a good reason for this. The parent that does most of the caring for the babies doesn't want to attract attention to herself or her tasty baby morsels. As the female bird is frequently the one to incubate the eggs, blending in rather than standing out helps to avoid the attention of predators. Although it's often the blokes doing the showing off, this is all reversed if the species is polyandrous, whereby the female has more than one male and has to compete with the other females to get the best mate. In this case, the females are bigger and brighter, as seen in the phalaropes (genus *Phalaropus*), a family of shorebirds. Phalarope males provide most of the parental care and their more modest plumage helps them not be seen by predators when they're sitting on the nest.

The male Lady Amherst's Pheasant (*Chrysolophus amherstiae*) is another one that goes out of his way to impress the ladies. The scientific name is from the Ancient Greek meaning 'with golden crest'. The common English name was given as a nod to the wife of the Governor General of Bengal, Sarah Amherst. Although this bird relies on an impressive display, it is mostly shy, secretive and rarely seen. The male is about 1.5 metres (5 feet) in length, of which the tail accounts for approximately two-thirds. The feathers on his neck comprise the showy black-and-white 'cape' that is raised during displays to females, and on his body he shows a rainbow including red, blue, green, white and yellow plumage. In contrast the female has mostly mottled and barred brown feathers. Brighter males, as a fairly general rule, do not make good fathers. Most of these exciting characters disappear after they've got what they came for: sex.

Conspicuous showy males are a common feature in the natural world. The strongest, brightest, most distinctive males are frequently the most attractive to the females. The more testosterone he has on board, the more vibrant his colours will be, which increases his sex appeal. The most colourful males sire the majority of offspring. Interestingly, once such a male loses status and position his brightness fades.

APPEARANCE ADVICE FOR THE HUMAN MALE

Male humans have definitely been known to employ this tactic too. A flashy Rolex watch can have an impact in the right places, a stylish suit of the right cut and fancy new shoes may all help to make a man look like a good catch. A gold tooth, prominently displayed, can be a bonus in some cultures. Some special moves may enhance the overall picture. It is no surprise that anywhere there's dancing is also an excellent spot to pick up a potential mate. Looking better than other men in your cohort can be done in a variety of ways and contexts.

The peacock drops his elaborate tail once the breeding season is over. This can be observed in human societies too. The flashy suit may become a tracksuit that more comfortably accommodates the middle-age spread once a mate has been secured. However, most animals scrub up again for the next breeding season. As humans do not have a specific breeding season it may be advisable to always look your best to keep the pair bond reinforced!

SOUNDING GREAT

Most nocturnal species don't employ a visual display as it can't be seen. The dark can be a challenging place to use visual signals to attract a mate. Until recently we knew about fireflies and bioluminescent fish, but now science has discovered more secrets of the dark. An accidental discovery by a scientist in the United States revealed that platypuses glow under UV light. Further tests by Australian scientists show that other mammals and marsupials glow too. Marsupial moles and wombats glow. So do echidnas and bilbies. How and if this is used in courtship is not known but it sure would help finding each other in the dark.

Unless they glow, animals living in dense dark habitats or under water face the same issues – how to advertise their wares? Most use sound signals to their best advantage. Dolphins and whales sing long complicated songs to communicate with each other over distances of hundreds of kilometres. Humpback Whales (*Megaptera novaengliae*) use sound to keep in touch with their mates in the deep dark oceans. They have a huge range of separate sounds to compose communications that can last for 30 minutes or more and their song is said to be the most complex sound of any animal on our planet. Male Humpback Whales have been described as inveterate composers of songs that are strikingly similar to human musical traditions. It has been suggested that humpback songs communicate male fitness to whale cows.

Many insects, amphibians, birds and mammals use vocal communication as a way of contacting the opposite sex. Tree frogs send their loud nocturnal message through thick vegetation to advertise their availability. The White-lipped Tree Frog (*Litoria infrafrenata*) living in my garden cleverly uses amplification to sound more impressive. A hollow metal pipe sticking out of an old fence is his preferred spot from which to call, the metal post reverberating to amplify his call. I ponder sometimes if female frogs attracted to his booming call are slightly disappointed when they see him in the flesh and find him modestly sized rather than the giant he sounds. A bit like photoshopped pictures on Tinder.

Birds are the most obvious creatures to use sound in communication and courtship. Bird song is complex and varied and is extensively used in combination with a visual display, such as flashing feathers and hopping about. Small, plain birds often have magnificent and elaborate songs, perhaps to make up for their lack of visual attributes. Many species of tiny unadorned birds like reed warblers look just like each other and only their song sets them apart. Each bird species has its own signature song and even dialects of that song have been known to evolve in different regions. Songbird females will select a male for the complexity and length of his song, which is a good reason for a male bird to mimic other species and thereby increase his catalogue.

Mammals on the whole appear to have a small repertoire of sounds that include grunts, howls and barks that we can hear. Some mammal species' vocal range extends well beyond our hearing. Sound equals vibration and can span vast distances through oceans, over plains and in dense forests. Deep vibration, beyond our hearing range, is highly effective in other animals such as whales and dolphins. The nerve endings in the heads of these cetaceans can detect vibrations in a similar way to elephants feeling the vibrations with the nerve endings in their feet. Enabling these long-distance travellers to find each other when they are in the mood for love.

Koalas are also long-distance callers. Every so often I used to hear

The Koala bellows his low-pitched snoring inhalations and a loud roar as he exhales. This snorty roar can be heard up to 800 metres (2,600 feet) away across the forest to convey his availability to females.

the male Koalas in the zoo calling loudly near my office, telling any nearby females that they were ready and able. In addition, the Koala mating call, as in numerous other species, tells rival males that there's a powerful stud in residence and intruders better stay away.

A nocturnal sound many urban dwellers may be familiar with is the yowling of domestic cats. Fortunately, most people have broken the habit of letting domestic cats roam by day or by night. Male cats make harsh, loud cries called caterwauling. This is both a courtship behaviour to attract a female and a deterrent to keep other tomcats away. The call is not attractive or melodious in any way and yet it seems to work fine for the tomcat.

SOUND ADVICE FOR THE HUMAN MALE

Homo sapiens also use some advanced techniques when it comes to sounding attractive. A beautiful song can be very seductive. Being heard is like being seen, the wares are out on display and females can choose if they like what they hear. Although somewhat out of fashion, serenading a loved one under a balcony might still work if you have what it takes. These days, being a member of a successful rock band often proves to be a winning attribute to accessing sexual partners, while those who don't make the grade for stardom can still use their voice to groom a prospective partner with flattery, humour and engaging storytelling. Women on the whole love a sexy voice.

SMELLING WONDERFUL

Smell is one of the strongest senses in both the animal and human world. 'Love scents' signal sexual interest using odorous substances and occur throughout nature from plants to animal species ranging from insects to elephants. A male moth can smell an attractive female of his own species from over 1 kilometre (0.6 miles) away. He follows this odorous trail using his feathery antennae to hone in on her. Flying against the wind he can keep track of her perfume until he is close enough for courting and possibly mating. The female moths produce these chemicals, called pheromones, themselves. In the insect world, pheromones do more than just get the parties together. They appear to act as an aphrodisiac as well.

Mammals also rely on smell for communication as the olfactory sense in most mammals is better than sight or hearing. The male North American Porcupine (*Erethizon dorsatum*) takes this concept to a whole new level. After chasing his lady, he rears up on his hind legs and squirts a jet of urine directly onto her. By scent-marking the female in this way he sends a message to other porcupines that this female has a mate already. I strongly advise human males against using this strategy!

Attraction and signalling sexual interest is a first step in the courtship ritual. Female mammals like giraffe and antelope excrete pheromones in their urine. These fragrances are picked up by the males not through their nose but by a structure called the Jacobson's organ. This organ is usually closed but can be opened by curling the upper lip upwards (as if disgusted). This lip-curling has a German name, 'flehmen'. Flehmen can be seen in cats, marsupials and ungulates (hoof-stock). These scents not only attract the male but tell the story of the female's fertility status. The male can tell by flehmen how ready a female is for mating.

Sometimes a prospective father needs to add his aroma into the mix to get things going. Experiments with rodents and sheep have identified that a whiff of a male's urine can bring the female into oestrus. Pig breeders use synthetic male pheromones to help determine which of the sows is ready for mating.

ATTRACTED TO SMELLY ARMPITS?

A Swiss zoologist, Claus Wedekind from the University of Bern, found 49 volunteers to smell sweaty T-shirts for science. The T-shirts were worn by men for two nights. They'd avoided contamination with other smells such as deodorants, aftershave, sex and alcohol during this time. The shirts were each put in a box with a hole in it and sniffed at by women in their mid-cycle, when a woman's smell is particularly sharp. The women scored each shirt on the basis of the intensity of smell, sexiness and pleasantness. The results of the study were revelatory: women were most attracted to the shirts of men whose immune system's genetic make-up was most different to their own. The Darwinian explanation for this is that their combined immune systems would give any offspring 'hybrid vigour' and make them less prone to illness.

OLFACTORY ADVICE FOR THE HUMAN MALE

Do humans use pheromones? In short, yes. Humans use scents to appear more appealing. We obviously love fragrances and have been using the bouquet of flowers, animal pheromones and other aromas for a long time to hide our own body odours and be more alluring. Perhaps we are under the apprehension that our natural signals of sexual chemistry are undesirable. We wash and scrub all natural scents off our bodies and replace these with chemical substitutes.

Somehow we seem to think that using animal pheromones, which form the basis of many perfumes, is better and more alluring than our own natural bouquet.

Perfumes have been used in human cultures for many centuries. The word perfume comes from the Latin words, 'per fumus', meaning 'through smoke'. The oldest perfumes ever found were discovered during an archaeological dig in Cyprus. These perfumes were more than four thousand years old. Animal essences varying from the excrement of the hyrax (order Hyracoidea) to the gland of the musk deer (family Moschidae) have been and are still used in expensive human scents today. I wonder if people know where musk comes from. The mature male musk deer produces this substance which is stored in a scent gland in front of his penis. The stags are killed to get this gland for the perfume industry. We seem to value smelling to such an extent that we spend billions of dollars on scents every year. In the UK alone, overall estimates for the fragrance market totaled 1.8 billion pounds in 2017.

For the would-be-dad, my recommendation regarding scents is to keep perfumes and aftershaves modest. The era of pungent aftershave and open-necked shirts showing chest hair and gold chains should be left behind in the 1970s. On trend now is a clean, vegan aroma that's been produced free of animal cruelty or child labour.

TACTILE COURTSHIP

Touch can be used to great effect during courtship as described by David Laux, a reptile and invertebrate expert at Wellington Zoo in New Zealand. David and the team at the zoo have been able to document some fascinating courtship behaviour from an unexpectedly courteous lover. David is one of the few people on this planet who can describe the courtship of the Goliath Bird-eating Spider in intricate detail:

'We have recently bred the Goliath Bird-eating Spider, the largest species of spider in the world. One of the things that has been amazing to watch is the intricacies and the delicacies of the courtship and mating. To get successful matings we had to ensure as little disturbance as possible, so we would wait for our males to start wandering the habitat, which is a seeking behaviour as he now searches for sexually receptive females. Once wandering, I can have him safely walk onto my hand, then gently lift him out of his habitat. As far as he is concerned, I'm just part of his environment and as such he is relaxed. I then slowly introduce him to the female's habitat and the moment he touches the first strand of silk he picks up her scent. He stops dead in his tracks and begins to drum the ground with his feet like a tiny jazz musician. He has a rhythmic tune and the female on sensing this comes up from her burrow. She will then turn to face him and will begin drumming back.

They will drum for each other at intervals, the same rhythm, the same beat every time. They move slowly towards each other whilst drumming and maintaining this rhythmic conversation between the two of them. As they move closer and closer, the male will scoop her up, lifting her into the air whilst drumming on her legs. It's amazing to see such tender contact between two invertebrates. He strokes her legs with his, he drums on her and he is in constant communication with her, letting her know what's going on. She, meanwhile, is in a trance-like state, which is the purpose of his display whilst he is wooing her. Once the mating has taken place he steps back and she resumes normal spider demeanour which is when he is at risk of being bitten by her. Up until that point they are absolutely in sync and in continual contact with one another. It really is incredible to watch.'

Rhythm, music and a tactile approach puts a potentially volatile partner in a trance-like state where she's much more receptive to romance. Without his delicate drumming, his chosen female may eat him as an after-sex snack. This relaxing, appeasing approach can work for humans also. Embracing and swooning to music can bring people together and put them in the right mood. As a species, we're known to often find a mate on the dancefloor – a good reason to learn to dance.

BACHELOR PADS AND OTHER LOVE NESTS

Many human females have been turned off a bloke because his bachelor pad reeked of dirty socks, or the washing-up in the sink showed an interesting species of fungus. This happens to animals too. The male Little Penguins (*Eudyptula minor*) I looked after at the zoo were ultra-competitive for females once the breeding season started. The males compete for the best burrow and once they've claimed one, they stand proud in the opening of their breeding pad, loudly proclaiming ownership and attracting female penguins to their home with their loud braying voices. To my ears they sounded more like a donkey than a bird but the female penguins seemed to be impressed.

Jo Walker, an expert penguin breeder at Taronga Zoo, has overseen many successful breeding seasons in the Little Penguin colony:

'Before the breeding season starts the keepers get everything ready for the birds. They don't have access to the breeding area all year round, as we don't want them laying eggs out of season and wearing themselves out. In the past they had access and they started breeding as early as June. One year, Wallace and Oogy, a long-term pair who bred together each year, produced three clutches in a row. Poor Wallace was so exhausted that he just keeled over in the middle of a feed one day. He was old and that extreme breeding effort really pushed him over the edge.

We now give the colony access to the breeding area at the end of August. This allows them to still have two clutches if they are up for the challenge. They have wooden breeding boxes with a tunnel that mimics the burrows they use in the wild. Before we open the area up, the keepers collect a lot of nesting material so the males can use that to make a nest. In the wild they would find bits and pieces on the beaches and under the bushes. They love the tea tree clippings we leave laying around for them – maybe it makes for a nice-scented home to attract the ladies! It's nice and soft too.

They know it's time to get really excited as we get the area set up for them, they keep looking over as they see us going in and out. I think they're already planning which burrow they are going to make a run for and claim as theirs. They vocalise a lot during this time, chatting away to each other. The best nesting site will get them the best female. They run in as fast as their little feet can take them but there are so many good places, it's hard to choose. Once they do choose a site there's some brawling between the males because some want the same burrow. Males will try and claim the den they were successful in last season.

The fighting can be quite fierce. They peck and they 'flipper slap' each other like a couple of guys having a punch up. The females at the same time will be checking out who's got what. She might go back to the same partner she had last year if he was a good penguin daddy and helped her raise their chicks. But she may think 'you haven't done the best with the real estate this year and I'm moving on to someone with a better place.' Some of the females stick their head in the tunnel to have a look, others just like where it is or the male. There's even been the occasional ménage à trois.

It takes two to three weeks before we see the first eggs being laid. Once everybody settles down, Little Penguins are great dads. Penguins are some of the best fathers in the animal world.'

Like the penguins Jo looks after, getting a suitable nest to raise young is where it all starts for most species, whether that's a cave, a burrow, a twig nest, or a house, each species evolves to have a preference for the kind of place they'd like to bring up baby.

ADVICE FOR HUMAN WOULD-BE DADS

Most women like a bloke who keeps a clean house or is at least house-trained to a reasonable standard. If you bring back a date, make sure you hide the three weeks' worth of washing in a closet, air the place, wash up the dishes and generally tidy up. If you look like a filthy slob, the chances of sex are significantly diminished. If you look like you're handy around the house, all the better. Casually show off some well executed do-it-yourself projects or your own impressive artworks. Gives new insight into the pick-up line, 'Would you like to come up and see my etchings?', doesn't it?

BOWER TO IMPRESS

Male bowerbirds (family Ptilonorhynchidae) are impressive housekeepers. They are also artists, architects and superb dancers. Male Satin Bowerbirds (*Ptilonorhynchus violaceus*) have striking glossy blue-black plumage and a knack for stage-building. They construct an elaborate performance space from where they try to impress a female. The bower starts on the ground with two parallel sticks to which our bird architect adds more material, creating an archway. He paints the structure with chewed vegetation and saliva. The artist in him places the decorations – which are initially blue and yellow and may include shiny objects – in an aesthetically pleasing display in his courtship arena.

As the male matures, he uses more and more blue in his decorations. Some of the best-loved items in urban areas are blue clothes pegs, drinking straws and bottle tops. My colleague Libby Kartzoff tells the story of her friends in St Albans, a tiny historic village north of

Sydney, Australia, who have a resident bowerbird who adorns his bower with discarded blue condom wrappers. Makes me wonder what's going on in that small hamlet!

In more natural areas he'll be more likely to use blue parrot feathers, flowers and snail shells. The bower's construction and decoration are a significant determinant as to whom a female chooses as a mate. Females are a mottled olive-green with blue eyes of the exact shade of blue the male favours to decorate his bower. The male bowerbird puts in a lot of effort to build an impressive bower. He will steal things from another male's bower and even destroy his competitors' efforts. Females are only attracted to a male who has a lovely intact bower, so whilst the competition is rebuilding, the bower destroyer has freer reign.

Any bowerbird female inspecting the bower is treated to an impressive display. This is when the male brings out his inner dancer. He performs quivering movements as he struts and bows with outstretched wings whilst making buzzing, rattling calls interspersed with mimicry. He may carry one of the blue pieces in his bill. If she's impressed, she'll mate with him in the bower and then goes off to build a nest in the trees. After all the effort of courting, male bowerbirds do not help raise the brood. Although much discussed in the avian literature, males with elaborate displays coupling with picky females who end up as single mothers only occurs in about 3 per cent of bird species worldwide.

As I'm writing this, I've just seen a Satin Bowerbird raid the hanging pot plant outside the window of my study. He's snapped the heads off my yellow marigold flowers and carried *four* off in his bill. Although his preference is for blue, he will sometimes vary his palette. I know his bower is just across the road from our house and

I'm intrigued to see what he does with the flowers. I follow him a few minutes later and find he's casually dropped the flowers on the ground within a few centimetres of the bower. I suspect I've brought this upon myself: I've been enticing him with the occasional blue bottle-top or clothes-peg deliberately left in the garden. I check his bower every now and then to see how he's used my offerings. Often, it's been pilfered by a rival bird by the following day.

A NOTE TO FEMALE READERS

The world of animals tells a cautionary tale here. As a broad sweeping statement, a drab-looking male may make a more useful partner in the child-rearing game. Beautiful males may make beautiful babies but don't necessarily help out around the nest much. I'm generalising here, but in the natural world, the more effort any animal puts into courtship, the less goes into child rearing. Just saying…

A NOTE TO MALE READERS

Men and women have had conflicting sexual interests since ancient times. Women have always been more vulnerable than men and engaging in sex comes with higher stakes for women than it does for men. Her eggs are limited and his sperm is not. She can't make an unlimited number of children like men can and pregnancy is (or more correctly *was*) dangerous to women, especially before modern medicine when mothers regularly died in childbirth. Being 'choosy' about who to take this risk with is the result of millions of years of evolution which has shaped the sexual behaviour of women today.

COURTING DANGER

Some species have to tread carefully if the balance of power in a relationship is not equal. Anna Bennett, an experienced hyena keeper and Assistant Curator at Monarto Safari Park, South Australia, describes how male Spotted Hyenas (*Crocuta crocuta*) go about approaching a much more powerful female. She discovered that the male's courtship behaviour could point to important information:

'Spotted Hyena clans are notoriously hierarchical and all males rank lower than any female. If a female approaches him, he'll run away. To win her over to mate he must eventually lure her in somehow.

We never see any mating as they seem to do this under the cover of darkness. Courtship is important because the male needs to charm a female who ranks much higher than he does. Years ago, when we first housed hyenas, a staff member observed some behaviours we'd not seen before. Male Gamba was seen pawing the ground and touching his foreleg with the foot of his other leg in front of a female who seemed to be just resting there. His posture was interesting too, hunched over and displaying an erect penis.

Having noted this behaviour in our diary, we looked back when the cubs were born and saw that it was exactly 110 days later – precisely the gestation period for the species. The female did not look as if she was in season at the time, but Gamba evidently noticed something we did not. Hyenas can breed any time of the year and the female shows very subtle signs of being ready to mate. We now know we can base the pregnancy gestation around the male's tap-dancing behaviour to plan for the arrival of cubs.

Once the cubs are born, they have their mother's social status and the male ranks lower than any of his offspring. Cubs stay in the den and only come out when their mother sits outside and calls them. The male is not allowed near the den unless the cubs' mother permits it. If she trusts him, she may let the father of the cubs come close and sniff them even if they're only a few days or a week old. The male usually won't approach the cubs at all for a while and is more likely to interact with them once they're a couple of months old. He'll carefully play with them then but always under the watchful eye of a female.'

This just goes to show that a nice bit of courtship can put even the crankiest mate in a better mood.

GIFT GIVING

In some societies, the giving and accepting of gifts is strongly ritualised around courtship. Think of dowries and the 'bride price' in some cultures. The world of animal courtship also incorporates gift giving. Offering your love interest a tasty morsel is a common feature in bird courtship in particular. Ravens, kookaburras and grebes are all gift givers in their honeymoon period. Often the gift is more ceremonial than of great value unless, in the case of the Gentoo Penguin, it's a pebble.

The Gentoo Penguin (*Pygoscelis papua*) breeds on Subantarctic islands. They nest on piles of stones situated between tufts of grass. The male brings his partner these stones as nuptial gifts, as they are highly valued in a geography where such pebbles are a limited commodity. Many penguin species mate for life, coming back together again and again during each year's breeding season. The gift of a pebble is therefore like the renewal of marriage vows. The meaning behind the gift is clear to his intended, reaffirming their bond. Despite being jealously guarded there are many neighbourly disputes about pebble ownership.

Fidelity seems to be highly regarded in Gentoo society. Any males attempting to breed outside of their original breeding pair are violently rejected from the colony, regardless of the male's pebble-giving history.

COURTSHIP RITUALS

Animals have solved the problem of finding a partner with an infinite variety of courtship campaigns. In many cases, love is a battlefield and pursuit an exciting phase of courtship. First, the pair find each other by sight, sound or smell. Then the male may pursue the female for a bit to convince her to mate. This very much reminds me of my early teenage years when boys literally chased girls or rushed up and maybe pulled your ponytail. Nothing else happened, but in hindsight perhaps these boys too were practicing some animalistic courtship ritual.

Formalities in courtship help to balance the struggle between aggression, sex drive and fear, as readily seen in the courtship of many species. In big cats, for example, physical domination is a feature of courtship. It may start with sparring, some snarling, mock charges and tentative nuzzling, but all male cats eventually grasp the female's neck during copulation. Fortunately, they have some specialised muscles that prevent their mouth clamping down. In yet other animals, such as Greater Kudu (*Tragelaphus strepsiceros*) antelope, the pursuit is a rather more dignified procession where the

Like many birds, Western Grebes perform a courtship dance to confirm their relationship. In many human cultures newly-weds perform a solo dance at the start of the wedding celebrations.

male walks behind his quarry, keeping his head low and the lethal, pointy horn laying across his back. This way he does not frighten the female too much, showing he's a nice bloke, despite his fierce-looking armament.

BIG, BIGGER, BEST

Female bowerbirds choose a particularly clever and innovative sire for their offspring. The Great Bowerbird (*Chlamydera nuchalis*) does bower one-upmanship to great effect. Not only is he an architect and a dancer, but like a good artist he has a superior handle on perspective. Researchers Kelly and Endler found compelling evidence to suggest that the Great Bowerbird is able to use optical illusions by placing pebbles and stones in such a way that their bower looks bigger. By placing small objects at the front end and larger ones at the far end of the bower they create a 'forced perspective'. Far from random, the location of the pebbles has to be exactly to the artist's design. When the researches mucked up his design by rearranging things, he would spot the changes instantly and put the items back precisely as he intended for the visual effect.

There are many examples of ritualised displays where both males and females perform to show their best attributes. Many species find that repeat performances to re-enforce the pair bond are needed. Birds-of-paradise need to impress the female time and time again to remain bonded and reaffirm these bonds at the beginning of the breeding season. Howler monkeys and gibbons can be heard in the dense tropical forest long before they can be seen. Paired gibbons sing duets as a way to re-enforce their union, letting others know of the close bond and that this territory is taken. Humans sometimes renew their marriage vows after decades of being together. However, many of the small human rituals between couples, from kissing goodnight to maintaining a regular date night, continuously reinforce the pair bond.

COURTSHIP ADVICE FOR THE HUMAN MALE

Animals are quite clear about their intentions during courtship: they want to mate. Things are not always as transparent in the human dating scene. Most species don't get physically close to another unless it's to be eaten or to mate. Most animals instinctively keep some distance from others. Even the most social creatures, such as schooling fish or a herd of antelope, keep a precise distance from their nearest neighbour. In humans, maintaining personal space boundaries is crucial to feeling comfortable in the presence of others. Infringement of these boundaries is often met with aggression. In the animal world, getting close enough to mate also involves risking being injured by a non-receptive mate, so males need to gain the trust of a potential mate first. The following principles may apply when translating this to the human world:

- Put potential partners at their ease and make them feel safe.
- Feeling desirable is an aphrodisiac. Honest, well-intended compliments are great.
- Be honest. Don't string anyone along thinking they've found Prince Charming if you're after a one-night stand.
- Courtship is about attentiveness and getting to know each other. Ask questions. Don't just talk about yourself.

- Gift giving is a feature in some wild courtships. Gifts don't have to be expensive. A flower picked from the garden can work just as well as pricey offerings – it's the thought that counts.
- Impress with housekeeping skills, cooking and looking after yourself. All strong recommendations for any prospective father.

The role of courtship and how the mating game works in nature may give modern humans a few insights on the exciting journey to fatherhood. The next chapter looks at how *mate choice* influences who in the end pairs up with whom and who doesn't.

SNORTY ROAR GETS THE GIRL

Compared to birds, mammals are generally much more casual about courtship before mating. Birds often have the visually charming courtships we can observe. Mammals however widely favour pheromones to communicate their readiness and willingness to mate. As observers we aren't able to appreciate this sexual chitchat for what it is. Scent glands are a common feature for sharing sexual and territorial information. Male Koalas rub a scent gland on their chest on tree branches to attract females and mark a territory. Although mammal courtship may lack the visual display in many taxa, it does have a good range of male voices advertising their availability.

The soft cuddly toy lookalike, the Koala, bellows his low-pitched snoring inhalations and a loud roar as he exhales. This snorty roar can be heard up to 800 metres (2,600 feet) away across the forest to convey his availability to the females.

Chapter 4

SEXUAL SELECTION – CHOOSING A MATE

'Sex is a part of nature. I go along with nature.'

MARILYN MONROE

Courtship might begin with a bit of flirting but soon gets serious when it comes to choosing a mate with whom to have babies. Do we have a say in whom we choose or do our hormones and biological make-up determine the outcome? Finding a mate is initially a game of advertising. Generally, the males promote their qualities and females choose from what's on offer. But how exactly do females choose?

The idea of sexual selection driving evolution was first proposed by Charles Darwin more than 160 years ago in his book *On the Origin of Species*. Sexual selection in biological terms is the process whereby members of one gender compete for mating access to members of the opposite gender. Darwin fleshed his ideas out further in *The Descent of Man, and Selection in Relation to Sex* in 1871. He noticed that some behaviours and characteristics in an animal's life seemed to have little benefit to immediate survival. In fact, they may have a negative impact on survival. So why, then, do they exist?

Darwin used the example of the peacock's tail. The male Indian Peafowl is a good example of how a very pretty long tail can become a handicap as well as a chick magnet. The tail trails behind the male, making escape from a predator just a little harder than it would otherwise be. His extravagant tail shows an 'eye' with blue, gold and orange markings that tell the peahen 'Pick me. I'm so fit and strong that I can carry this heavy tail behind me.' During the breeding season this tail is so cumbersome that flying is a challenge.

Simply having the looks is not enough, though. The peacock not only has his amazing tail, he arches it over his back shaking the iridescent feathers as he prances in front of the female. When he shakes his tail-feathers it sounds like grasses rustling in the wind. We now know this also produces an infrasound, too low for human hearing but probably irresistible to a peahen.

Peahens show a distinct preference for males with the longest, most impressive tail. Sexual selection is therefore a significant driver of evolutionary change. If peahens keep choosing mates with the longest, brightest tail this exaggerated but otherwise useless appendage will continue to be passed down to other generations and becomes increasingly striking. In the case of the peacock, the fact that females mate with him preferentially is worth the burden of his tail. He balances the dangers of slow, cumbersome flight from predators against the increased opportunity to spread his genes. In effect he is advertising to females that he is so fit and strong he can squander energy at will. His tail says: 'Mate with me if you want sons and daughters as superior as I am.' Peacocks drop their magnificent tail-feathers after the breeding season as there's no need to impress anyone anymore.

The peacock's tail trails behind him, making flying just a little harder. However, this extravagant appendage tells the peahens he's fit and strong and likely to produce fit and healthy babies.

Biologists formally call this phenomenon 'mate choice'. The first thing an animal does to select a potential mate is to evaluate the quality of the potential sexual partner. In particular they look for aspects that may show how fit and healthy the mate is, both of which can equate to fertility. An estimate is then made of how beneficial these characteristics would be to any future offspring. If the female Blue-footed Booby has a strong preference for bright blue feet because they indicate greater health, then male boobies will develop bluer and bluer feet in order to come out a winner. There's a genetic component here too of course. If the bluer-footed boobies make more babies, then offspring will have increasingly bluer feet.

The species, over an evolutionary time-scale period, will develop brighter and brighter feet. The genetic benefit of choice to females is bearing healthy young that survive well and go on to reproduce themselves. This is a heritable benefit. Non-heritable benefits are general advantages such as access to good food, parental care or a good territory. A good provider in both genetic and non-genetic terms is what most females are after.

LOVERS' LANE

Mate choice happens in all species, including those that do not have extreme features pushed by sexual selection. Some species we look after in human care demonstrate how mate preference is their choice, not ours. Cheetahs in all-important global breeding programs were notoriously difficult to breed in the past. Over time they made it clear to us humans that mate choice is important to them and the choice is theirs, not ours. Unless we offer a variety of potential mates, there's likely to be no cubs at all.

Michelle Lloyd is the Cheetah keeper at Monarto Safari Park and has been working with Cheetahs for 17 years. She's been able to observe at close range how mate choice works in these felines:

'I've been able to try a lot of different approaches to get Cheetahs excited about mating. In the wild females are fairly solitary and would only come across males when they wander into male territory. Males are a little more sociable than females and may live in a male coalition. We brought in such a coalition of four males to provide choice for our females. To make choosing possible we keep the male yards away from the female yards, whilst a long raceway connects the two. Female Cheetahs stay in their familiar surroundings and need to feel safe and comfortable in their yard. If they are happy they will cycle naturally. The 'lover's lane' concept means that we can parade the males past a female and observe how they react to each other.

Being able to use the 'lovers' lane' idea means that we can try different combinations of animals, which seems to be really beneficial. The females always seem to show a preference for the more confident males. The dominant male always gets the female.

I will vary how the males are introduced to the female. Sometimes it's the whole coalition, sometimes only two or even one. We look at the reaction of both the males and the females to each other, but more so from the female perspective. I grade some key indicator behaviours from one to five and when she scores five on the key I will introduce her to that male. If she likes the male she will get all flirty. With a fence separating them she rubs against the barrier, flagging her tail, lowering her hindquarters and lifting her tail high are all good signs that she's receptive to his advances.'

Cheetah females won't take any old male as a sire to their offspring. Breeding Cheetahs in human care was extremely challenging until enclosures were built to allow the individuals, specifically the females, to choose. Parading boys in this way is not dissimilar to the dance halls of old.

LIONESS'S CHOICE

We do not always understand why females favour a particular male. Anna Bennett, Assistant Curator at Monarto Safari Park, recalls what happened when the lionesses in her care made their choice known:

'We had an original pride of two males and four adult females. All was well for a long time and cubs were born and grew up. Then the old male died leaving behind his brother who'd always been the subordinate one of the two. A few weeks later all the females turned on the brother, effectively pushing him out of the pride. I thought they were going to kill him but they stopped short of that, giving him only puncture wounds and scratches. We managed to get him out in one piece before the lionesses did more damage. They did not like this male and certainly did not want to have his babies now the dominant male was gone. It seemed the dominant male held the pride together and without him it fell apart.

A new male would kill any young cubs to be able to sire his own more quickly. The lionesses had no young cubs at the time which allowed them to be selective with the male they wanted to sire their offspring – a clear demonstration of mate choice in action.'

It seemed that the lionesses at Monarto didn't want the genes of the subordinate brother to flow in the veins of their future cubs and did something about it. Lionesses have good reason to be fastidious in their mate selection. They are the ones who are left with most of the childcare. In addition, a female is born with a fixed number of eggs which are not replenished in her lifetime. Males can replenish their gametes, producing about twelve million per hour. Sperm comes easily, eggs do not. This is the main reason females are selective.

Being picky is not the sole reserve of females however – in cases where females maintain a harem of males, the males become the fussy ones. As soon as there is an oversupply of one gender in a social group, the other gender can afford to be selective in their choice. Male Green-and-black Poison-arrow Frogs (*Dendrobates auratus*) are excellent dads who do most of the parental care. These males are in hot demand but availability is limited. Females therefore compete for the chance to leave their eggs in a male's nest. The male inseminates the eggs and takes the burden of defending and caring for the young until they are independent. Just as in economics, supply and demand determine value in the competition for a mate.

LEKKING TO CHOOSE

A lek is a gathering of males performing competitive displays to attract a female. It is also the perfect place to see sexual selection and mate choice in action. The word 'lek' comes from the Swedish word *lekställe* or mating ground (*lek* meaning 'mating' and *ställe* 'place'). Lekking is a very serious business where showing off impresses not only the females but marks out territory in front of other males.

During the breeding season, male Black Grouse (*Lyrurus tetrix*), a large Eurasian gamebird, will perform at a lek at dawn. The males, who are much more impressive than the 'greyhen' females, strut around making distinctive mating calls, showing off their red wattles and flashing the white patches in their wings and tails. Their performances are energetic and include tail fanning, posturing, jumping and the occasional short flight. Dominant males position themselves in the central lek arena while juvenile males are relegated to the outer spots. Females choose the best dancer based on the 'fittest' performance. There is no pair bond and after copulation the female is left on her own to raise any resulting chicks. Her dull appearance is a camouflage to keep her nest safe so she's no sitting duck for predators.

Other males that use leks include the New Zealand Kakapo, the appropriately named cocks-of-the-rock from South America, some birds-of-paradise and also some mammals such as Fallow Deer, Waterbuck, some seals, bats, frogs, reptiles, insects and even humans.

The lek reminds me of the bars and clubs I used to hang out in during my teens and twenties. Boys would come to display and girls would look at what was on offer. The boys would show off for the judging females, hoping sex might result. Sporting fields and gyms, as well as bars and dancefloors, are conceivably the human version of a lek.

GENDER DIMORPHISM

Nature provides males and females with the 'look' they need to perform in the drama of their sexual life. In many species, the difference in appearance and behaviour between the genders is pronounced for reasons of sexual selection, as mentioned above. Differences can include size, colour, markings, extra adornments and behavioural differences as well. These variances may be subtle or exaggerated. The greatest degree of sexual dimorphism occurs in animals where males have more than one female and compete with other males. This can take many forms, from the distinctive red comb on a domestic rooster – which depends on hormones produced by the testes – to the impressive antlers of a Fallow Deer (*Dama dama*) which are shed each autumn and regrown in time to attract the females during the next breeding season.

Lions are much larger than lionesses and proudly advertise this masculinity with an impressive mane. The mane was thought to help protect the male's neck during aggressive interactions with rivals. Dr Craig Packer, one of the world's leading lion researchers, believes that the mane may instead be a token of strength or status and conducted an intriguing experiment. He had a plush-toy company produce realistic life-size lions with manes of varying length and degrees of darkness. He called them Romeo, Fabio, Lothario and Julio. He enticed the real lions to the decoy lions with the calls of hyenas at a kill. Lions will scare hyenas off their kill to steal their food. The lionesses were mostly attracted to the darker-haired manes. At the same time, male lions avoided the dark-maned dummies.

Further research showed that males with short manes had more injuries and illnesses than darker-maned lions, who tended to be older and have higher testosterone levels. A lush, dark mane therefore seems to signal to females and other males that a male lion is strong and healthy.

Size is frequently an observable feature that separates the males from the females in the natural world. Male baboons are about twice the size of females and sport an impressive mane. Whenever males initiate a fight with other males for the chance to mate, they tend to be bigger and stronger. Additionally, they may have some extra fighting gear like horns, antlers or tusks. Research looking at which carnivores have the largest canine teeth for inflicting damage shows that there is a direct correlation between tooth size and breeding system. Monogamous pairs and multi-male, multi-female groups tend to have smaller canine teeth than males who have to compete to maintain a harem.

In the majority of cases, it's the male who shows off and the female who is duller and more modest by comparison. If you look after vulnerable young things that could be eaten by a predator, it's best not to attract attention to yourself. However, it is not always true that males are the larger, stronger gender. In some species where females dominate, such as the Spotted Hyena, the females are larger. In many birds of prey, the females are also larger than the males but the jury is still out on exactly why this is so.

Dimorphism makes it easier to recognise a potential mate and impress them. In many monogamous species, sexual dimorphism is not very pronounced. According to Clark Spencer Larsen, an American biological anthropologist, modern humans show an average body mass difference between the sexes of about 15 per cent. Human males being generally larger than females may be a further indication that in our ancient past men may have been harem masters, needing to fight off other males over 'possession' of females.

In addition to a size difference, distinctive markings are used in many human cultures to display masculinity or femininity. Tattoos and body paint are still used by indigenous people around the world and most of these markings are gender specific. Hair, clothes and jewellery are used globally to differentiate the sexes. All these clever tricks to stand out help when it comes to being seen and maybe being chosen as a potential mate.

HERDING POTENTIAL MATES

Some males behave like aggressive sheepdogs, herding females into their territory and keeping them there for as long as they can whilst excluding other males. Seals are particularly prone to use this strategy. Despite the bullying of some harem masters, females of the species are frequently in a more powerful position than we think because, more often than not, they do get to choose. Although, once she chooses a male or perhaps his territory, she may have to put up with him as a harem master.

Big boofy male sea lions are not averse to bullying the females and keeping them confined on the stretch of beach he's claimed. The bulls arrive early to fight other males for a section of beach they will establish their harem on. They claim their domain ahead of the arrival of prospective mothers, some of whom will already be pregnant. The better the territory, the more cows he can attract to his ocean-view home. He displays his masculine bulk and sharp teeth to good effect, keeping other males at bay. Once he's established his territory, he can't go to sea and eat. For several months, sex is more important to him than food and during this time he'll use a significant amount of blubber to stay alive.

Sea lionesses, pregnant from last year's breeding season, are ready to pop as soon as they arrive. The cows choose what looks like a safe beach for their young to be born and grow up a little before they head off for an ocean life. As a rule, females are more likely to join a large harem in favour of a small one. As they come ashore, the bulls round up as many cows as they can into their harem. After giving birth to their single pup the new mother is immediately mated by the harem master. This phenomenon is called post-partum oestrus and is common in animals that only get together once a year. It's a case of getting birthing and mating done all in the same yearly visit! Through a process called delayed implantation or embryonic diapause, the newly fertilised egg lies dormant in the mother for some months. The foetus will be full term next year at the same time so that all pups will be born within weeks of each other at the next annual beach orgy. Beach masters may father a dozen or more young in a breeding season, but don't contribute to their upbringing in any way. If a mother can manage on her own, there is no evolutionary pressure on the dad to help.

Zebras are herders too. The Plain's Zebra (*Equus quagga*) lives in groups of five to twenty individuals where the stallion controls a few mares and their young ones. These basic groups stay together even when they congregate in larger herds and families can have the same members for years. Within the bigger herd, the stallion will spend a lot of his time chasing off males who have come to sniff out his females. When a mare has a foal, she benefits from the protection of the stallion who will defend the family from predators such as lions.

As only a few herding males control the females, it means that there are always a number of males living in bachelor groups.

BACHELOR GROUPS
In many animals, bachelor herds form because the species to which they belong has a harem social system. Many young males that leave the natal group form bachelor groups or herds until such time as they are able to change their fortunes and score a partner. These

males are also known to form long-term bonds, some of which are sexual bonds. They are either too young or too old to manage a harem, or else not fit or strong enough to overthrow a harem master. Bachelor groups exist in dolphins, lions, seals, elephants and many hooved animals such as horses and deer. Sticking together gives some protection against predators. Bachelor groups can be short-, medium- or long-term depending on opportunities presented. Some males exist in bachelor herds all the time except during the breeding season when they become competitive.

PANDAS AND MUTUAL ATTRACTION

It's notoriously difficult to get Giant Pandas to reproduce in breeding programs in China or in zoos around the world. This mammal is not 'in the mood' very often. The female is in heat only once a year, in spring, and only for 24 to 72 hours. A male panda needs to make a quick move or they miss out on the annual chance to make whoopy.

To save the species, attempts have been made to breed them in human care in order to augment numbers in the wild. To pair the pandas, scientists select the least related male and female to minimise inbreeding. It now seems that the pandas are keen to make that selection themselves. If they get a chance to pick their mate, pandas are more than twice as likely to copulate with an individual they have shown an interest in. Additionally, if a female mates with a partner she chooses she's twice as likely to conceive and give birth to a cub. The best results come about when both parties chose each other, increasing the chance of a cub being born to 75 per cent.

Young male gorillas are a typical example of a species that leaves the family when they're adolescents of around eight years old. At this point they are called blackbacks – too old to be a juvenile and too young to be a silverback. They usually leave the family voluntarily once they reach blackback status but sometimes they may need a little push to leave home. Once on their own, they will band together with other blackbacks and maybe an older male to form a social group. Gorilla bachelors are not able to manage a harem of their own until they are fully grown, which is at least 20 years old or even older.

Elephants also form bachelor herds. Elephant bulls have different social needs than females. Adult male and female elephants only come together for reproduction. In the wild, like gorillas, elephant males leave or are driven out of the family group by the older females when they reach puberty. They may join or form bachelor groups once they leave the maternal herd. Bachelor elephants can be quite sociable when they are not competing for dominance or females and they form long-term friendships. Young male elephants chill out with other males and play-fight from a young age. As they play they begin to test their strength and learn the fighting skills they will need as older males. A dominance hierarchy exists among the males when they hang out in a group. Dominance depends on age, size and sexual condition. When they are in groups, males follow the lead of the dominant bull. The older, more experienced males appear to control the aggression of the younger bulls. By the age of 25, males are twice the size of females and will often stay close to female herds when there's a cow in season.

SEXUAL SELECTION IN HUMANS

Compared to most other terrestrial mammals, with the exception of the Naked Mole-rat (*Heterocephalus glaber*) and a few others, humans are pretty hairless. Charles Darwin postulated that the relative hairlessness of humans is the result of sexual selection as being hairless does not increase our chance of survival. As women's bodies are almost completely hairless, he suggested that in prehistoric times males may have overwhelmingly selected women with less hairy bodies. Over time, this affected men's bodies too as the women passed on their hairlessness to their baby boys also. It's also suggested that men's beards and the genital hair of both sexes have evolved as a result of sexual selection.

Darwin also studied the Khoisan women of the Kalahari Desert and observed that 'the posterior part of their body projects in a most wonderful manner.' This is known as steatopygia and it is characterised by a substantial level of tissue on the buttocks and thighs. Darwin considered this feature an expression of sexual selection as the features appeared to have no advantage to survival. Perhaps this casts new light on Kim Kardashian's booty?

Geoffrey Miller in his book *The Mating Mind* draws on Darwin's ideas about human behaviours that do not have a clear benefit to survival but may help in getting you laid. Traits like being funny, playing a musical instrument, or being an artist can be advantageous for sexual selection. Miller also suggests that we have a far greater vocabulary that we need purely to survive. We may use language to show how smart we are and thereby demonstrate a fitness to potential mates.

Despite the research of the last centuries, attraction in humans continues to have that little bit of mystery, a certain je ne sais quoi! The sparks that ignite between people, be they pheromones or hormones, work in peculiar ways.

ADVICE FOR THE HUMAN MALE

The importance of sexual selection in our lives remains as pervasive as it does in the animal world. Many males of myriad species put on impressive shows during the breeding season. They are composers, choreographers and fashionistas, all in order to find a mate and have sex. I'm yet to be convinced that animals actually know that sex leads to offspring, but I have no doubt that sex is what drives a huge proportion of behaviour in animals and humans alike.

A demonstration of courage, skills and stamina goes a long way for a male trying to impress a potential mate. In our society, the occasional reckless behaviour or extreme risk-taking in young males is an expression of their animal nature. Risky behaviours are largely male mating displays designed to make women want to have sex with them but are also about competing with other men who want to mate with those same women. Resources contribute to mate choice too. A male who holds a good territory with plenty of food for offspring is likely to be a better choice than one without.

It's important to heed Darwin and Miller's observations. Intelligence, humour and use of language are all very sexy attributes. How to stand out from the crowd is highlighted in the chapter about courtship. When it comes to mate choice though, think about supply and demand. My husband tells me he went to Scottish dancing lessons as a teenage boy, not because he loved Scottish dancing, but because there were hardly any boys amongst plenty of dancing girls. A diminished supply meant he was in hot demand.

FEATHERED FIDELITY, OR MAYBE NOT ...

Some 90 per cent of birds will pair up for the entire breeding season or even for life. In these pairs both genders will usually help to feed and care for the young. These monogamous pairs have previously been held up as models for true fidelity. Since the advance of DNA, paternity testing has demonstrated that 'extra-pair mating' is a common feature in socially monogamous species in the animal kingdom. Very few pair-bonded species are now considered to be exclusively sexually monogamous.

Zebra Finches (*Taeniopygia guttata*) for example are certainly socially monogamous but not sexually monogamous given half a chance. They'll have 'something on the side' if the opportunity arises. Extra-pair copulation as it's called is much more common in nature than once thought.

Chapter 5

WILD SEX — MATING SYSTEMS

'Everything in the world is about sex except sex.
Sex is about power.'

OSCAR WILDE

To become a dad, you have to 'get it on' first. All species have developed a particular way they get together and make whoopee. Some have to rely on chance for their eggs and sperm to come together, while others just 'put it out there' and hope for the best.

Species can be grouped by the nature of their sexual relationships or the bond they form, known as a mating system. These mating systems are influenced by competition for mates and tend not to be very flexible. If your species is polygamous for example, then that is what you do. A species that lives a monogamous life would not suddenly have one individual trying to keep a harem. Alternatively, a lot would need to change in the circumstances of Chimpanzees before they would consider monogamy in their best interest. In humans there appears to be much more flexibility with our mating system incorporating monogamy, polygyny and polyandry, with promiscuity always being an option.

In contrast to monogamy, three types of polygyny are usually recognised: polygamy, polyandry and polygynandry. The kind of fatherhood we see in animals is strongly influenced by the mating system the species uses. The natural histories of different species are used to illustrate how and why the mating system affects how a male feels about his offspring and what role he plays in bringing them up.

POLYGAMY – FROM THE GREEK 'POLY' (MANY) AND 'GAMOS' (SPOUSE)

In most mammal species the male has no parental duties. His success as a father is measured by how many females he can get pregnant. This largely depends on how many females are around, which in turn depends on the resources available. If there aren't many females around, the male has two choices: he either defends the resources or the females. If the resources are thin on the ground, the suitor will be more likely to defend the females directly.

Polygamy is more prevalent in species where one sex is freed from parental duties, usually the male. In this breeding system, a male monopolises two or more females and mates with them when they are in season. In most cases, it's the female who is left in charge of the kids. Gorillas use this mating system with several females thought to be in an exclusive sexual relationship with the one male. Eighty per cent of sexual relationships in mammals follow this system. Amongst non-mammals, however, it is a rare occurrence and only found in about two per cent of bird species.

In this system the female is responsible for child rearing as the male can't possibly provide for all his progeny. His job is to provide and maintain a territory with the best resources. Females who come into his territory are drawn to the rich resources and to 'catch' a male who is a good provider. The other important role these prospective dads play is as the protector of the young and vulnerable.

African Lions, the only social cat species, are a typical example of a polygamous animal society. Nearly all felines grow up in single-parent households, except for lions. The size of a pride of lions varies, but the average is about 14 or 15 individuals. The lionesses live in groups of related individuals and their descendants. The lionesses do most of the hunting for the pride. Sometimes there's even more than one male in the pride, although one will be dominant over the others and will get to sire all or most of the cubs. What, then, does a male lion contribute that makes him earn his keep? His main job is to make babies. As the strongest, healthiest male around, his genes are worth propagating. Important too is his role as the protector of the group, shielding the lionesses and their offspring from any danger, particularly the advances of rival males keen to take over. If a new male succeeds in taking over leadership, the young cubs will be killed and any adolescent cubs expelled from the pride. Although the adolescents escape infanticide, life outside an established pride is tough and starvation a significant risk. Given that a male has a harem of females with whom he mates exclusively and birthrates are 50 per cent males and 50 per cent females, there are a lot of males who never get to join a pride as an adult.

The top job in a pride is challenging and takes a toll on the harem master. To make sure his genetic lineage gets passed on he has to constantly fight off other males. Lionesses, on occasion, will support the alpha male in helping to fend off a challenging male outsider. The females are clearly invested in their cubs' survival. Raising cubs is hard work for a lioness, who does so without input from the male. She is pregnant for four months, then feeds and raises the cubs for up to a year and a half. The lioness's enormous maternal investment means that the role of the father as protector of her cubs is really important to her. Lionesses prefer the strongest, most confident male to sire their litter and he will have the best genes to pass on.

THE POLYGAMOUS DAD

There are examples of committed and caring fathers in polygamous relationships, but they are usually not as committed as fathers who truly bond in other ways with their mate. We do not have the same expectations of polygamous fathers as we do from the more monogamous types. After all, if you have many wives, you probably have many offspring and looking after multiple children is more problematic than looking after a few. However, some polygamous dads do look after their offspring as sole parents and with dedication. Several ground-dwelling birds such as emus, ostriches, rheas and tinamous have a paternal style that they appear to owe to the dinosaurs. This group of terrestrial birds includes single dads who look after an ambitious brood from several females. It's not a common strategy in the natural world, but researchers have found that it runs in this particular ancient avian family and goes back millennia.

Over 90 per cent of birds do co-parent but it's only in these birds of prehistoric lineage that both polygamy and sole paternal care co-exists. In a 2008 study, researchers connected this behaviour to their extinct dinosaur relatives. Large numbers of dinosaur eggs were found in the same nest – too many for one female, suggesting that several females laid eggs and a single carer looked after them. The bones on top of the nest were determined to be male, thereby proving that this unusual behaviour has been around since the dinosaurs.

However, most polygamous dads fall into the harem master category. They might be protective, defending the territory and even providing food, but many males in seasonal polygamous systems, such as the seals, never see their offspring again.

DADS WITH HAREMS

In human culture, a harem is traditionally a house or a palace where the women of a king or ruler live. The women may be a man's wives, his concubines, his mother, unmarried daughters, female servants and other unmarried or widowed female relatives. In previous times, some harems were guarded by eunuchs, the only men allowed inside apart from pre-pubescent boys and of course the ruler of the harem. Eunuchs were castrated male servants who could guard the women without the possibility of having sex with them. I suspect this wasn't a job servants or slaves volunteered for. Harems were once the norm in affluent Mediterranean and Middle Eastern societies who still reflect this in the traditional architecture of the indoor courtyard – a place where women could be outside but remain unseen by other males.

Harems are a popular reproductive unit in nature. In a harem situation, males have control of several females. A harem usually has one or two males and a number of females and their offspring in the group. The dominant male is usually the only one to father children. It's a stressful job as he has to drive off challenging males as well as keep track of all his females and prevent them sneaking off to join another harem.

Females in the animal harem are commonly related, but not always. The dominant male gets to mate with all the females if he's not too tired from all his exertions keeping it all together. Most harems are of a temporary nature. Eventually, when the male is no longer a peak performer either sexually or physically, he will be replaced by a challenger. Males who take over a harem may commit infanticide to get the females back into breeding condition quickly.

In the short term, the main beneficiary of the harem is the male. He has exclusive mating rights but must pay dearly for that pleasure. He must constantly fight to keep his position and protect his unit and he could be severely wounded or even killed by a challenger at any time. The benefit for the females in the harem is living in a stable social group with other females, whilst a strong male provides protection for their offspring

Several species in the primate family live in harems. Gorillas, Hamadryas Baboons, Golden Snub-nosed Monkeys, Guinea Baboons and Grey Langurs all use this mating system. It's also seen in bats, birds, fish and insects.

Zebras and Impalas (*Aepyceros melampus*) defend their harem from intruders all year round, whereas other species such as Red Deer and Elephant Seals only bother when it really matters, during the breeding season. Many harem holders ignore their offspring but some are caring, protective fathers. Ostrich fathers take turns to sit on the eggs at night, while his main or major female takes the day shift. It's a good distribution of labour as she's paler and therefore camouflaged in daylight and he melts into the night with his dark plumage. Once the eggs hatch, dad is the one to do most of the child rearing and teaches the youngsters how to feed.

The adults in some non-seasonal harems can remain unchanged for many years. As the father has an important role as the protector of females and offspring, trust exists between the members of the group. The lion pride or a gorilla or baboon troop can be stable for many years. But anyone thinking this is only about privileges and having lots of sex is wrong. It takes a lot of work to be a good harem master. These males must rise to the challenge and be able to handle pressure.

Allan Schmidt, an expert gorilla carer in Taronga Zoo, looked after one such harem master and comments on the pressures a silverback experiences while heading up the family troop:

'Male gorillas take fatherhood responsibilities very seriously and suffer for it because they are more stressed than anybody else in the family. They die younger as they shoulder the stress for the entire group and they worry for everybody else.

Kibabu, a silverback I looked after for many years, was everybody's favourite. He was a magnificent silverback, the epitome of a strong dedicated gorilla male. He lived with three adult females, Mouila, Frala and Kriba, and their combined offspring. I always felt that he took his responsibilities as the leader of his family very earnestly. The life of a male gorilla is not an easy one and they do not live as long as the females. These animals have massive bodies, basically at the limit of the primate body structure and they often experience physiological trauma such as arthritis and heart trouble because of their size. Their organs have to work hard to keep that enormous body mass going. Add this to the pressure of having sole responsibility for the family group and it makes for a stressful life.

If a plane or helicopter flew low overhead, Kibabu would freak out and become anxious on behalf of his whole family. Meanwhile the females would simply keep doing what they were doing, just hanging out. They were not stressed at all because it was Kibabu's job to worry for all of them. He always solved whatever danger they might be faced with so it was not their problem. Kibabu would regularly freak out in these situations, whereas the females were happy knowing he was onto the problem.'

Harem masters of a variety of species live hard and fast for the prime years of their lives. This takes a rapid toll on their bodies as they age but by then they have usually contributed a substantial number of offspring to the next generation, ensuring their genes will perpetuate in the future.

POLYANDRY, FROM THE GREEK 'POLY' (MANY) AND 'ANDRY' (MALE)

This is the female-dominated version of polygamy, meaning one female has two or more male mates. The word comes from the Greek meaning many husbands. This mating system is known in insects, reptiles and frogs, a few bird species, a small number of mammals and most famously in some seahorses. Although it is much rarer than polygamy, through a process of evolution polyandrous species have developed a system that balances the costs and benefits to both genders.

Polyandrous behaviour is popular in many insect species, including honey bees. Around one per cent of bird species, including jacanas and Dunnocks, are polyandrous, as are some primates, such as marmosets. There is a generalisation among humans that all females are choosy and all males are promiscuous, but these examples in the natural world disprove this. In many polyandrous species, the female has multiple sexual partners and is the easy-going one, whilst the males are choosy. This system is much rarer than either monogamy or polygamy, however. In certain circumstances, it makes good sense for females to court several males as this allows her to select more than one sire for her offspring. Females of some species, such as the Australian Brown Antechinus (*Antechinus stuartii*) are able to store the sperm of several males at the same time. These are, by the way, males who literally shag themselves to death (discussed in more detail in Chapter 7). A female antechinus who has several partners is three times more likely to have surviving young than one who had a single partner.

Polyandry tends to be more common when males take care of the progeny or where there are a lot more males than females. A well-known example of a polyandrous mating system is demonstrated in pipefish, which are relatives of the seahorses. Females compete for access to the males. He receives eggs from the female, fertilises them and looks after them in his pouch. Pipefish live in densely populated resource-rich environments. The male pouch is the limiting factor in the baby-making business, so females seek out as many as they can and compete with other pipefish females for a good pouch.

Not all polyandrous female societies leave the child-rearing to the male. Spotted Hyenas are a polyandrous female-dominated carnivore group. However, it is the mother who lavishes maternal care on the pups, which she raises without the help of any of the males she's mated with. Her mate choice does not buy her paternal care for her litter but gives her the best genetic lineage for her pups.

POLYANDROUS DADS

Polyandry is a mating system that not seen often in nature. In birds, two parents caring for young is the standard approach. Fathers in the polyandrous system are usually excellent at their job though. That's why they are there in the first place. Fathers in polyandrous relationship tend to look after the offspring so that the mother can either rest up, put some weight back on, forage for nutritious food to lactate, or maybe even have some additional affairs with other males.

Polyandrous societies are found amongst the New World monkeys of South America. New World monkeys are those that live in the region from Mexico to Argentina, whereas the Old World monkeys span Africa, Arabia and Asia. The Callitrichids, which includes the marmoset and tamarin families, both have devoted fathers who care for tiny twin infants. Social groups of tamarins and marmosets are typically made up of three to ten individuals. The group usually includes only one reproductively active female, a couple of males who are sexually active and a few non-reproductive helpers of either gender. All members of the group help to raise the young. The father and any helpers share the carrying and grooming of the infants.

The fathers in these groups are nature's poster child for paternal devotion. Perhaps it's to be expected that males in polyandrous families make excellent fathers. After all, the entire system probably evolved because they had the ability to be really caring and devoted to their offspring so that mum could get her strength back for milk production. Cooperative polyandry is not the only system found in these families, however. Under different circumstances, the group may change to a monogamous or polygynous mating system. This flexibility is likely because these species' typically give birth to twins. Regardless of what system is used, the mother can do with a bit of help to raise two infants. This makes Callitrichids the primates with the most flexible mating system other than humans. Individuals can even swap between systems depending on their options. However, polyandrous males and females have a higher success rate in raising young, when compared with monogamous pairs of the same species. This suggests that in this species, two dads may be better than one.

DADS IN A POLYANDROUS HAREM

In general, biology predicts that females are the quiet, modest partners in the reproductive system. This is obviously not the case for polyandrous females such as the jacanas, which are bigger and have brighter plumage than the males they court. Jacanas are amongst the small percentage of birds where the female is bigger than the male (this is also seen in shorebirds and birds of prey). Although polyandry is rare in birds, jacanas provide an interesting example of fatherhood. Jacanas are also called 'lily trotters' or 'Jesus birds' – nicknames earned due to their long toes which allow them to spread their weight over aquatic plants such as water lilies, giving the impression that they walk on water.

The female Comb-crested Jacana (*Irediparra gallinacea*) from Asia and northern Australia keeps a male harem and mates with several males. Once she's mated, she's off for more sex with another male. The males are hard-working stay-at-home dads, solely responsible for building a flimsy nest on floating vegetation, where they incubate the eggs and rear the chicks.

A particularly endearing feature of the male jacana's fathering style is that when danger looms he picks up the chicks, tucks them under his wings and takes them to a safe place. These are African Jacanas.

Galápagos Hawks (*Buteo galapagoensis*) are also known to use this breeding strategy. The male starts his seduction by making fake attacks on the female by dive-bombing her. (I've known teenage boys in my youth who also thought this was courtship behaviour). As the female hawk flies down, her suave suitor then follows his chosen one to a tree. Interestingly, the males of this species are thought to be monogamous whilst she will mate with up to seven partners. Throughout the nesting season, the female and her band of males take turns in protecting one to three eggs in the nest, incubating them and feeding the young once they hatch. This mating system can potentially foster good paternal care for the young as well.

Tamarins were once thought to be monogamous but studies of Emperor Tamarins (*Saguinus imperator*) in the wild show that one dominant female mates with multiple males. The males all think they could possibly be the father and work cooperatively with the other males in the harem to raise the infants. Parental care is an all-important factor in infant survival in this species. Multiple caring fathers are more likely to be able to give the constant care the twin babies need. Infant carrying has a fairly high energy costs and a female recovering from giving birth to two fairly large babies is able to forage, eat and regain her condition whilst these fathers take the load off her. Male Emperor Tamarins are very protective and attentive to the youngsters, reacting faster to the call of a baby tamarin in distress than their mother. On the whole, males in a polyandrous mating system make great dads.

FIRST TIME FATHERHOOD LESSONS

A young stallion Przewalski's Horse, also known as the Takhi or Mongolian Wild Horse, I knew in Taronga Western Plains Zoo became infatuated with the mare who gave birth to his firstborn foal. He seemed to have forgotten about polygamy in his species and was heading for monogamy. Stallion Nicolai only had eyes for the female who made him a father for the first time. He completely forgot his duties to the rest of his harem. His role as the stallion is to take his harem to food and water and to protect all the mothers and all their foals. As a relatively inexperienced stallion and perhaps overwhelmed by first time fatherhood Nicolai only cared for his main female and their offspring, neglecting his duties to the other members of his harem once they started dropping foals too.

Nicolay was very protective of his favourite mare and his firstborn foal. He tried to keep all the other females in the herd at a distance from her, shooing them away. He forgot the concept of a harem and having to look after *all* his mares. His attempt to protect his best-loved ones had a negative impact on the herd. He was rough on all others in the harem, kicking out even to his other foals to keep them away from his chosen ones.

After a few weeks the lead mare Gengis and her helper, both experienced mothers, set him straight. They drafted him away from the group and gave him a good hiding. Something they would also have done to a stallion in the wild if he wasn't doing his job. Somehow Nicolai understood the lesson and paid much more attention to all the females and foals in his harem. A couple of wise old mothers pointed out a few home truths to the new dad.

HUMAN SOCIETIES PRACTICING POLYANDRY

Polyandry has been known in a few human cultures, including in Nepal, Tibet, Sri Lanka and India. Between 1962 and 1980, George Murdock published successive instalments of his 'Ethnographic Atlas' in the *Journal of Ethnology*. He lists a total of 1,231 human societies, of which he found 186 to be truly monogamous, 453 had occasional polygyny, 588 had frequent polygyny and four had polyandry. Fraternal polyandry is practiced by Tibetans in Nepal and in parts of China. Under this system two or more brothers marry the same wife and the wife has a sexual relationship with both. Polyandry is more likely to be practiced in societies with fewer resources. The marriage of brothers to the same wife allows the family's land to remain undivided. If both brothers married different wives the land might become too small to sustainably feed two families. In Europe, the solution to splitting the land was to have only the oldest son inherit property and encourage the rest of the boys to be celibate and enter the priesthood.

According to a recent article by Anna Fifield in *The Washington Post*, polyandry has been controversially proposed by a professor at Fudan University in Shanghai as a solution to overcome the effects of the China one-child policy and as a way to encourage women to have more babies. For more than three decades China's Communist Party advocated that couples should have one child only. As a result, today there are some 100 million people under the age of 40 who were born in a one-child household. The preference for sons led to baby girls frequently being aborted, resulting in some 34 million more men than women of marriageable age.

'If you have a couple of husbands you may be more likely to have two children,' Professor Yew-Kwang Ng suggested in the face of an imbalanced gender ratio. To date I do not believe it's been adopted as a formal policy.

POLYGYNANDRY

A variation on polyandry is called polygynandry. This is where plural breeding happens within a social system. In this system, two or more males have an exclusive relationship with at least two or more females, but not necessarily equal numbers on either side. Often the number of males is lower than the number of females. Polygynandry may be advantageous from the female's perspective because it causes paternity confusion, which decreases infanticide and allows her to potentially have several males to help her raise the youngsters. For the males it means access to females without having to fight other males and risk injury or even death defending them.

PROMISCUITY

Promiscuity is the most prevalent reproductive system in mammals. This term can carry a moral judgement in our society. Exactly what is considered promiscuous differs amongst various cultures. Different standards are frequently applied to the different genders. Whereas a promiscuous man can be considered a 'stud', a promiscuous woman may be called a 'slut'.

Stories of promiscuity have both scandalised and titillated society for centuries. Still a favourite subject in the media now, we seem to love hearing about a conservative politician having an affair after having been elected on a platform of family values. Even in more conservative times, reading what went on in other people's sex lives has held an interest. Made famous and notorious through his autobiography, *Histoire de Ma Vie*, Giacomo Casanova described the sexual exploits common amongst the nobles of the 18th century. The Italian adventurer's writing provides an authentic insight into the flirtations, bedroom games and short-term affairs that were de rigueur amongst his contemporaries. European nobility at that time married for social connection rather than love, which left the door wide open for extramarital liaisons. Despite being essentially known as a socially monogamous species, we seem to do promiscuity rather well. But then this is a family trait we share with our animal relatives.

Our closest relatives in the great ape family, the Chimpanzees and Bonobos, subscribe to a promiscuous mating system, both sexes mating randomly with a variety of partners. Females mate with multiple males and males with multiple females. Chimpanzees live in large social groups and one dominant male can't prevent all other males from mating with a sexually attractive female, even if he may try. Promiscuity is common where a single male is not able to dominate a group of females and keep tabs on them. This has advantages for both genders. For female chimps there are advantages to an occasional hook-up with a male who is not the alpha as it provides varied genes to sire her offspring and creates a relationship with another male. The official term for this stolen mating is 'kleptogamy', although a more universally used term is the 'sneaky f*cker strategy' given to this phenomena by the evolutionary biologist John Maynard Smith.

Bonobos, with whom we share 98.7 per cent of our DNA (as we

do with chimps), are hyper-sexual beings. In most mammal groups, females are sexually receptive for a couple of days around ovulation. Bonobos, however, are known to engage in sexual activity as a greeting, to resolve conflict, to reduce tension and to form bonds. Before Frans de Waal studied Bonobos in San Diego Zoo in 1983, we thought ourselves to be the only species on the planet to have sex for fun and bonding and not just for conception. De Waal reported Bonobos performing tongue kissing, fellatio and a whole *Kamasutra* of sexual positions. Sexual encounters in Bonobos take place in all combinations of ages and genders. The only taboo appears to be between mothers and their sons, whereas young Bonobo females leave their natal group as teenagers so is no chance of conceiving a

Most animals mate when the female is 'in season', that is, she is ovulating and ready to make babies. Humans and Bonobos, a great ape closely related to us, sex for pleasure as well as reproduction.

baby from their father or brothers. When each female mates with a number of males, paternity becomes clouded. This serves to protect infants from infanticide, which is not evolutionarily advantageous.

Promiscuity is also a common strategy in species of pelagic fish who need to take their chances when they can in the big open ocean. If you see another fish and they are the right gender, go for it. It is also a quite widespread strategy in amphibians where there are large populations in small ponds. The sexual contact is opportunistic rather than carefully considered.

THE PROMISCUOUS DAD

In promiscuity there are no pair bonds. Promiscuity is more likely to happen in environments where the conditions are unpredictable. If you come across someone of the opposite sex and one of you happens to be in oestrus, well then take advantage! The random quality of mating in promiscuous species does not make committed loving fathers. Not all promiscuous dads should get a bad rap, for there are cases of promiscuous males who are also great fathers. It has long been thought that promiscuity excluded any fatherly involvement because how could a male be sure his efforts were lavished on his own child and not some other male's? However, research by Carson Murray and colleagues seems to suggest that males in some promiscuous species at least recognise their descendants. In Chimpanzees, it was found that fathers hang out with their own genetic offspring more often than could be expected to happen by chance. This did not result in that male being more likely to sire the mother's next baby. The researchers therefore concluded that a capacity for paternal care is possible independent of long-term mother-father bonds and may have existed in early hominin evolution.

Chimpanzees and Bonobos, on the whole, do not get a lot of medals for the best father in the promiscuous animal kingdom, however. Devoted wild fathers are more commonly found in species with a monogamous mating system and we'll meet some in the next chapter.

GENDER FLUID – THE NATURAL SEX CHANGE

Many species have same-sex encounters but there are also many that are gender-bending, changing how they look or even their biology. We can't know if an animal is 'transgender' or how it feels about its gender identity, for that we need to know what it's thinking. It is clear though that some animals such as the cuttlefish can change their sex, or at least change their appearance, to look like another gender.

In some animals changing sex is a normal anatomical process, this includes many species of coral reef fishes such as moray eels, wrasses, gobies and clownfish. Whereas in the clownfish the sex change is from male to female, in the wrasses (family Labridae) the change is from female to male. If the dominant male dies or disappears, the largest female in harem changes into a male and takes over as harem master.

Natural sex change is also known in mushroom corals (they are animals too!) which can change either way just to be convenient to each and every situation. This changing gender at will is not a party trick or a folly. It happens for reasons such as a lack of the opposite gender in the population. The ability to do so is called sequential hermaphrodism.

Chapter 6

MONOGAMY – JUST YOU AND ME BABE

'I reject monogamy as an affront to evolution.'

DAN BROWN

MONOGAMY

We expect fathers in monogamous relationships to be caregivers. There are many interesting and faithful fathers amongst the monogamous pairs: Mandarin Ducks, swans, many penguin species, pigeons and doves, gibbons and many more. A strong bond and mutual fidelity can have advantages. Fathers can be more confident about paternity and mothers can count on help raising the young. Monogamy frequently only occurs in species who work cooperatively in several aspects of their lives, such as hunting or defending the territory against predators or intruders. This is the case with beavers who can't build a dam on their own, or African Wild Dogs who need each other to bring down large prey. These animals may pair for life.

Monogamy is more typical in birds than in mammals like us.

It is of course often debated whether we humans are in fact as monogamous as is stated. Only a small proportion of all mammals are monogamous, compared with nearly all birds. The number and needs of the offspring a species has determines what kind of sexual strategy evolves. Monogamy and involved fatherhood are regularly found together in the natural world and seems to be a likely reproductive strategy when food is scarce and predators are many. In such a situation, the care of both parents is necessary to find enough food and protect the young.

Birds, like this male Eurasian Golden Oriole, tend to be more involved fathers than mammals. Defence of the nest against predators requires constant vigilance. The demands of feeding many hatchlings is also a job that needs both parents to help the youngsters reach independence.

Baby birds hatch out of the egg in one of two ways: altricial or precocial. Precocial birds, like chickens and malleefowl, get up after hatching and start to feed themselves pretty soon after. Altricial birds hatch as helpless, naked and blind creatures. Both parents are therefore needed to bring up altricial young as they demand a lot of attention. The parent birds must build the nest, keep the eggs at the right temperature constantly and protect them against predators, while the chicks need warmth and a continuous supply of nutritious food. Monogamy or at least serial monogamy is therefore an effective strategy in birds with altricial young as it takes two adults at least to raise such helpless fragile little chicks. For parents of such helpless critters, two individuals on the job is essential, therefore monogamy or at least serial monogamy is the right sexual strategy for so many bird species.

Non-monogamous bird species usually have precocial young. For example, Emu young, once hatched, are well developed and one parent can do the work. The other parent is now free to have more sex, lay more eggs and produce more offspring. Similarly, when young mammals, such as antelope and giraffe, are mobile and capable enough of getting straight up on their feet and following mum and the herd, they are less likely to need a dad.

Monogamy clearly evolves as a sexual strategy when both parents are absolutely essential to the successful rearing of one or more young. Closely related species generally have the same or a similar social and reproductive system. Humans are part of the great ape family along with chimps, Bonobos, gorillas and orangutans, but there's no monogamy and little paternal care to be found in any of our cousin species. So why are we so different?

There must have been a good reason for our ancient ancestors to evolve in such a dramatically different manner from our ape relatives. For our closest practicing monogamist in the primate family, we need to look at the lesser apes, the gibbons and siamangs found in South-East Asia. In these groups we find monogamy as the norm. The two families, the great apes and the lesser apes, are related and share many a common trait, but faithfulness, only found in our more distant cousins the lesser apes, is not amongst those.

When I first worked as a zookeeper at Taronga Zoo in Sydney, I looked after Müller's Gibbons. Gibbons are strongly monogamous and in the wild live in family groups occupying a large territory in the forest. They are thought to mate for life and together the pair defends their home against other gibbons, the conflicts being ritualised with noisy mock battles between rivals. I looked after a gibbon called Mary who was middle-aged and lived alone after she lost her mate of many years. As gibbons mate for life, we worried that Mary might be lonely and brought a young male from another zoo as company for her. She would not have a bar of him. Despite our careful, gentle introduction she refused to share her space with the new male. In fact, she resorted to domestic violence in an attempt to make him leave her island. We found a new home for this rejected suitor at the earliest opportunity and later found a more welcoming partner for him with whom he lived in matrimonial bliss ever after. After careful consideration, we decided that Mary preferred the life of a merry widow rather than becoming the gibbon version of a cradle snatcher.

She did however show a distinct preference for male zookeepers. Allan Schmidt was her favourite, a carer she sought to comfort her when something startled her. She jumped on him for a hug when a loud truck passed by her island home. On another occasion, Allan fondly remembers her 'saving him': 'One day she seemed really agitated as I came onto her island. She quickly approached me and swiped at my chest. Knocking off a large huntsman spider on my shirt that I was clearly unaware of. As I'm slightly arachnophobic I appreciated the help when such a large specimen was on me.'

One of my own favourite memories of Mary is her melodious sunrise call. Normally, gibbon calls are characterised by a duet performed by the loved-up couple. After her partner's demise, Mary kept up her haunting solo hoots each morning, ringing out over the zoo grounds as keepers arrived at sun-up to start their shift. Quite a few of us would call back to Mary, mimicking gibbon calls as best we could, just to make her feel that her efforts were appreciated. Mary demonstrated that 'pairing for life' meant something to her. Our favourite merry widow lived for quite a few years on her own before old age caught up with her.

MONOGAMY AND FIDELITY

Monogamy and fidelity are held in high regard in many human cultures, yet divorce rates are sky high, which seriously questions the idea that humans can stick to one sexual partner for life. Sexual fidelity is tricky for most species. Males are genetically programmed to mate with as many females as they can whilst they benefit from absolute commitment from the ladies. Females are evolutionarily hardwired to find the best, strongest, fittest male to sire their progeny. That can take some fooling around too. Monogamy is a huge risk for both partners as they bet their entire parental investment on the fitness of their chosen one. The pressure to pick the right one, as we humans know too well, is enormous.

Although monogamy is more frequent in birds, it does exist in mammals and humans may gain more insight from looking at the small proportion of mammals which form life-long bonds. Of the approximately 5,000 mammal species on the planet, only about 5 per cent are thought to be monogamous. Wolves, beavers, foxes, otters and a few others are amongst the romantics that commit to each other for the long haul. Even so, they may occasionally have affairs on the side. If one of the pair dies, the remaining partner may replace their mate as soon as a suitable candidate shows up. Many animals are serially monogamous. They stay with a partner for a breeding season or even meet up again the next breeding season.

Monogamy is found even amongst reptiles. The Australian Shingleback skink is almost unique in the lizard world in pairing up with the same partner each year.

Others are monogamous 'until death do us part'.

Many mammals are territorial, regardless of the sort of mating strategy they use. Defending resources against rivals is a common way animals secure food, water and shelter – all the essentials for survival. A territory with resources makes a potential mating partner more desirable. Monogamy tends to go hand-in-hand with territoriality. The males are in competition for territory *and* females, defending both from the competition.

Not all monogamy is the same. In nature we see both sexual monogamy, whereby partners only have sex with each other, and social monogamy, where pairs mate and bring up progeny together but may have flings with other partners. A combination of these is probably the norm in humans and many other animals. Swans have long been celebrated as a beautiful and elegant prototype of fidelity but are now known to cheat and have a 'bit on the side'. Once it became possible to use DNA to determine paternity, it was abundantly clear that social monogamy and sexual monogamy are different notions.

LOVE HORMONES

Animals which practise monogamy also seem to have an ancient neuropeptide called oxytocin as part of their biology. The Prairie Vole (*Microtus ochrogaster*), a small rodent from (you guessed it!) the prairies of central North America, has been of interest to scientists because it commits to one partner for life. The voles build their nests together and share the parental role equally, which makes them appear a worthy poster child of true monogamy. What scientists have discovered is that Prairie Voles have enhanced receptors for feel-good hormones, causing an addiction to the close social contact the pair maintains. These hormones are released during embracing and spending quality time together. Nature's lesson here is that cuddling is good for us. People in love have more of this hormone on board than those who are not in love.

Oxytocin is sometimes called the 'cuddle hormone' or the 'love hormone' because of the association with pair bonding. This hormone reinforces the bond between mothers and infants and the bond between starry-eyed lovers. Gibbons, our monogamous ape cousins, cuddle a lot, not simply grooming like other primates. Scientists report that humans have higher levels of oxytocin after orgasm than before. Our oxytocin levels are increased by cuddling, hugging and having sex. Robert Sapolsky in his book *Behave: The Biology of Humans at Our Best and Worst*, states that:

'According to lore, oxytocin makes organisms less aggressive, more socially attuned, trusting and empathic. Individuals treated with oxytocin become more faithful partners and more attentive parents. It makes lab rats more charitable and better listeners, makes fruit flies sing like Joan Baez.'

Oxytocin is also released by the pituitary gland during birth and whilst nursing a baby. This neuropeptide is often given to help the birthing process along in humans and it is this oxytocin that helps maintain the pair-bond. Research has shown that men in committed relationships choose to keep their distance from attractive women when given oxytocin in a nasal spray. Oxytocin therefore seems to play an important role in monogamy and fidelity.

The Prairie Vole mentioned earlier has a close relative, the Meadow Vole (*Microtus pennsylvanicus*). The two closely related vole species have vastly different social dynamics and reproduction. The Meadow Vole is promiscuous whereas the Prairie Vole is an icon of fidelity. Prairie Voles have significantly more oxytocin receptors in their brain than their Meadow Vole cousins. Before you think that a nasal spray might bring your cheating partner into line, further research on the Prairie Vole shows that despite producing high levels of the 'love hormone', the male Prairie Vole does have the odd illicit affair.

THE MONOGAMOUS DAD

The Wandering Albatross (*Diomedea exulans*) is thought to pair for life. As they can live for over 50 years, that's an impressive effort in the fidelity stakes. Pairs of Wandering Albatrosses breed in alternate years on Subantarctic islands. Although they live quite separate lives outside the breeding season, flying long-haul to search for food, once the biannual breeding season arrives, they find one another again. They manage to hook up after all that time, and without the need for mobile phones or email!

These large seabirds rebuild and reinforce the pair bond by courting as if it were the first time. They spread their wings, wave their heads and clack their bills whilst braying loudly. That's enough for both of them to renew their marriage vows. A mounded nest of mud and vegetation is placed on a ridge with a good view of the sea. An egg is laid and both parents take turns to incubate it, giving their partner a chance to go and fish at sea. Once the single egg hatches, both parents hunt to feed their precious chick. The parents appear to work together successfully as studies confirm that more than 31 per cent of albatross fledglings survive. Research also shows that dads bring back more food for their offspring than females do and that male chicks receive more of it than female chicks do. An unexplained bias, perhaps?

A MONKEY MODEL OF MONOGAMY

There are critters that are truly monogamous rather than just socially monogamous, which is a lot more common. Azara's Night Monkeys from South America are thought to be monogamous on all counts. In animals, as in humans, social monogamy, or living as a pair, does not equate to sexual monogamy. True monogamy is also called genetic monogamy, meaning that if you check the paternity of offspring, the mother's usual partner is indeed the father. Unlike many humans, this little nocturnal monkey truly is faithful to its mate. Night monkeys live in small groups consisting of a pair of reproductive adults, one infant and one to two juveniles. The male protects his female and prevents other males from mating with her. According to Maren Huck from the University of Derby in England, the fact that both partners are faithful suggests a link between joint parental care and less sexual cheating.

One night monkey infant is born each year and dad is the primary carer. From an evolutionary perspective the theory is that this male has more to gain from shepherding his offspring to independence than sewing his seeds more widely and leaving his babies to an unknown fate. These little primates are unusual in several ways. As they are nocturnal, their big eyes have adapted to seeing better in the dark forest at night. The mother carries the youngster for a week or so and then hands over to dad. The father's care for the infant is thought to increase its survival chances because the mother can put her energy into producing quality milk which makes the baby strong. After the father takes over, he carries baby up to 90 per cent of the time. He supports his partner by sharing food with her when she's lactating. If a lactating female is depleted from pregnancy and birthing, she may be too weak to forage for herself and stop nursing the child. By sharing his food, dad ensures milk production for the youngster, but this kind of resource-sharing by primates is only observed where the male is quite sure of his paternity. After all, you wouldn't want to be giving tasty morsels to your partner if she's been playing away from home…

HOW DID WE BECOME MONOGAMOUS?

Robin Dunbar, in his book *Grooming, Gossip and the Evolution of Language,* defines evolution as 'the outcome of a successful solution to the problem'. Our existence today in our current form is the result of predecessors successfully having solved problems of survival and adapting to challenging circumstances. Our forebears survived at least long enough to have babies and pass their genes on to us and we continue to evolve today and into the future, adapting as we go.

Charles Darwin hypothesised that our ancestors left the forests in Africa in favour of the open plains. Along the way, our early relatives developed the ability to walk on two legs, a more suitable way of moving about on the savanna. A study by Michael Sockol found that walking upright could have been more energy-efficient than the quadrupedal knuckle-walking of early ape-like humans. Exactly why and when early humans stood upright and started moving around on two feet is still being speculated.

Once we did not need arms and hands for locomotion, we could use them for other things, such as holding weapons and making and using tools. This in turn may have encouraged the growth of a bigger, better brain, although a more recent theory is that increased socialising and language development required a larger brain. Yet another theory suggests that our more advanced brain is the result of sexual selection. A big brain means intelligence and intelligence is sexy as it aids survival. The human brain is unusually large. Our brains have tripled in size from those of early humans and are almost six times larger than expected for a placental mammal of our size.

On the plains, our forefathers changed their largely vegetarian diet to include more meat. While a little meat is eaten by other primates, we added a lot of protein to our diet. Our evolution from mostly vegetarians to carnivorous predators is therefore quite unique in the primate world. Desmond Morris in *The Naked Ape* illustrates the way our predecessors transformed:

'His whole body, his way of life, was geared to a forest existence and then suddenly (suddenly in evolutionary terms) he was jettisoned into a world where he could survive only if he began to live like a brainy, weapon-toting wolf.'

Our predecessors took to hunting for meat on the open plains with gusto. They now had their hands free to carry weapons. The larger brain facilitated the making and use of tools and our communication skills helped us to hunt cooperatively. At this time there were already some very accomplished hunters filling this ecological niche on the plains of Africa. Lions, African Wild Dogs, Cheetahs and hyenas all competed for game. These carnivore species were eminently better designed for the job, having superior hearing and smell. On top of that, both these large cat-like and dog-like species seemed to have an enhanced physical design for sprinting and long-distance running. Humans at this point had only just managed to walk upright. We needed that bigger brain to outsmart them all. Our progress from a forest-dwelling primate to a hunter-gatherer is a long one, an evolutionary path for which we did not seem to be very well designed in terms of speed, hearing, smell or teeth. It seems that our brain, not our body, was a determining factor in our success.

As we evolved from arboreal primates to walking upright, our hips narrowed and as a consequence the birth canal in females followed suit. At the same time, we started to develop the bigger brains we're proud of. If we combine a narrow birth canal with a bigger head, you can see that a problem emerges. Something needed to change and that was giving birth to large offspring. Our babies needed to be born much less advanced than other primate babies. Essentially, human offspring are born very premature, even if they are technically full term. A baby monkey can walk a couple of hours after being born and their brains are fully grown, whereas human babies need another 12 months to reach the same stage of development as their primate cousins. If our babies were to be born with their brains as developed as monkeys at birth, women would need to be pregnant for another 12 months. This would total about 21 months of pregnancy, about the same length of gestation as an elephant.

Chimp and Bonobo babies are perfectly capable of clinging to their mother for dear life as she climbs trees and swings through the branches, but a human newborn can do little more than grip their mother's finger. Even so, women have more painful births than other primates. We evolved to deliver babies with big heads that are difficult to push out and these underdeveloped offspring need so much attention that the mother can't go out hunting and gathering for quite a while. Humans are still born with a hole in their head, the fontanelle, covered only with a bit of skin, because their brain needs to grow a lot more and the skull must adapt to that growth. These are some good reasons to explain why humans need fathers to be involved in looking after both the offspring and the new mother.

TRUE LOVE

Love is what keeps people bonded. From a Darwinian point-of-view, love evolved to keep people together for long enough to raise their children at least to sexual maturity. Because childhood is so much longer in humans than in other species, both the mating bond and parental bond have to be exceptionally strong. Human progeny rely on their special adults to teach them the things they need to know to live independently and successfully. But having fallen in love, how do humans stay in love? In other primates, females are not interested in sex whilst breastfeeding and the male is not attracted to a lactating female who doesn't ovulate. The human great ape, however, is not focussed on producing more offspring, but has sex for the sake of cementing the pair bond. We see more complexity in the human sexual act because a rewarding experience for both partners, using variation and novelty, will prevent boredom in a long-term bonded pair.

DEMANDING EXTREME FIDELITY

As a male what do you do if you want to be extra sure that you're not being cheated on? You lock up your partner! That the solution that the Rhinoceros Hornbills of South-East Asia have come up with. When in pairs they have an enchanting duet. Performing this helps to keep the love alive. He calls out a short note 'hok' to which she replies with a short 'hak'. Together they celebrate their special bond with a 'hok, hak, hok, hak, hok, hak' song.

After mating the female climbs inside a nest cavity in a hollow tree trunk and together the pair seal the entrance with mud and excrement until there's only a small slit left. She now completely relies on her mate for her survival. The faithful father-to-be feeds her and the hatchlings through this narrow slit. The mother also uses the slit to expel her and the nestlings' faeces. The mud wall is removed before the fledglings are ready to leave the nest.

The monogamous mating system may not work very well if the female is off-line for extended periods preoccupied with raising our big-brained slow-growing little people. For this bond to last the distance, there have to be trade-offs to reward fidelity. Humans have evolved a number of external signs to make us the sexy ape that we are. The special time we take before copulation to stroke and caress far exceeds anything we see in other primates. We even have specialised organs such as lips, nipples, earlobes and genitals that are sensitive to tactile stimulation. Females have evolved enlarged, protruding breasts which are often thought of as a maternal necessity rather than a sexual feature, but there is not a lot of evidence to support this. Breasts are more likely noticeably sexual flags to attract the opposite sex. The number of breast enlargement surgeries worldwide seems to attest to this theory. The American Society of Plastic Surgeons reports that over 300,000 breast augmentations took place in the US in 2018 alone.

Our species has found a rather unique way of keeping the pair bond strong over the long haul: continuous sexual attraction. This is why we do not have a distinct breeding season like so many other animals. Mating can and does happen at any time of the year, despite the fact that the human female is only fertile for a few days each month. However, the human pair-bonding system is not foolproof as we know and things can go wrong. Our pair-bond system was grafted onto the old primate system which is rather more promiscuous or polygamous and this still surfaces now and then. If the pair bond is temporarily weakened, earlier primate urges may flare up. This is coupled with the fact that our evolutionary development includes an increase in childlike curiosity being extended well into adulthood. Both these factors endanger the pair-bond.

The advantage of frequent sex is that we get close, touching, hugging and cuddling, which all help to stimulate the release of the feel-good hormone oxytocin. Sex is what bonds initially, but bonded couples develop a deep love and attachment to one another. Love is what keeps couples close. Without love, it's hard to see how the human species could have lasted this long. In species that pair up for the long haul, the relationship is constantly reinforced and the couple renew their commitment through grooming, feeding or communicating in species-specific ways.

BABY-BRINGING STORKS

The European legend of the White Stork (*Ciconia ciconia*) is historically intertwined with the arrival of a baby. When the baby arrives, many new parents put an image in the window or a statue of a stork in the garden with the details of the new baby. Date and time born, gender, name and weight. This way the neighbours know the baby is born.

Well-wishing cards depict the long-legged bird as the creature delivering the baby, with a cloth bundle carried in the bird's long red bill. Storks are monogamous and caring parents and they are large and conspicuous, often nesting close to people in villages and towns. This myth about storks as the bringers of babies spans a wide area covering Europe, the Americas, North Africa and the Middle East. Myths are hard to trace but popular culture pinpoints the origin of this folklore to ancient Greece. A vindictive goddess, Hera, was jealous of a beautiful queen named Gerana and changed her into a stork. Gerana, now stork, went to get her baby and the Greeks depicted the queen as a stork carrying a baby in her beak. The story of the stork has become popular too perhaps as a way of obscuring the need for sex to have babies. For parents, embarrassed to explain the fact of life, the myth is a useful tale to maintain prudishness.

MONOGAMISH?

Marriage vows in most Western countries include something like 'until death do us part', whereas divorce rates disprove this vow time and time again. None of the other great apes are monogamous. It is therefore possible that our common ancestor was polygynous or promiscuous. There is no anatomical evidence for monogamy, whereas there is for the other mating systems. Where monogamy exists in animals the pair is usually the same size and shows no sexual dimorphism. There's still a size difference between men and women, perhaps suggesting that the early human social system was polygamous or promiscuous like the other African apes. Our canine teeth also add to the story here. In early humans, males had canine teeth some 25 per cent larger than females – another sign of sexual dimorphism pointing at polygamy. The size of human male canines has been getting smaller and smaller and they are now only ten per cent bigger than females. Robin Dunbar, in his book *Grooming, Gossip and the Evolution of Language*, states that the sexual dimorphism seen in humans implies a shift over time from a strongly polygamous mating system towards mild polygamy.

One of the main reasons we're at least socially monogamous is because we need both parents to raise our freaky little hole-in-the-head babies. Some scientists suggest that monogamy developed because our diet changed: the fact that food was more spread out meant that males could only mate-guard one female at the time, or perhaps a male could not hunt enough meat to feed more than one female. However it has come about, very few animal species have proven to be truly monogamous. Many human societies aspire to be socially and culturally monogamous, even if the reality is imperfect with occasional lapses in fidelity. Maybe it's more accurate to say humans are 'monogamish'.

SERIAL REPTILE LOVE

The Australian Shingleback (*Tiliqua rugosa*) is almost unique in the lizard world by pairing up with the same partner each year. These skinks are very long-lived and stay in touch with their preferred partner through scent trails to find each other again and again every spring for 20 years or more. The male is thought to stroke and lick his partner. The young of these lizards do not hatch from an egg but are born as fully-formed miniature adults. If it all works out, the female gives birth to two live young each year.

Unfortunately, the scaly lovers are separated for human 'entertainment' as described in this article in *Reptiles Magazine* by Karl-Heinz Switak:

> 'An event took place that was definitely to our liking. It involved a 'stumpy race,' with excessive betting on the side. An Aboriginal boy had been sent out to collect about a dozen Shinglebacks earlier, and now, each animal was marked with white paint so that you knew which beast you were betting on. One had a bar across the back, another two bars, one a large dot on its head, and so on. A large area next to the pub had been cleared of obstacles and surrounded by a rope configured into a circle. In the centre, the young boy now dumped all of the lizards at once, and from then on, the coaxing, screaming and swearing began. Once the fastest lizard reached the rope, the race was over. Believe it or not, Shinglebacks are capable of moving fairly quickly (about

the same speed as a blue-tongued skink). Now bets were either collected or paid off, and within minutes there was standing room only in the pub. The stumpies were placed back into a large box, about three layers deep, and released nearby.'

This 'outback tradition', for a few minutes of drunken amusement, is a tragedy for the bonded pair. They're unlikely to ever find each other again. After the 'races' the animals are let go and many are killed on the roads near the pub as they try to get back home.

MONOGAMY: JUST YOU AND ME AND ME

Chapter 7

TOOLS FOR THE JOB

'Sometimes a cigar is just a cigar.'

SIGMUND FREUD

FATHERING EQUIPMENT AND PENIS ENVY

Sigmund Freud thought that the necktie was symbolic of the penis. Sigmund did think that many things were symbolic of the male appendage, including dreams about church steeples! But clearly when we talk about fatherhood, the penis is an all-important attribute. The penis is an essential bit of kit for the prospective mammalian father in particular.

Some animals treat the penis in peculiar ways. A curiously frequent phenomenon in nature is males using their literal manhood as a sword to combat other males. Bonobos are famous for their legendary penis fencing. They have been observed crossing swords whilst hanging upside down in trees and seem to do so to be friendly, to resolve conflict or just because they are excited about something.

Most other species treat their member more respectfully. All backboned animals, including humans, rely on sex for continued existence. Early in the fathering business, the penis is a significant piece of paraphernalia. It puts the sperm where it needs to be. There are so many different designs for the penis that it seems like evolution has never-ending resourcefulness in thinking up new designs. Snakes, for example have two appendages, other animals have penis bones, while still others have phalluses as long as your arm or like a corkscrew. Sexual selection has shaped the genitalia of every species on Earth and the variation is startlingly impressive. Humans too have evolved to have the genitalia we have because these have also adapted to the kind of sex we have.

Mating can be a tricky business for many species. Some use hooks, spines, darts and syringes to bring eggs and sperm together. If you've ever agonised about whether your penis is 'normal', you can stop wondering now. Unless it has four heads and you're not an echidna, you most likely fit the norm for your species. The diversity both between species and within species is much greater than most of us imagine. Some creatures have a hydraulic form of penis with small muscles to make it function. Humans and horses have a vascular penis that takes a bit longer to become erect, while cats have spines on their glans and pigs have a corkscrew shape. There are literally thousands of different blueprints for the key mammalian fathering tool. Once early life evolved and left the oceans, animals had to come up with a way to get the sperm to the eggs whilst remaining moist and being able to swim to their destination. Like a salmon swimming upstream, this little bundle of DNA often has to cover an enormous distance to meet an egg, even if it is deposited as close as it can go.

For all mammals, the fertilisation of the eggs by the sperm happens deep inside the female's body. Human sperm swim almost

1,000 times their own length through the cervix and into the uterus to reach the fallopian tube. Only a few are fit enough to ever make their destination. This is one of the reasons why males produce large amounts of sperm compared to the limited number of eggs a female produces. There are many casualties along the way and only the fast, strong swimmers have a chance.

DELAYING NEW FATHERHOOD?

When's a good moment to become a father for the first time? In *The New York Times* Nicholas Bakalar reports that humans in the Western world are delaying fatherhood more and more. The average age to become a newly minted father is now 30.9 years in the US, up from 27.4 in 1972. Researchers at Stanford University in the USA looked at data for live births between 1972 and 2015 and found that the age of new fathers had increased for all ethnicities and for fathers with different educational levels. In Japan, the age for first-time dads has increased even more and is up from 30.7 in 1972 to 36.3 in 2015.

The same study also found that first-time fathers over the age of 40 jumped from 4.1 per cent in 1972 to 8.9 per cent in 2015.

THE LONG AND SHORT OF IT

Length and frequency of mating has just as many variations in animal species as penis designs. Rodents only insert their penis for a second or two while a rhinoceros's intromission may last 30 minutes or more. Copulating carnivores generally collapse during intercourse but the swollen tip of the penis makes sure that withdrawal is not possible until the transfer of sperm is completed. This prolonged union gives the swimming sperm a better chance of reaching the egg.

Domestic rams and bulls are even quicker to climax and are known to have one ejaculatory thrust that lasts merely a second. So much for being as fit as a Mallee bull! Baboon copulation lasts about 15 thrusts, roughly 30 seconds, whereas the Australian dasyurids of the genus *Antechinus* can copulate for hours on end. These small marsupial mammals are semelparous, meaning that they only mate once and die not long after. An individual antechinus has been clocked mating for almost 14 hours straight, while a 12-hour mating session is not unusual. After that sterling effort, the male's immune system gives up and it dies soon after. Dasyurids literally live by the motto *live hard and die young*.

When it comes to frequency or stamina, there are some impressive examples in the animal kingdom. During Lion mating time at Taronga Zoo, I would regularly hear mating roars ringing out across the zoo for days on end as I worked quietly in my office. Females are polyestrous, meaning they cycle throughout the year and heat lasts about four days. This means they can often be found mating every 15 minutes for four days straight. Quite a feat. No wonder the females do most of the hunting – the male, as the sire of the pride's cubs, is no doubt too busy or too tired to do much more than 'service' all his females. The constant call of mating lions when you're trying to finish up a report can be a tad distracting! Add in the huffing and puffing of copulating giant tortoises and it's almost impossible to escape the noises of procreation when surrounded by wild animals.

DOES SIZE MATTER?

There is a saying, 'Big man, big cock; small man, all cock'. However, the animal world does not support this theory. The mighty gorilla, weighing in at about 200 kilograms (440 pounds), has a penis that measures a mere 6 centimetres (2.4 inches) when erect. So does size really matter in humans? The penis, as a sexual organ, has evolved under the influence of sexual selection and we have learned that sexual activity is important for reinforcing the bond between a monogamous pair.

Perhaps a larger penis can result in greater stimulation that makes sex more enjoyable, which therefore aids in reinforcing the pair-bond. In the gorilla, however, sex may only be for procreation and usually only happens once the female has weaned her last offspring. Theoretically there's no great advantage for a gorilla in developing a large member: as a harem master, he has no competition. Human males can take heart in the knowledge that amongst our ape cousins *Homo sapiens* has the thickest and most flexible member. If it were a competition, the awe-inspiring gorilla would lose as he has the smallest penis of all the great apes, followed by the orangutan. Humans are pretty much on par with Bonobo and Chimpanzee for length and all have appendages which are up to three times longer than a gorilla's wiener. Chimpanzees and Bonobos proudly display their penis to females and presumably a larger penis makes for a better display.

The fact that, biologically, the size of the human penis exceeds its functional requirements may indicate that display was, in ancient times, a possible reason for the length. Humans however will and do get into big trouble if they show off their members to passers by, although it is interesting to note that with the advent of smart phones and 'sexting', 'dick pics' have emerged as an equivalent sexual display and might be seen as a courtship ritual. Perhaps the mobile phone is becoming a tool that can be used in sexual selection?

It is sometimes postulated that humans are well-endowed so they can perform a wide range of sexual positions to prevent boredom during their long-lasting monogamous relationships. Orangutans, however, still manage to perform in a range of positions that easily outdo humans and they do so with a pecker measuring only 8.5 centimetres (3.3 inches)! In conclusion, men have a penis length similar to our closest primate cousins, chimps and Bonobos, although somewhat thicker and more flexible, but the purpose of the length may be more to do with sexual selection 'displays' rather than functionality.

Other species, less closely related to humans, have interesting accessories as well. An excited male Brazilian Tapir (*Tapirus terrestris*) is so well endowed that he can accidentally step on his penis causing him to yelp in pain. The size makes his romantic overtures quite ungainly and getting it into position means lots of swinging about to get into the female's reproductive tract. As this species spends a lot of time in water, a nifty adaptation is a couple of large flaps near the end of the penis that makes a seal inside the female and allows for mating to happen whilst submerged, as well as on land.

When mentioning tapirs recently to an old colleague, Libby Kartzoff, formerly the manager of Exotic Fauna at Taronga Zoo, she shared her memory of a Brazilian Tapir called Toby:

'The ungulate keepers' office was in the old Giant Panda building for a while, complete with large windows that looked into the adjoining dens. It had become a South American exhibit, occupied by three Capybara males and a male Brazilian Tapir. In his solitary state, the tapir occasionally entertained himself by masturbating through his front legs. Although a rather off-putting element to morning tea, there was a collective awe that evolution had created such an elaborate appendage. Not only can a tapir's penis seek its way some distance forward (for reproductive purposes) but it can also accurately spray urine several metres backwards (as a territorial statement).'

Not all appendages are as functional as tapir Toby's. If there is a problem with the penis there are now surgical solutions. Inflatable penile prostheses have been around since the 1970s and are considered a good cure for erectile dysfunction as they involve only a one-off procedure. Some 25,000 patients annually have surgery for such prosthetics in the USA alone. Furthermore, pharmaceutical companies have developed a good many drugs for any number of rectifiable dysfunctions. As an aside, my email inbox is full of offers of penis enlargements based, no doubt, on my recent search history for this book!

ODD PENISES

Not to be outdone in the penis department, the Lake Duck (*Oxyura vittata*) from South America has a member that corkscrews into the female duck's vagina, which threads in the opposite direction. This gives the female some control over who she wants to be the daddy of her ducklings. As if that was not special enough, North American scientists consider the Lake Duck the winner of the award for the longest bird penis of all time, with an organ measuring 42.5 centimetres (17 inches) – as long as the duck itself. Dr Kevin McCracken and colleagues at the University of Alaska measured this part of the anatomy of the otherwise modest duck. The penis of this bird is unusual as most male birds, except for some ratites and waterfowl, don't have one at all, mating instead by cloacal kissing (a brief touch of genital openings to pass on sperm). Researchers of the Lake Duck speculate that this rather long member may be an example of sexual selection driving anatomy in an exaggerated direction, just like the peacock's tail.

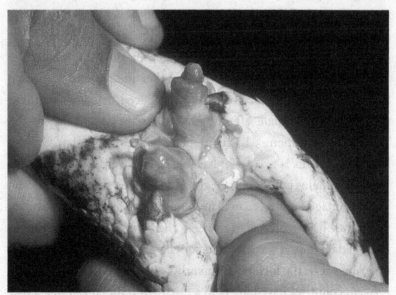

A penis is an essential bit of kit on the path to fatherhood. Snakes and lizards have two, called hemipenes.

Snakes and lizards are interesting in that they have two glans, called hemipenes. These are held inside the body and everted when needed. If your natural mode of movement is sliding on the ground, a dangling penis would be a hindrance indeed, so it's tucked away for greater comfort. Once they do come out to play, these penises have many shapes and are ornamented with hooks and spines. But why two, you may ask? They are not really two penises but two heads on one stalk and studies have found that snakes alternate which one they use in successive matings. Some think that by having two heads, one can be used to make a sticky gel that is used as a sneaky mating plug, the reptile version of a chastity belt (see Chapter 8 for more about such sexual trickery). It's therefore possible that by having two penises, a snake can literally keep the competition out more effectively. It has also been noted that snakes in preference use the right head over the left one. Once again, you have to marvel at how dedicated these researchers are in getting their information.

In mammals, the Tiger's penis is rather unique and has some fascinating adaptations. Female cats are induced-ovulators, meaning that they only ovulate after vaginal stimulus. This is where the Tiger's 30 centimetre (12 inch) penis comes into play. On the head of his penis is a cap that has lots of backward-pointing barbs. Vaginal stimulus by this barbed apparatus causes ovulation to occur. The advantage of induced ovulation means the females only ovulate when they have a chance to mate, so there's no wastage of eggs – a handy adaptation if the species is solitary and only comes across the opposite sex in the forest infrequently.

Asian countries have long held a fascination for consuming Tiger penis as an aphrodisiac. There is no scientific evidence, however, to support the notion that the ground bone of a tiger's penis does anything for erectile dysfunction. The only outcome of consuming Tiger penis is the continued poaching of Tigers, which has driven them to near extinction in some parts of the world. Luckily, in Asia, the use of pharmaceutical erectile disfunction medication is now increasingly sought instead of Tiger penis.

Another remarkable penis owner is the Australian Short-beaked Echidna (*Tachyglossus aculeatus*), which is already known for its many unusual characteristics, such as its hedgehog-like spikes, duck bill and long sticky tongue like an anteater. Echidnas are monotremes – a mammal that lays eggs which the female incubates in a pouch like a fold of skin. Once they hatch, the puggle, as the baby echidna is called, suckles milk from an oozy patch of skin on mum's belly. If that was not weird enough, males have a four-headed penis. Yep, four heads! All on one shaft. This seems like an oversupply, given that the female has a reproductive tract with only two branches and when the male gets close to ejaculation he retracts two of the 'rosettes' leaving the other two to do the job. Once again, I'm fascinated to learn how researchers managed to discover this. The echidna alternates the use of his four penises, somewhat reminiscent of the hemipenes in reptiles, indicating a distant common ancestor. If that was not fancy enough, echidnas also appear to have an adaptation for sperm competition. Echidna sperm forms bundles that can swim faster than solitary sperm cells. I imagine them to be like the training squads in the swimming pool, egging each other on to go faster, or like a bicycling peloton, the leaders setting the pace for the group. The male echidna may only use two of his penis heads at a time, but it seems prudent to have evolved to have some spares of this essential gear.

Echidna courtship and mating is noteworthy in its own right. The males form 'trains' behind a female in season. These male trains may have ten or even more males following one female. When the female is ready to mate the males dig a trench in the ground around the female and compete for the right to mate by pushing each other out of the trench. The last echidna in the trench wins and gets the girl.

BONERS

Whereas some mammals rely on simple hydraulics, some penises have a bone. The Red Panda, Snow Leopard, Brown Bear, Meerkat, Tiger, Honey Badger, European Otter, Golden Jackal, Fossa and many more all have this feature in common. The penis bone is called the baculum or os penis and runs along its shaft. These bones have all sorts of unusual features like ridges and grooves, curves and curiously shaped pointy ends. In the Arctic, the penis bone of Walruses (*Odobenus rosmarus*) can reach 60 centimetres (24 inches) long and is pretty solid.

Bacula have been studied since at the 1880s and became a tool with which to classify animals. Some bat bacula have curves, others

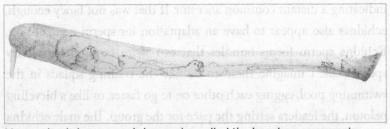

Many animals have a penis bone, also called the baculum or os penis, which is absent in humans. In the Arctic, the penis bones of Walruses are often carved and sold as tourist souvenirs.

look like little arrows, whereas some have lobes, each identifying a different species. In shrews and some other insectivore animals, the penis is so long that the bone is hinged and the penis folds when not in use. Perhaps a folding penis would be rather handy for male ballet dancers or Olympic swimmers trying to get everything into their lycra? Shrews also have interesting decorations along the tip of the glans. These rows of hooks and spines prevent the penis from slipping out when it is not wanted.

FAKE ONES

The penis can seem like such a great attribute to have that some species have evolved to have one on both genders. The evolutionary war between the sexes has resulted in some drastic adaptations in Spotted Hyenas. Perhaps the strangest thing about female Spotted Hyenas is their fake male genitalia. On the inside there are the normal female mammal reproductive organs but externally there is no vaginal opening – a totally unique feature in a mammal. Instead, the clitoris is so elongated that it forms a fully erectile pseudo-penis. This multi-tasking organ is used to urinate, copulate and as a birth canal. That all sounds fine until you get to the 'give birth' part. The cubs - usually one or two, rarely three – exit through the clitoral birth canal which is only about 2.5 centimetres (1 inch) in diameter. Ouch! The female's full cooperation is needed even for proper coitus to occur. Apart from a clitoris that looks like a penis, the female's labia are fused to form two fatty pads that look like a scrotum.

True hermaphrodites, such as flatworms, can go either way in the reproductive game. They can also reproduce both sexually and

Perhaps a case of severe penis envy? The Spotted Hyena has evolved to have one on both genders. In females the clitoris is elongated to form a fully erectile pseudo-penis.

asexually. Hermaphrodite flatworms (*Pseudobicoros hancockanus*—an interesting scientific name) can engage in penis fencing, just like the Bonobos, although this is a more serious game that includes fertilisation. They coil around each other and wrestle head-to-head with their penises exposed. The flatworm who wins the battle stabs the other in the head with its member, thus forcing the loser to become the receiver of his sperm and the bearer of the eggs. Producing sperm is easier than eggs and less energetically costly.

For centuries people speculated that Spotted Hyenas were hermaphrodite, having both male and female sex organs. They can be observed with both swollen mammary glands for milk production and what looked like a large phallic erection.

The individual who wins the battle takes on the male role, then tries to find another flatworm to have a penis fight with and start the process all over again.

Another hermaphrodite flatworm, *Macrostomum hystrix,* inseminates itself if it fails to find a partner. Lots of animals can inseminate themselves, but this flatworm stabs itself in the head with a hypodermic appendage. More commonly, however, flatworms prefer to fight it out to see who gets to do the stabbing.

Human sex organs start to look decidedly plain compared to the plethora of reproductive gear out there.

THE BALL'S IN THEIR COURT

Testes are also essential fathering tackle and come in a great variety of shapes and sizes in the animal world. In most placental mammals, the testes drop into the scrotum or lower abdomen helping to keep them cool and not fry the little swimmers inside. The testes of our ape relatives come in a variety of sizes. Species in which males have a lot of sex with ovulating females need bigger testes. The basic theory here is that they require more room to store the copious amounts of sperm needed to impregnate large numbers of females. The gorilla male again comes in on the lower end of the size scale. His nuts resemble a pair of kidney beans tucked up in his body. His evolution has geared him towards fighting off other males, but his size and bulk does not translate to his genitalia. Once he's taken over a harem he does not get to mate all that often. He may only have a few females in his troop and once they are all pregnant or lactating his work is done for a few years.

Chimpanzees and Bonobos, both promiscuous species, have sex on a more frequent basis and possess testes roughly the size of chicken eggs. Human testes may almost match this size but the human body weight to testes ratio falls well beyond those of the polygamous gorilla or the monogamous gibbon. Christopher Ryan and Cacilda Jetha, in their book *Sex at Dawn*, also support the theory that humans, in this case on the basis of their testicle size, may not always have been the monogamous species we think we are.

Research has been conducted that suggests men may be better off without testicles at all. A study done by an American scientist called Hamilton managed to get data on jailed males, castrated for sexual offences. The longevity of these castrated men was compared with non-castrated prisoners and results found that the castrates lived on average 13 years longer than their intact cell mates. Raging sex hormones make males compete with other males, the stress of which can impact the immune system and make male animals more vulnerable to wounding, illness and disease.

WHAT THE FAMILY JEWELS SAY ABOUT PATERNAL CARE

There's a trade-off in primates between mating opportunities and making sure the offspring produced survives. It seems that testes size can predict the kind of mating strategy males employ and how much care they give their young. Chimpanzees are super promiscuous and have testicles twice the size of those sported by humans. Chimps make a lot of sperm but do little or no fathering duties. Gorillas have the smallest testes of the great apes and are very protective of their progeny.

Studies that presumably have measured a lot of human testes (great topic of conversation at a party: what do you do for a living?) suggest that humans have a variety of testicle sizes and exhibit varying levels of parental care. Fathers with smaller testes are said to be more involved with looking after their children. However, the size of one's marbles is only one variable amongst other factors that affect the kind of father one becomes. The social environment a man grows up in himself, along with whether he has looked after younger brothers and sisters in his youth, are also likely to impact the paternal role performed in addition to the size of the family jewels.

NOBODY WINS – IT'S A DRAW

To conclude, humans have less outrageous adornments than other species but evolution has adapted our genitalia according to the sex we have. Penis envy becomes meaningless when we consider the startling variety of members out there. It may be more appropriate to stand in awe of evolution and its many creative solutions to a problem. Amongst our greater ape family, humans can stand proud that they have evolved the appropriate equipment for the task of procreation and recreation.

ARE MEN'S TESTES THE CANARY IN THE MINE?

Sperm counts from America, Europe, Australia and New Zealand have all declined by more than half over the last four decades. The rate of decline has not slowed during this time, which should be a wake-up call for health authorities as this points to a possible decline in the overall health and fertility in men. Studies suggested that the reason for the decline may be smoking, stress, obesity and exposure to certain chemicals and pesticides. Men's testicles may indeed be the canary in the mine, pointing to a wider health risk.

CHAPTER 8

SEXUAL TRICKERY ON BOTH SIDES

'Anything worth having is a thing worth cheating for.'

W.C. FIELDS

Sex and deception are close bedfellows. Many reproductive strategies rely on some form of deceit as males and females of all species have different desired outcomes. Many animals try to outsmart the competition when it comes to conception and mating and, as with all battles and warfare, there are defensive and offensive strategies in play. Some males try to prevent another male from mating by mate guarding the female until she's no longer fertile or has conceived with his sperm. Others literally put a barrier inside or around the female to prevent access to her. Similarly, females of many species use a form of trickery when selecting the sperm they want to sire their babies – the so-called 'cryptic female choice'. This chapter is all about the trickery used in the sexual lives of animals and humans.

MATE GUARDING

Sexual jealousy causes mate-guarding behaviour, a strategy employed by both males and females. The aim is to keep the relationship going a bit longer and fend off same-sex rivals. This strategy is common but most interestingly exemplified by the devil itself!

The female Tasmanian Devil, a carnivorous marsupial, is polyoestrous, meaning she can have more than one oestrus in a year until she falls pregnant. During the mating season, females will try to mate with as many suitors as they can and she can end up giving birth to a litter fathered by several males. The male devil tries to prevent this from happening by keeping her captive after mating for as long as he can. The manner in which he does this is not so subtle: he literally drags her by the neck into a den by clinging to the roll of fluid on the back of her neck which she develops precisely for this purpose during the breeding season.

After mating the male Tasmanian Devil tries to prevent any opportunity for the female to mate with another male, keeping her prisoner for around nine days.

Once mated, the male may keep the female prisoner for around nine days, during which time she does not get to eat. The male, meanwhile, is busy fending off other males who have come to sniff around, as well as preventing the female's escape attempts. I used to look after Tasmanian Devils in the breeding program at Taronga Zoo and always got the feeling that the females were utterly over any affection they originally had for that male. A few days after mating, she would try to make a run for it, attempting to sneak out of the burrow when he was momentarily distracted by me bringing food. Female devils get quite tired of the male hanging around long after the business has been concluded. Males usually carry a few battle-scars around the face and the neck after the breeding season – injuries not just from rivals but from females making it clear they want their space.

If the female devil is not pregnant after this mating, she will come into oestrus again, mate with another suitor and be mate guarded again until she conceives. If she is pregnant, chances are she carries babies from a couple of different males. Despite his diligence in guarding her after mating, the female regularly manages a sneaky copulation.

Tasmanian Devils sound quite romantic compared with some species which take even more drastic action. After mating, some male butterflies pass on an aroma that is an anti-aphrodisiac, making 'his' female less desirable to other males. The preference of these male butterflies is for virgins. They wait beside a pupa until a female emerges, then mate with her instantly. She will be pregnant before she's even taken her first flight. Some flies show even more impatience, fertilising unborn female pupae through the skin so they'll be born expecting.

THE NATURAL CHASTITY BELT

The use of a 'chastity belt' type of strategy is rife in the animal kingdom. References to chastity belts for human use have been found in texts from as early as the first century, mostly in religious tracts. Medieval historian Albrecht Classen purports that these items may actually be more mythical than real. According to Classen, the belt was more of a metaphor than an actual practice. At any rate, the natural world is full of examples of genital blocking mechanisms, proving that many males go to extreme lengths in the war of 'gene continuation', preventing rivals from impregnating their female. The longer a male has access to the female without competition, the more likely it will be his sperm and not some other candidate's fertilising her eggs.

Some snakes secrete a liquid substance during mating which solidifies in the female's reproductive tract. This is where a second penis (the hemipenes) comes in handy. When the next Romeo arrives, he finds the portal closed. Animals routinely use copulatory plugs, a physical barrier inserted into the female's vagina after sex, to prevent another male from inseminating the same female. I used to find these plugs regularly in the kangaroo yards at the zoo as all macropods seem to use this method. These copulatory plugs are made of an amorphous material secreted in the male's ejaculate. Rats and guinea pigs do the same. Most female spiders have three genital openings – two for mating and one for egg-laying. This way she can lay eggs whilst she is otherwise plugged up. Knowing what the male has done to her perhaps makes us somewhat more sympathetic to those female spiders who eat their lovers after sex! Although inserted into the female, copulatory plugs are really a weapon between males in the 'gene war'.

Dragonflies also use trickery in the mating game. They physically remove any other sperm from the reproductive tract of the female before mating with her. As if blocking a female's bits with sticky stuff wasn't enough, some animals take this a step further. Copulatory plugs can contain a substance that decreases the female's interest in sex and are a clear sign to other males that someone else has got there first. Female ground squirrels (family Sciuridae) are known to groom-out mating plugs and eat them. I have seen this in kangaroos as well. These plugs contain protein so it's a nice little snack after sex. Males will also remove mating plugs left by others and then deposit their own stopper after mating.

Dogs use the adaptions of their body to prevent another male taking advantage of mating opportunities. A dog's penis has some erectile tissue called the *bulbus glandis*. This tissue helps the dog maintain a large erection after mating and keeps both parties tied together for half an hour or so after ejaculation, allowing the sperm time to travel to the egg.

Females in some species are not always entirely able to choose their sexual partner – there may be some male intimidation involved. Just to even things out, there's something biologists call cryptic female choice. It's a phenomenon that occurs in internally-fertilising species both before and after mating and involves a female using chemicals or a physical mechanism to prevent a male's sperm from fertilising her eggs. This allows these females some control over who becomes the sire of her offspring.

Cryptic female choice is not fully understood yet, but recent research has shed some light on how such a mechanism may work.

Chemicals are important in reproduction and chemical signals often ignite the first spark between sexual partners. More chemical signals become involved when the sperm is about to meet the egg. Swedish research into female cryptic choice found that when sperm reach the ovaries and enter into the follicular fluid which surrounds the egg, they change the way they swim subject to the female's chemical signals. If the egg likes the sperm, the female's chemicals tell it to swim faster. If she does not like the sperm, she sends a go-slow message. This means that the follicular fluid from one woman can be better at attracting sperm from a particular male in preference to others, allowing her to subconsciously select the fittest sperm.

IS MARRIAGE THE VIRTUAL CHASTITY BELT?

The first recorded evidence of a wedding ceremony between a man and a woman was in Mesopotamia in about 2350 BC. Weddings, dowries and divorce can all be traced back to ancient times. Marriage, in some form or other, has sprung up in cultures all over the world. Curiously, in some ways it reminds me of the mate guarding found in animal societies. Rather than physically guarding the female, a visible symbol of the marital status is habitually placed on the woman, signaling her unavailability. Women are most frequently the ones to wear this recognisable, culturally-determined symbol. It may take the form of a certain hairstyle, jewelry, tattoos, or clothing. In India, for example, a woman applies *sindoor* (vermillion) on her hair parting to tell the world she's not available for flirtation, courtship or, heaven forbid, sex. Perhaps that's why another word for marriage is 'wed*lock*'?

The markers of marital status tend to be gender specific. In Western societies, males may display fairly low-key symbols that can easily be removed, such as a ring. In other societies, such as the Amish and the Hutterite of Canada and the USA, men only grow a beard once they are married. Single men must shave. An Ashkenazi Jewish man may wear a Tallit – a prayer shawl – once he's married, often given to him by his bride's father as a wedding gift. In return, Orthodox Jewish women, once married, cover their hair with a scarf, hat or wig when they are outside the home.

In the past, in many places in the world and even today in some countries, married women had few rights and were considered the property of their husband, along with any children from the marriage. In the United States and Europe, this started to change in the late 19th century when the rights of women slowly improved. There are, however, still countries where the legal status of married women is significantly unequal to that of their husbands.

Having an affair or committing adultery is a crime in many jurisdictions and is considered legal grounds for divorce. In some parts of the world, women and girls suspected or accused of sex outside marriage run the risk of becoming victims of 'honour killings', a horrific crime committed by the girl's family in order to save the reputation of the family. In some countries, if your family does not kill you for adultery, the state will organise to have you stoned by outraged members of the public. If that is not enough to deter women from having sex outside marriage, some societies adopt a more physical form of discouragement through genital mutilation. Sadly, this crime continues to be committed in some cultures, even after being outlawed.

In the human world, males have developed ways of mate guarding females by enforcing social, religious and cultural norms. Yet, despite compelling discouragement by state and church in some countries, humans continue to have an undiminished interest in sexual intercourse both within and outside marriage.

SNEAKY F*CKER THEORY

Charles Darwin was right in so many of his theories, but his arguments about sexual selection have developed some caveats as animals began to be studied more closely. Darwin's theory on sexual selection assumes that animals will have better success with the opposite sex if they can outcompete others. However, zoologists and biologists have since observed plenty of 'sneaky f*cker' mating or kleptogamy among species, which shows males from outside a social group or lacking in status within the group, mating with females by means of deceptive behaviour.

Evolutionary biologist, John Maynard Smith, is thought to have coined the term 'sneaky f*ckers' to describe subordinate males taking advantage when dominant males are busy fighting or otherwise engaged. Males who have low status, a small stature or are immature, find a way to take advantage of mating opportunities as they arise, sometimes even disguising themselves as female in order to approach without suspicion. Some fish, for example, hide on the margins of a male's territory and while he's busy courting the interloper rushes in to fertilise the eggs before the territorial male gets the chance to do so. It's a dangerous strategy, but for males who do not quite measure up to the big boys it may be their only chance.

Many animals resort to cheating in order to become a father. While large males are busy fighting other large males, smaller males will regularly take on the appearance of females in order to 'sneak' past the fighting males and successfully mate with females.

For a long time it was thought that in species with a big bully male, only the dominant alpha got to mate successfully. However, through field studies and more recent DNA analysis, we now know that sneaking mating behind the alpha's back is more common than once believed. Darwin did not have the benefit of DNA analysis to test his theory. He's still right on almost everything else, however.

SPOTTED HYENAS – THE ULTIMATE SEXUAL CONTROL

In some species, we must take a longer evolutionary view on the war between the sexes. Already an enigma in evolutionary terms, hyenas are neither canine nor feline. They are carnivores but often behave like primates. They have the most beautiful eyes, doggy-like wet noses and teeth that can take your leg off in one bite. People have strange beliefs about these curious creatures. It's been said that they have magical powers and that witches once rode on their backs.

In addition, biologists propose that infanticide by males in their evolutionary past pushed females to take action. So, what was their solution? Female hyenas evolved their own penis, got bigger and became more aggressive. In fact, hyenas have masculinised the anatomy of their genitalia to the point that the females get to choose their partner as the pseudo-penis makes sexual non-consent impossible. As a result of these significant evolutionary adaptations, females control all sexual activity. Males have to work extremely hard to father offspring. Males disperse from their natal clan at puberty. Once they are on their own in the big world they have to beg for acceptance by another clan. Even if successful, they are kept on 'probation' for a period of time. Biologists call this 'endurance rivalry'. If the male sticks with it for long enough, he may eventually be rewarded with a female to mate with. His probation can last a couple of years, after which the lowest-ranking female may allow a mating. Being a male Spotted Hyena is very tough.

Females choose their partners according to several criteria. They prefer immigrant males over those born within the clan – a measure that prevents inbreeding. Male rank does not necessarily influence their reproductive success, but females do show a preference for males that are of similar age, are submissive and less aggressive. The selection of less aggressive males may further perpetuate the difference between the sexes.

Females copulate with several males when in heat, possibly to let them all think they are the father and further minimise the potential for infanticide. They can choose the sire of their offspring because of their pseudo-penis and cubs in one litter may therefore have several fathers. The females have evolved to ensure cub survival by being bigger than the males, more aggressive and therefore able to eat first.

For centuries people speculated that Spotted Hyenas were hermaphrodite – having both male and female sex organs – or alternatively, that they were male for part of their lives and then female. They were observed with both swollen mammary glands for milk production and what looked like a large phallic erection. One theory to explain this is that the females of the species, through evolution, have been naturally selected for a larger size and aggression. Nearing the end of gestation, high-ranking females flush their embryos with androgen, a male sex hormone linked to aggression. The high levels of this male hormone during embryonic development could make their genitals develop their unusual features.

Developing a pseudo-penis is not exactly cheating but it certainly is about taking control over any sexual activity.

BUT THAT'S CHEATING

The tendency to covet what others have exists in most humans. This particularly applies when it comes to mate choice. I've heard girlfriends say that all the men they like are either married or gay. Somehow, this seems to signal that if someone else has chosen that particular male or he's not available, he must be a good choice. This inclination is exploited by some animals. Female Three-spined

Sticklebacks (*Gasterosteus aculeatus*) appreciate endorsements from other females before making their mate selections. These small fish prefer to lay their eggs in the nest of a male who already has a clutch. They judge a male who has already been chosen by another female as a better sperm donor than one who has not yet scored – a definite case of 'I'll have what she's having.' The not-so-stupid stickleback male who has an empty nest will even go and steal some eggs from another male to make himself look worthier and more attractive. On the positive side, the more eggs a male has to guard in his nest, the more committed he is to see it through.

SEXUAL DECEPTIONS

We have seen that trickery is rife in the sexual lives of most animals, as many reproductive strategies rely on some form of deceit. Male Topi (*Damaliscus korrigum*) have an imaginative scam going. Males of this antelope convince females to stay in their territory by making them believe there is a predator. When the female looks like she's about to leave, he makes a fake alarm call, telling her she's about to encounter a predator. The longer she stays, the more mating opportunities he has with her. Perhaps this ruse becomes transparent after a while, but in the meantime it gives the male time for another round.

When I looked after the Chimpanzees at Taronga Zoo, the alpha male, Snowy, maintained a rule of fear and intimidation rather than the cooperative behaviour many good chimp leaders prefer. He was a particularly jealous chief and would not stand for any other male copulating with his females. If he saw or heard any (literal) monkey business, he would run the length of the enclosure to severely punish the couple having sex. Some of the female chimps clearly liked some of the other chimp males more than they liked Snowy and the male chimps thought a sneaky mating was worth the risk if they could get away with it. The chimp enclosure at Taronga has visual barriers planted in it, allowing amorous couples to get out of Snowy's line of sight. Normally, chimp matings incorporate excited vocalisations, but cleverly the sneaky pairs also knew to curb the noise they made lest Snowy would hear and retaliate. Every baby chimp born at Taronga had a paternity test and these showed that quite a range of male chimps had been able to father offspring even in this tightly controlled troop.

Other primates are also smart enough to know how to hide sneaky unions. Geladas – a baboon-like monkey – habitually emit a 'copulation call,' except when a male has convinced a female to sneak away from her usual consort. Then he's silent throughout.

Another way sexual trickery is used in nature is as a lure for food. Bolas spiders (*Mastophora* species) have worked out how to reproduce the pheromones of female moths so they can lure moth males on the look-out for a receptive female into their sticky trap. Different moth species are active at different times of the night. The bolas spiders are so clever in their mimicry that they will try to replicate the pheromones of other moth species throughout the night, based on their common activity patterns.

Yet another trickster is the katydid *Chlorobalius leucovirdis*. This green bush-cricket has evolved to imitate the female cicada's wing-flick song, thereby attracting horny male cicadas who become a tasty snack. Similarly, *Photuris* fireflies mimic the flashing pattern of their prey – another firefly species. The male *Photuris* poses as a snack to meet more females, presumably hoping she'll be more horny than hungry. It's a risky move, but one that has obviously been worthwhile or it would not have survived the evolutionary process.

SNEAKY F*CKER – CUTTLEFISH

There is a mating theory intriguingly called the 'sneaky f*cker strategy'. This mating strategy is cleverly demonstrated and successfully employed by Giant Cuttlefish *(Sepia apama)*. The largest of all cuttlefish has a number of tricks - it can change colour in an instant as well as shape and texture. Some of these attributes come in handy too during the mating season. Breeding begins at the start of the southern winter. Males change from being camouflaged to using rapidly changing forms with bright and striking patterns to impress the polyandrous females, who are out to mate with multiple males. The males in the upper Australian Spencer Gulf population have developed some delightful sneaky strategies. While large males are busy fighting other large males, smaller males will regularly take on the patterns and appearance of females in order to 'sneak' past the fighting males and successfully mate with females.

NATURE'S CHEATERS

A cuckold is a man who, unaware of his wife's infidelities, raises a child that is not his own. It is a word which derives from the word cuckoo, a family of birds that are masters of trickery, laying their eggs in other birds' nests to be raised by foster parents. Cuckoos are nature's poster child for tricking others into bringing up their progeny. There are many separate cuckoo species around the world and nearly 60 of these are so-called 'brood parasites'. True brood parasites only ever breed this way, by tricking other unsuspecting nesting birds.

Raising a clutch of helpless birds is a full-time job that fully occupies both parents. Cuckoo brood parasites have evolved to avoid this hard work all together. The Common Cuckoo (*Cuculus canorus*), a ubiquitous European bird, is one of the species to have managed to dodge all parental responsibility. More than 100 host species are known to be used as foster parents by the Common Cuckoo to raise its offspring. The cuckoo lays its egg immediately after the host mother has laid the last of her eggs. In Great Spotted Cuckoos (*Clamator glandarius*), the male may help by luring the host parents away from the nest so that the female can lay her egg undisturbed. The hen cuckoo usually pushes out one of the foster parent's own eggs, leaving the original number in the nest. Her egg will look just like one of the host's. She flies off straight after, her 'mothering' efforts taking little more than about ten seconds. She may repeat this procedure up to 50 times in one breeding season. A hen cuckoo follows the adage of 'not putting all her eggs in one basket' quite literally.

The imposter egg will develop much faster and will hatch some three to four days before the legitimate eggs. The newly hatched cuckoo will deal with the remaining eggs, pushing them over the edge of the nest to crash to the ground. It will make begging calls that mimic the begging calls of the host birds, keeping them motivated to feed this super chick.

Some host birds get wise and develop 'signature eggs'. They notice that the cuckoo egg is a bit different from their own and throw it over the edge of the nest. The best egg mimicry has adapted in cuckoos who have hosts that can spot impostor eggs. And on and on it goes, this evolutionary arms race between the cheaters and their victims.

An abundant cuckoo species in eastern Australia is the Eastern Koel (*Eudynamys orientalis*). Arriving from its northern wintering grounds in spring, the male's presence is noticed instantly as his piercing call starts to ring out over the landscape well before first light. They have just arrived for this year's breeding season and like an early alarm clock they wake me up at least an hour before sunrise.

SEXUAL DECEPTION IN HUMANS

In a study by David Buss, interviewers asked male participants if they had ever exaggerated their feelings for a woman just to have sex with her. Over 70 per cent of men admitted to having done so compared with only 39 per cent of women who were asked the same question. Participants were also asked if they had ever been deceived in this way themselves. The outcome was that more women than men claimed to have been deceived by a sexual partner. This seems to suggest that some men pretend to have a long-term emotional attachment in order to have a short-term mating opportunity.

On the flip side, men reported being deceived by women who are sexually appealing, spending time, energy and money on them with the expectation of a sexual pay-off that failed to be delivered.

Other studies of online dating sites found that both genders enhanced their dating profile, the women by saying they were on average 7 kilograms (15 pounds) lighter than in real life and the men claiming they were several centimetres taller.

GREAT BALLS OF FIRE

Red-sided Garter Snakes (*Thamnophis sirtalis parietalis*) from North America come together in one great orgy. Tens of thousands of snakes emerge from the limestone caves where they've been hibernating over winter and have only one thing on their mind: sex! Garter snakes communicate with pheromones and they can find one another by following scented trails. Male and female pheromones are quite distinguishable but male garter snakes sometimes can produce both varieties. This can then make other males think they are dealing with a female. Female Red-sided Garter Snakes are swamped by multiple males as they exit the cave, wrapping themselves around the female trying to be the first to mate with her. As they wrap the female, large twisting snake balls form. Males pretending to be females make other males wrap around them which gives them an instant advantage: heat. Snakes rely on the sun to warm up, particularly after hibernation, allowing them to be more active once warmed up. This fooling other male snakes into thinking they are a female means they can warm up faster. This cheating behaviour is called kleptothermy.

Pheromones are also used to find females. The male gives the female a quick lick with his forked tongue. With that brief flick of the tongue a male can tell the reproductive condition, size and age of his potential partner. Larger and older females seem to be preferred by male snakes because they can make more babies. These older female snakes produce a slightly different chemical signature in their individualised pheromone. The younger and smaller female snakes also have their suitors, just not as many.

After the deed is done, female snakes secrete a different pheromone to let other males know mating has happened already. The other males then lose interest and move on to find unmated females.

ADVICE FOR PROSPECTIVE HUMAN FATHERS

For most animals, sexual trickery has evolved in males to increase their chance of becoming a father. For a human in a normal, loving relationship, becoming a father usually does not require mate guarding, sperm plugs or chastity belts. Monogamy or at least serial monogamy is a good insurance policy for most male *Homo sapiens* to commit time and energy to raising young. Paternal security tends to make males perform better as fathers.

Chapter 9

AWARD-WINNING WILD DADS

'I cannot think of any need in childhood as strong as the need for a father's protection.'

SIGMUND FREUD

Some wild animal fathers stand out from the crowd, demonstrating admirable commitment and paternal care. We have the opportunity to find out about these dads in nature through the efforts of some remarkable people who go out into the jungles, the deserts and the sea to bring us stories about awesome animals. My colleagues in zoos around the world dedicate their lives not only to making sure the animals they look after are happy, but to learning about and documenting what they can about the biology of the species. Often this information is difficult to gather in the wild. Questions about who exactly builds the nest, how often a father sits on it and whether dads contribute food and childcare can all be studied by zookeepers. Around the world these people share their knowledge about the special creatures they know, allowing us to get to know them too.

The planet is full of magnificent animals, some of which make good fathers who are remarkably committed. There are male animals that would, if there were such a thing, make strong candidates for an 'Animal Father of the Year' award. These fathers show ways of parenting that speak to us humans. The care and love they lavish on their young is recognisable and palpable to us and their dedication admirable. In this chapter, I've selected my favourite candidates for the imaginary 'Animal Father of the Year' awards.

THE ROLE-MODEL DAD – THE GORILLA

My old friend Kibabu, in Taronga zoo, was a Western Lowland Gorilla (*Gorilla gorilla gorilla* – yes really!). He was a quintessential silverback who was also a role-model dad. A silverback gorilla's day-to-day job is about control, organisation and discipline, but Kibabu was very much a benevolent dictator of his troop, a protector who would risk his own life to defend members of his kin. His job as the head of the family was to make babies, resolve conflict and to defend against any threats – not necessarily in that order. A gorilla male is the one to decide everything for the group: when they move, when they feed, when they rest. It's a tough job and male gorillas in the wild only lead a family group for a few years in their early adulthood when they are in peak condition.

Libby Kartzoff, formerly the Manager of Exotic Fauna, looked after Kibabu and his family for many years and accompanied them from a zoo in the Netherlands to their new home in Australia. She tells the following story about what happened when they arrived in Taronga Zoo:

'By the time Kibabu, the silverback, his harem of three females and their six young arrived in Sydney, they were spent. As the leader of his family, Kibabu was the first to be released into the network of indoor rooms where they were to rest and recover. One by one the mothers were also released, each carrying an infant and with a juvenile in tow.

For Kriba, the most highly-strung of the mothers, the new circumstances proved momentarily overwhelming, to the point where she put her tiny baby on the floor and walked away in a daze. Worse, the more her abandoned infant screamed, the more disorientated and distressed Kriba became. We looked on helplessly, dreading the possibility of her permanently rejecting her baby.

This was the first instance where we witnessed Kibabu's leadership and fathering expertise. Tenderly, he scooped up his tiny offspring in one hand and approached the anxious Kriba. Placing the palm of his free hand between her shoulders, he gently pressed her baby to her chest and waited. Decisive and firm, his intent was clear and the effect on Kriba was immediate. She came back from disorientation and distress as if she had found her anchor.'

This example of rock-solid support during a crisis illustrates why a good silverback is such an asset to a gorilla family. Kibabu could not afford to lose his head as his family all relied on him to keep calm – they looked to him for direction.

Typically, a family of gorillas consists of a strong adult male, a harem of three or four females and their combined offspring of between three to six youngsters. Gorilla males between eight and twelve years old are called blackbacks as they don't yet have the silver hair the adult male develops on his back and legs. This age is an important time of learning for young gorilla males. Their father demonstrates what it takes to be the leader of a harem. A good gorilla dad knows how to keep a harmonious family group safe and well-nourished. These teenagers are subordinate to their father and help out with protection of the clan in times of trouble. Young males need a strong male role model to show them how to live life as an adult and fully grown male gorillas are the ones the young males watch.

Not every male gorilla gets to be a father. There are plenty of bachelor groups as the gorilla social structure has only one silverback monopolising a harem. This results in many males with no harem to lead. As few males have a lot of females and most males none at all, competition for access to female gorillas is fierce. Once the males leave home they hang out with other males. The young and the very old form bachelor groups. They have friendly interactions and socialise with the other bachelors through play and grooming. Occasionally they engage in homosexual interactions. Some junior males stay in proximity to family groups biding their time until they believe they have what it takes to become the leading silverback.

Kibabu's boys Haoko and Shabani, once grown up, went to live in other zoos to father a new generation of gorillas. Each of these males demonstrated a paternal style reminiscent of their dad. They too managed their family groups with a firm but gentle hand. They've been seen playing tenderly with their infants, their massive hands as big as the entire baby, yet their movements careful enough to make sure they don't hurt the little one.

Animals who are harem masters are usually much bigger than the females in their harem. Gorillas display significant sexual dimorphism. The size difference between the male and his females is enormous. The male may weigh around 180–200 kilograms

(400–440 pounds) whereas females are at least 50 per cent smaller and usually weigh around 70–90 kilograms (150–200 pounds). A typical gorilla male has the strength of several grown men and he's prepared to use that physical power to defend his family and his position. Competition is the likely reason males are so much bigger than females, with natural selection favouring notable physical differences between the sexes. The females are likely to prefer a bigger bloke who can prevent a takeover by a rival male who could put their babies' lives in jeopardy.

This size difference is shared with many other polygamous mammals, such as seals and lions, where one male dominates several females. A silverback uses his size to scare off any challengers and to appear impressive in case he needs to keep control of his harem.

This harem master is a true authoritarian and makes all the decisions. He closely watches the members of his group all day and will correct their behaviour if he thinks it is wrong. Usually, a stare or head jerk from him will be enough to keep the peace. If two females or young are fighting, he will immediately jump in to separate them. Sometimes he punishes the culprit but mostly he reprimands both, as if he does not much care who started it as long as the bickering stops. An experienced male gorilla will be gentle but firm in managing conflict resolution.

The bond that a dominant male has with his females and his offspring is the core of gorilla social life. These bonds between the male and his females are maintained by grooming and sitting close together. The silverback is at the centre of everybody's attention because he takes responsibility for the safety and well-being of the entire troop. Kibabu, despite being ruler and enforcer, also had his

A father, gorilla or human, sets an example for his offspring by respecting their mother. Show your children how a good man cares for and respects his partner so your daughter will choose well and your sons will follow your example.

softer side, however. He could often be seen playing games with the youngsters in the group. Playing games with dad is how a gorilla male learns to control his strength and can model becoming a good silverback one day.

Silverback gorillas, with their cool-headed leadership skills, their care and responsibility for their families, and their tenderness and patience with their young, are therefore the worthy winners of the 'Role-model Father' category in my 'Father of the Year Awards', given in memory of my old friend, Kibabu.

WHAT CAN WE LEARN FROM THE AWARD-WINNING ROLE-MODEL GORILLA FATHER?

- You're always watched by your children and they will do what you do, not what you say.
- Research in humans confirms that the same sex parent has the greatest influence on the future adult. Gorillas seem to confirm this.
- Despite their enormous strength, gorillas are gentle giants when playing with the infants in their family. Kibabu and other male silverbacks demonstrate that fathers can show a soft and gentle side without losing respect.
- The bond between the father and the mother of his children is of utmost importance in safely raising offspring.

THE COOLEST DAD – THE EMPEROR PENGUIN

Nearly all warm-blooded creatures have the challenge of feeding their young and keeping them warm. Many animal dads use nearly all the energy they can muster to raise their youngster, none more so than the Emperor Penguin of Antarctica, who is literally the coolest dad, bringing up baby in the coldest place on earth. The first part of the Latin name of these penguins, *Aptenodytes*, means 'wingless diver' and *forsteri* is taken from the father-and-son team of German naturalists G. and J.R. Forster, who shared a ride with James Cook on his second voyage around the world.

The Emperor Penguin is the only penguin to breed in the Antarctic winter, perhaps not an entirely smart evolutionary development, but there it is. They can trek 50–120 kilometres (30–75 miles) over ice to reach the breeding colony, where several thousand penguins will be getting ready to have sex. Before he can become the cool penguin dad he will be, the male Emperor Penguin has some rituals to complete. Courting starts at the beginning of the winter when the temperature is around -40°C (-72°F). Flirting begins with the male standing still, his head on his chest, inhaling deeply to produce an ecstatic courtship call which he repeats a few times. The courting pair then stand face to face with one stretching the head and neck and the other mirroring. This seems enough to seal the deal. Once paired up in this way, the couple steps out and waddles around the colony together. Before the actual deed, the male bows deeply to his chosen one, bill pointing to the ground. His mate does the same.

After the female lays, the delicate operation of the egg transfer begins. Fortunately, the eggshell is quite thick to prevent breakages. Male Emperors don't sit on the eggs like most birds would. Instead they have a brood-patch on the belly – a flap of skin that serves as a kind of pouch for the egg and later the chick. The skin flap folds over the egg and transfers heat from the father's abdomen to the egg. After the female lays the egg and catches it on her feet, the male with difficulty rolls it gently onto his own black feet. The delighted couple now sing together once more before the female goes off to sea to replenish herself. She will come back with a belly full of fish to feed the newly hatched chick in a few months' time.

The male, meanwhile, does not eat, standing on ice in freezing temperatures and gale-force winds for a few months caring for that year's one and only offspring in the coldest place on Earth. He alone broods this single egg for up to 75 days as temperatures drop and blizzarding winds reach over 150 kilometres (100 miles) an hour.

The Emperor Penguin dad does not eat for up to 75 days in the least hospitable place on Earth. All this time, the brooding father has to hope that his partner will faithfully return from her time at sea.

Although he's bulked up to withstand the deprivation of not eating and hardly moving for three months, he's set to lose almost half his body weight. He moves as little as possible to conserve energy and joins the expectant fathers' club in a scrum of tightly packed bodies. Although an Emperor Penguin's plumage has adapted to be waterproof and windproof as a protection from the bitter cold, the combined body heat of thousands of others in the scrum further helps the dads' survival.

The expectant fathers stand shoulder to shoulder, graciously moving in a circular motion to ensure that every bird gets some time in the heat of the central scrum. Thousands of penguins all politely take their turn to benefit from this life-saving strategy in these harsh conditions. One other trick used by these cool dads is to lower their metabolic rate while brooding to help save more energy.

All this time, the brooding father has to trust that his partner will return from her time at sea. When the egg is about to hatch, he is well and truly ready for some food. He's fasted for so long that by now he is emaciated. However, if for some reason she's delayed, dad has another trick up his sleeve. He is able to feed the chick on penguin 'milk' which is secreted from the lining of his oesophagus. This can sustain the hatchling for another couple of weeks.

The Emperor dad places huge amount of trust in his mate. She needs to come back to relieve him so their offspring can live. The returning female has to frantically search for her partner and their egg or chick in a colony of several thousand breeding penguins by relying on vocal calls alone. She has a belly full of food to feed the chick and can suspend digesting that food by 'walling' it off from the digestive juices with mucous. She can now feed the chick if it's hatched and dad can go to sea to have a good feed himself.

Emperor Penguins are some of the most dedicated dads on the planet and are a worthy winner of the 'Coolest Father' category in my 'Animal Father of the Year Awards' – not only in terms of literal temperature, but due to their unflinching care in extreme conditions. Truly a heart-warming dad.

WHAT CAN WE LEARN FROM EMPEROR PENGUINS ABOUT BEING A COOL DAD?

- Mirroring during flirting, a behaviour whereby one animal imitates the gestures and speech patterns of another, builds rapport, not only in penguins. Mirroring shows attentiveness to the pair-bond and a willingness to follow the pace and emotions of your partner.
- Have unwavering faith in the mother of your child.
- Patience and self-sacrifice pay off and can be much-admired qualities in dads when faced with extreme situations.

THE PREGNANT DAD – THE SEAHORSE

Many women have wondered what the world would be like if men could be pregnant and give birth. Nature has given us seahorses to take a closer look at that idea. These gender-bender dads make excellent mums. They have a head and a neck like a horse and swim upright. If that weren't special enough, they also have a curly prehensile tail which they use to hold on to things like seagrasses or the tail of their chosen one during courtship. These little creatures

Seahorses like the Denise's Pygmy Seahorse are gender-bender dads and make great mums. Seahorse dads are the sperm producers and the ones to get pregnant. The male fertilises the eggs as they are laid directly into his pouch by the female.

are really exceptional in that they can camouflage, grow spiny appendages depending on the habitat they're in, have a crown on their head which is distinct in each species, and they can move their eyes independently like a chameleon. Most exclusively, they have a pouch where males carry their eggs. There are incredibly good reasons to award male seahorses with the 'Pregnant Father' category of the 'Animal Father of the Year Awards'.

Seahorse dads are the sperm producers *and* the ones to get pregnant. The male fertilises the eggs as they are laid directly into his pouch by the female. Seahorses are actually a bony fish and there are 46 species of them that all follow this unique reproductive pattern. So why are the males the ones to get pregnant? One theory proposes that males may have donned this role because the females take a while to produce the eggs. If he incubates them she is able to spend her time working on the next batch of eggs – teamwork in action. The survival rate of some species of newly hatched seahorses is only around 0.5 per cent, but that's better than a lot of other fishes. This tag-team approach reduces the time between clutches and favours lots of offspring in any one year, in the hope that some will make it to maturity.

Before getting down to the business of sex, seahorses have a complex courtship that may go on for several days. This courtship gets hormones racing and helps to synchronise the pair's readiness for action. During this flirtatious period, they change colour and, sweetest of all, they swim side-by-side holding tails and wheeling around in unison. After this, an even more serious courtship dance begins, which may last some eight hours. The 'sea-stallion' pumps water through his egg pouch which shows the 'sea-mare' that it's empty and ready to receive eggs. Depending on the species, the female may deposit dozens of eggs or indeed thousands.

As she releases her eggs she visibly slims down while his body swells up. She then swims away leaving him pregnant! The fertilised eggs are embedded in his pouch wall. What makes it like a real pregnancy instead of simply 'cargo carrying', is that daddy supplies the eggs with prolactin, a hormone that's responsible for milk production in pregnant mammals. There's oxygen in the pouch and a controlled environment for the eggs to develop in a safe place. The pregnant male also secretes all sorts of energy-rich lipids and calcium to help his babies build a strong skeletal system. The eggs hatch in the pouch where dad can regulate the salinity of the water, carefully preparing the newborns for the salty sea.

Males and females of the Australian White's Seahorse

(*Hippocampus whitei*) are faithful to each other at least during the entire breeding season. Throughout the incubation, the female pays her partner a daily visit just to see how things are going and to have a dance. As the sun rises, they greet one another and perform an elaborate dance that goes on for some six minutes. This little bonding ritual never fails, according to researcher Amanda Vincent.

The number of baby seahorses born varies for each of the species but anywhere between five and a couple of thousand may be released. Their birth has similarities to mammalian births, with the male having strong muscular contractions to expel the young. While he was pregnant, the female has been getting ready to lay more eggs. He often gives birth during the night and by the next morning he can potentially do it all again if his partner visits for the daily greeting and she's ready to lay more eggs.

Although the survival rate of the young is low, it's higher than for most other fish species as a result of the father's protection during the gestation period. Most other fish fertilise their eggs and that's the end of their parenting job. In the practical but evidently romantic seahorse there are sunrise greetings with ritual dancing, as well as taking on the bulk of the parenting responsibility. Therefore, the 'Pregnant Father' category of the 'Animal Father of the Year Awards' goes to all the sea-stallions in the ocean.

WHAT CAN WE LEARN FROM THE SEAHORSE?

- Paternal care will increase the survival rates of offspring.
- Daily dancing with your partner is a romantic gesture that reinforces the pair-bond.

- Fathers are capable of much more hands-on child-rearing than they think.

THE PRACTICAL DAD – THE EMPEROR TAMARIN

Tamarins belong to a family of small primates called Callitrichidae. The callitrichids are the only non-human primate to practice polyandry. As a group, these little monkeys have a lot in common. They are territorial and all weigh less than 1 kilogram (2.2 pounds) as an adult. Another significant characteristic is that 80 per cent of births are twins, making them the only primate to routinely produce twin offspring. The Emperor Tamarin *(Saguinus imperator)* is not only impressive looking with his long, white military moustache, but is an icon of paternal care. Their resemblance to the German Emperor Wilhelm II is thought to be the reason for the name. The Emperor Penguin has nothing in common with its namesake tamarin, other than the fact that both species have a regal bearing and are excellent, noteworthy fathers.

A native to Peru, Bolivia and Brazil, this petite critter makes its home in lush forest south of the Equator and takes parenting duties extremely seriously. It was once thought that these tamarins were monogamous as paternal care is often more prevalent in monogamous relationships. However, detailed studies in the wild have discovered they are in fact polyandrous. The dominant female mates with several males who then do a great deal of childcare. This mating system ensures greater paternal investment in the offspring, which is needed because the female typically gives birth to twins. The males then all think that there's a possibility that one of the twins carries their genes to the next generation. When I say 'think' here, I obviously don't know what a monkey thinks. I don't believe there's a conscious process going on but an overwhelming instinct to do these caring things, programmed, like a blueprint in the brain that must be followed. This mating system ensures greater paternal investment in the offspring.

Carrying young about has a high energy cost to the parent doing the carrying. Tamarin babies are born relatively heavy. The average weight of a newborn primate is around eight per cent of the mother's body weight. In callitrichids this increases to 18 per cent and she has two of them to carry. Not surprising, then, that she needs a hand from at least a couple of possible dads. Adult males even help her with the birth, performing as practical midwifes. They take the newborn immediately and clean it up. The helpers give the mother

The Emperor Tamarin is often the father of twins. The male is the one most regularly seen carrying both infants, giving the mother the opportunity to forage and eat enough food to keep up the milk production for two babies.

the opportunity to forage and eat enough food to keep up the milk production she needs to feed the twins. Male Emperor Tamarins are the ones most regularly seen carrying both infants whilst their mother provides food. The fathers are very observant and protective, often being the first to react when a twin utters a distress call.

Any male already on the scene when a second male arrives benefits from the additional help with the kids. If that means he has to allow sexual access to the female, so be it. Being the one and only male trying to raise two babies is simply too difficult. If he were on his own he could sexually monopolise the female but potentially have no surviving offspring as infant mortality is high with only one male doing the caring. If he shares the female with another male at least half the kids raised have a chance of being his and his genes are carried forward.

Emperor Tamarin dads are both practical and nurturing because evolution has adapted them to forfeit sexual jealousy in favour of infant survival. The young they care for are loved and cherished, whether their own or another male's genetic offspring is the outcome. They carry and cuddle and groom that infant as if it's their own. The Emperor Tamarin is therefore winner of the 'Practical Father' category in my 'Animal Father Of the Year Awards'.

WHAT CAN WE LEARN FROM EMPEROR TAMARINS ABOUT BEING A PRACTICAL FATHER?

- These fathers put infant survival above sexual jealousy.
- They carry the babies so mum can feed in peace, get her strength back and make more milk.

- They care for infants regardless of whether they are their own offspring.

THE TEACHER DAD – THE WOLF

Wolves in myths and legends have been portrayed both as nurturers and as predatory enemies – the 'big bad wolf'. The first wolf-as-nurturer story dates to the fourth century BC. Romulus and Remus were the twin sons of a Vestal Virgin, Rhea Silvia. King Amulius saw them as a threat to his power and he ordered them to be killed. Abandoned on the bank of the River Tiber at the site that would become Rome, they would have died but instead were saved by the Father of the River, the God Tiberinus, who intervened, having a she-wolf suckle the twins. Since antiquity, the she-wolf has been a powerful symbol of Rome, representing imperial power, papal authority, greed, good politics and excessive female sexuality – quite a list of competing qualities.

Turkey's legendary founder, Tu Kueh, was reportedly suckled by a wolf, as was the Teutonic hero Siegfried, the religious reformer Zoroaster and several babies in Navajo and Aztec legends. There is also an Irish legend about a young king who was raised by wolves and later returned to reclaim his right to reign. All these stories link wolves to child-rearing and stress their nurturing nature.

However, there are also plenty of early European fairy tales about the cunning and deceit of wolves, the most famous wolf story being that of Little Red Riding Hood, which was thought to have originated in the 1600s. This story focuses on the cunning of the wolf, as well as having some sexual innuendo.

Despite their fearsome reputation as top predators, male wolves are caring and fiercely protective dads who live with their females for life. Wolves maintain a tight family group called a pack. A wolf pack varies in size but tends to have around eight members that are related to each other. The alpha pair does most of the breeding and are the leaders of the pack. The special bond between the breeding pair can last for many years as they produce a litter of pups each year in succession. Wolves are generally considered monogamous. It is the norm that only one pair in the pack gets to breed during the annual breeding season. During late winter and early spring, a wolf pair starts courting. They whine at each other, touch noses and may do some mutual grooming, nibbling each other's fur. The male sometimes bows to his female and lays his legs across her neck. They will mate once the female is in full oestrus and five or more pups may be born a couple of months later. Their pair-bond is reinforced each breeding season as they raise their offspring together.

A wolf father cares for his pups by preparing the den where his female will give birth. After a wolf gives birth, she stays close to her vulnerable pups and doesn't leave the birthing den for several weeks. Dad defends his pups and delivers food both to the nursing mother and the pups. During the daytime he may find a high point in the landscape from where he can survey the scene, scanning for possible threats to his kin. There are reports that when humans approach, the alpha wolf will howl and move away from the den, repeating this alarm call while moving further and further from the den. By drawing attention to himself, he risks his own life rather that his mate's and their pups. Wolf males make generous, caring fathers.

Once wolf pups get mobile at three or so weeks of age they start

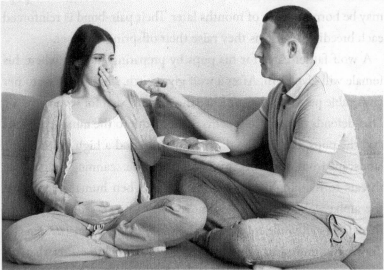

Wolf dads look after their partner, bringing food and protecting her. Looking after the mother of your cubs helps to build a strong family with healthy offspring.

to interact with their father and other adults in the pack. At this time, they have to learn the rules of their community and build their emotional bonds with the family. Around week four, pups start to eat pre-digested food disgorged by adults. The father and other pack members are greeted with enthusiasm by the pups when they return from a hunt. They will lick the adult's face and lips and the adults, in return, will oblige by regurgitating food for the pups. Cleverly, they deposit the food in separate little piles so that the kids don't squabble. Only once the pups have had their fill will the father of the pups eat. Growing pups are hungry and finding food to satisfy them takes time, energy and dedication. Eminent wolf researcher L. David Mech in his book *The Wolf: The Ecology and Behavior of an Endangered Species*, describes several occasions where male wolves have been observed bringing food to the den over a great distance. One male was quoted to have carried caribou meat in his stomach from 28 kilometres (18 miles) away.

As a young pup grows, dad takes on the role of strict, sometimes playful teacher, integrating each pup into the pack. Play is essential to socialising young wolves. Play provides the rules for complex social relationships later in life. It also helps the pups develop stamina, build muscles and practice hunting techniques. Once the pups are between four and ten months old they join the hunting school as they are now mobile enough to follow the adults. Even hunting needs to be learned. This gives the pups plenty of opportunity to see the adults in action and hone their own hunting skills.

Wolves, like all social species, enjoy much friendly contact. They nuzzle each other frequently and even lick the wounds of an injured pack member. Touching strengthens the bonds between individuals and may help to reduce stress. Studies of humans and their dogs reveal that touching and petting reduces the blood pressure and heart rate in both mammals.

Wolf puppies experience what it is like to be fathered in a selfless and nurturing way. These experiences will serve them well when it is their turn to be a dad. Good parenting is learned. Wolves communicate, working together to share knowledge across generations. Older wolves are experienced hunters to have survived as long as they have. They share their hunting strategies and techniques with the younger generation, maintaining a culture unique to that pack. However, good wolf fathers do more than taking care of their pups and teaching them. They look after their mate too, not unlike good human fathers. Because of all these qualities, the 'Teacher Father' category of my 'Animal Father of the Year Awards' goes to all wolf dads everywhere.

Male wolves make great fathers – they are selfless and nurturing, in complete contrast to the reputation of the species.

WHAT CAN WE LEARN FROM THE WOLF FATHER ABOUT BEING A TEACHER DAD?

- Looking after the mother of your children helps to maintain a healthy family life.
- Providing for your offspring requires energy, dedication and some self-sacrifice.
- Teach your offspring what you've learned, so experience is passed down and continues to grow.
- Socialise your young ones and teach them how to be a good member of society.

RAISED BY WOLVES

Wolf fathers are devoted protectors of their young. Some domestic dogs still show these ancestral traits in dedicated protection of all those in their human 'pack'. My first memories in life are about a beast as close to a wolf as a domestic dog can be, a German Shepherd. Despite male domestic dogs not being significantly involved with their puppies, they will take care of human children in their 'pack'. Growing up in Holland, sunshine was highly valued for the vitamin D that it delivers. Parents shove even their young children out in prams on the street to get some rays of sunshine after the long winters. My guardian and protector was a jet-black German Shepherd called Peter, who would sit next to my pram, not letting any strangers approach. Peter and I became inseparable for the next 12 years. The earliest memories I can retrieve all have Peter by my side.

Chapter 10

REMARKABLE SINGLE DADS

'Your children are not your children. They are the sons and daughters of life's longing for itself.'

KAHLIL GIBRAN

Raising kids is tough and even harder when you're doing it on your own. Some animal dads do all the hard work of raising the next generation – a commitment exemplified by some special single dads. In the human world, being a single dad may come about for a variety of reasons. They may have chosen to foster, adopt, have separated or their partner may have died. There are some impressive single dads in the natural world who have chosen, or rather have evolved, to do all the hard work of raising the next generation alone. They may carry their young, incubate the eggs, or keep their brood chamber at the right temperature – lifestyle changes all made to accommodate the kids. Outstanding single dads who have evolved to be sole parents are found amongst insects, fishes, amphibians and birds. Reptiles have never been documented as single dads although some biparental care may happen in certain crocodiles. Wild mammals are rare in this group too for understandable reasons: lactation. Feeding the young can't be done with a bottle unless you're human. In animals, lactation pretty much means that the one with the mammary glands does all the feeding, at least early on in a baby's life.

Men do have breasts though because we all begin life as a ball of cells that's initially female. These cells then divide and differentiate into different body parts. By six weeks a human foetus starts to develop arms, legs and face and even a tail which we lose some time later. At this stage a foetus with a Y chromosome will produce testosterone that turns a couple of buds into testes. Since the foetus is already female, without the testosterone they continue to grow ovaries and a vagina, but the breasts and nipples are already in place at this point of development, so that's why men and male animals have nipples and mammary glands.

If our tail falls off before we're born, why then don't breasts and nipples do the same for boy babies? Evolution tends to focus on getting rid of the body parts we don't need *and* are a potential problem for survival. Clearly, unlike tails which can be attacked and grabbed, male boobs are not a threatening feature and are retained as fairy inconsequential appendices. As male boobs have the right plumbing, they can under certain circumstances produce milk. The hormone that makes male lactation possible is prolactin, which, produced by the pituitary gland, stimulates the mammary glands to produce milk. Male lactation has been observed in a couple of fruit bats: the Dayak Fruit Bat (*Dyacopterus spadiceus*) and the Bismarck Masked Flying-fox (*Pteropus capistratus*). Male goats are also known to lactate occasionally.

Single dads might be thanking their lucky stars that their lactation plumbing doesn't start working in this way when mum is absent and they can stick to warming up a bottle. Raising a child on your own is hard enough without leaking boobs. To all the dads doing it tough out there, just remember there are some animal dads who are doing it even tougher than you.

Involved fatherhood is the successful reproductive strategy that has evolved in humans to help a male's genes survive to the next generation. However, in reality, paternal involvement ranges from complete absence to being the primary carer. Only in humans do we see this huge range of fatherly involvement.

THE TALL ORDER DAD - THE EMU

The Emu has an important place in Aboriginal mythology, including a creation myth that tells the story of how the sun was made by throwing an Emu's egg into the sky. Emus are one of the world's tallest birds, standing proud at up to 1.8 metres (6 feet). This was one of the first birds to be 'discovered' by Europeans when they arrived in Australia, while they have been 'good tucker' to indigenous people for millennia.

In science the Emu is rather special, belonging to a group of ancient birds called the ratites. These flightless birds are grouped with the ostrich, kiwi, cassowary and the rhea as being very closely linked to the time dinosaurs roamed the world. Additionally, they are masters of sole parenting in the avian world. A good father can be hard to come by and female Emus compete for the males. Some females will try to court a male who already has a partner and the incumbent will deter the competition by chasing and giving the interloper a good kick. Sometimes a fight over a male can go on for hours, especially if he's still single and has not chosen a favourite yet.

Emu courtship is a sight to behold. The female Emu courts the male enthusiastically. In the breeding season, small patches of bare skin just under her eyes and near her beak turn a flirtatious turquoise. The hen struts around fluffing out her neck feathers whilst calling him with seductively low drumbeat sounds. Once she has his attention, she starts to circle closer, turning her neck but keeping her chest facing him. If he's impressed he will move towards her. If he becomes more interested he will erect his neck feathers and rub his breast against hers, then rub his neck on the hen's mane. She meanwhile makes a drumming, booming sound and grunts alluringly. This unforgettable sound comes from inflated throat pouches and can be heard over long distances. Suddenly, the female plops to the ground so the male can mount her.

The pair mates every day or so until the hen lays a huge green thick-shelled egg. She does this every second or third day until there are about a dozen eggs in the nest. He gets broody as soon as there are half a dozen or so and starts to sit on them. Once he's got what he was after, the male becomes aggressive to his mate. She wanders off and leaves him to incubate her eggs. She may find another male and do it all again.

Emu males are great dads. Good fathers can be hard to come by and female Emus compete for the males. After hatching, dad looks after his fast-growing stripy brood for another six or seven months.

During incubation, the male hardly eats or drinks and loses a great deal of weight. He only gets up briefly some ten times a day to turn the eggs. He sits on these charges diligently for eight weeks, living off his stored body fat. If the eggs hatch successfully, there's a 70 to 80 per cent chance the chick will reach adulthood.

The newly hatched cream-and-brown striped chicks stand some 12 centimetres (5 inches) tall and leave the nest within days. They are able to feed themselves but dad guards them and teaches them what to eat. The father is very protective during this vulnerable stage of chick development, defending them if needed. He takes an aggressive pose towards other Emus and even the mother should she return. He ruffles his feathers, emits cranky grunts and kicks belligerently to protect his offspring. At night the chicks are wrapped in dad's feathers, protected and warm as they sleep. They stay close to him whilst they slowly lose their camouflage stripes and get that shaggy Emu look.

Dad looks after this fast-growing clutch for six to seven months – a considerable part of the year. He's so emaciated when he finishes looking after his brood that he's literally at the end of his body's endurance and close to death. He is physically depleted and must eat almost constantly to return the condition he's lost before the next breeding season begins. If he can get back in top form, he will do it all again the following season.

FATHERING FROGS

Frogs are fascinating to most people, as they are present in much folklore and many fairy tales, one of the most popular being the

Grimm Brothers' tale, *The Frog Prince*. In ancient Egypt, frogs were symbolic of fertility and in antiquity the Romans and Greeks linked frogs with harmony and fecundity. The transformation from egg to tadpole to frog is mesmerising. In usual frog reproduction, the male clasps the female and she lays eggs which he fertilises. But some species have evolved in more novel ways to have babies. Frogs may not be the first animal you'd think of when listing the most dedicated single dads in nature, but the variable amphibian mating system throws up a few pearls.

For most frog species, breeding takes place in the water. Male frogs croak at night to attract a female to their bachelor pad. If he's loud he's more likely to attract a mate. As he mounts her, his thumbs swell to become the aptly named 'nuptial pads', allowing him to hold on to her slippery skin. He has no penis, therefore fertilisation is external: as she lays her eggs, he releases sperm. He holds on to her until all the eggs are fertilised. This might take hours in some species, while in others the pair clasp each other for months. No wonder she's off as soon as he lets her go, her mothering job done.

Rheobatrachus – the gastric-brooding frogs – is a genus which consisted of two species found in the state of Queensland in Australia. Both are now presumed extinct. These frogs were rather special due to their unique form of care for the young. The female would swallow the eggs after they were fertilised and once they'd grown and hatched in her stomach, they'd be spat out as tiny froglets. She clearly did not eat during this time.

Meanwhile, on the other side of the world in Chile, another frog evolved a notably similar reproductive system. Darwin's Frog (*Rhinoderma darwinii*) is named after Charles Darwin, who first recorded it in Chile during his voyage around the world on the *Beagle*. This frog has a most unusual form of parental care with the uniquely brooding male keeping his babies in his vocal sac until they are ready to emerge. Firstly, Mr Darwin's Frog leads Ms Darwin's Frog to a sheltered site where they court for a short while. She then drops some eggs which he fertilises in normal frog fashion. He guards the eggs for about 20 days until embryos start to wriggle inside the eggs. His defence strategy during this time is based on camouflage: he lays on the ground looking like a fallen leaf when predators threaten.

Once the embryos start to wriggle, the male Darwin's Frog starts to differ from other frogs in terms of parental strategy. He now takes as many as 19 embryos into his vocal sac, using his tongue to move them there, where they hatch about three days later. After hatching, metamorphosis takes place inside the male's vocal sac. Initially, the embryos feed off their yolk sac and secretions produced by the wall of their father's vocal sac. Some six weeks after being gathered, small frogs hop out of their father's mouth. One assumes that the froglets' dad has not eaten anything during this time and probably not croaked either.

The Common Midwife Toad (*Alytes obstetricans*) has also come up with yet another novel way to carry out its parental duties. Females are larger than the males, but she selects the biggest male she can find as she has considerable work planned for him and she needs him to be strong and fit for the job. The male caresses the female for about half an hour before he squeezes her sides and she obligingly ejects a mass of eggs embedded in strings of jelly. The male releases her to fertilise the eggs and then proceeds to unravel the egg mass,

The male Common Midwife Toad has a unique method for looking after the eggs until they hatch, by wrapping strings of them around his back legs.

wrapping the strings around his back legs. The male is able to carry up to three clutches at once on his legs and looks after them until they hatch in three to eight weeks' time. Meanwhile, the rest of his body is free to mate again.

He keeps the eggs moist by staying in damp places and going for a swim whenever the eggs start to dry out. Once they are about to hatch, he finds a nice cool ditch or a pond to let them go. There they will become tadpoles and eventually little toads.

Many readers may not have given much thought to the parental qualities of male frogs, but now realising what devoted and hard-working fathers they are, it's going to be difficult to order frog legs from any menu in future!

THE PROMISCUOUS SINGLE DAD – THE AUSTRALIAN BRUSH-TURKEY

An ancient lineage of birds includes both the Malleefowl and the Australian Brush-turkey. In both species the male alone provides parental care by incubating the eggs. He constructs a mound by scraping leaf litter into a huge pile to create an incubation chamber. The Australian Brush-turkey (*Alectura lathami*) is promiscuous by nature and trades sex for chick-rearing duties. These single dads belong to a group of birds that are collectively known as mound-builders, incubator birds or megapodes (referring to their noticeably big feet).

Brush-turkeys have an innovative fathering style. This mound-builder is a sole parent and dad does all the work once the eggs are laid. They don't incubate the eggs with their own body heat, as most birds do, but use a sophisticated alternative: they bury the eggs. He gathers huge heaps of organic matter, the rotting of which creates heat which makes a great incubation chamber for the fertilised eggs. Dad then steadfastly manages the conditions inside this rotting mound of vegetation, adding and removing leaf litter to control the temperature inside it. The male brush-turkey will spend hours and hours each day maintaining his mound to the right incubation temperature of 33°C (91.4°F). A mound is usually about 2–4 metres (6.5–13 feet) wide and about 1 metre (3.3 feet) high. The male takes a large mouth full of the mound's contents to check the temperature using heat sensors in his upper bill. He will add or remove material as needed. This skill is what gets him the sex he's after.

Brush-turkey females visit a male's mound and if the mound is at the right temperature and she's ready, she will lay her eggs. After

This promiscuous bird trades sex for egg incubating duties. Australian Brush-turkey males are single dads and provide dedicated parental care by incubating the eggs. They construct a mound by scraping leaf litter in a huge pile to create an incubation chamber.

that, she mates with the mound-builder. She may or may not come back to his mound to lay the eggs now fertilised by him. A number of other females may visit his mound and deposit eggs, depending on how good he is at managing the temperature. He will only allow her to lay the eggs when the conditions in the incubation chamber are exactly right and he gets to mate with her. That's his condition and motivation for being such a great 'groundsman'. The mound may have up to 50 eggs being incubated at the same time. Essentially, the male brush-turkey exchanges sex for child-rearing duties, even if the eggs have been fertilised by another male. The female trades sex for sperm from a fit male who also possesses top real estate, after which she divulges all responsibility for the eggs and chicks. Everybody is happy.

Megapode chicks do not have an egg tooth. That's what most chicks use to break out of their shell. Instead, they use their strong legs and claws to crack the shell and tunnel out of the mound. Dad does nothing to help. The chicks lay on their backs, kicking away at the sand and leaf litter until they reach the surface. These super-precocial hatchlings emerge with their eyes open, fully feathered, ready to fly and start life without any further parental care. Brush-turkeys are among some of the most independent hatchlings. However, many don't make it to adulthood due to their parents' lackadaisical attitude to rearing once hatched. It's estimated that only one in 200 chicks makes it to adulthood.

It is interesting that all the work the male puts into constructing and maintaining his mound and then incubating the chicks does not guarantee the paternity of those chicks. Research by Sharon Birks used DNA fingerprinting for 65 brush-turkey chicks and found that almost 30 per cent were not sired by the mound-tending male. So, what's in it for this hard-working bird? I suppose he has to maintain a mound for his own brood anyway and a few more eggs don't cause any extra work. He also gets to fertilise eggs that the female goes on to lay in another mound, to be cared for by another dedicated foster dad, balancing out any perceived disadvantage.

DOUBLE DADS

Studies show that stable dual-parent families offer good outcomes for children growing up in same-sex households. It appears that the family unit's habits and behaviours are more important than the gender of the parents and study results do not support the notion that children need both male and female parents. Australian Black Swans (*Cygnus atratus*) support this notion. Like other swans, the Black Swan is largely monogamous, even if they do seem to have extramarital affairs quite frequently.

Almost a quarter of Black Swan families are headed up by two cobs, or male swans. Sometimes, one of these two males mates with a female (called a pen), only to chase her off the eggs once she's laid. His male partner then helps to brood the eggs, hatch them and raise a family of their own. The male pairs are also largely monogamous, staying together for years, even for life, except for needing a female once in a while to produce the eggs. Another way such swans get a family is to drive another couple off their eggs and commandeer the nest and its contents. Fortunately, the heterosexual pair can quickly lay more eggs. They are able to produce more cygnets carrying their genes whilst some devoted foster parents raise their earlier clutch.

Despite the rather harsh way these families are initially created, the chicks could not ask for more loving, caring dads. Black Swans are fierce and frankly a little scary when they rush another animal or a human they consider a threat. Their threat display looks quite aggressive and usually shoos predators away quickly. The advantage of two males is that collectively they are a little larger than a male-female pair and are able to defend the best territory in the pond or lake. They take turns sitting on the eggs and their overall breeding success is higher than in the heterosexual pairs. On average 80 per cent of same-sex parents successfully raise young cygnets, compared with only about 30 per cent of the heterosexual swan pairs.

WHEN DAD'S A MUM

Finding a mate can be tricky and having the ability to change gender is a popular option in some species. Clownfish (subfamily Amphiprioninae) are so named because they are very active and perform acrobatics, but equally it could be said that the name is appropriate due to their fooling around with their gender assignation.

Clownfish live around sea anemones (order Actiniaria) which, although they may look like pretty flowers, are actually predatory animals. Sea anemones tend to sting but for some reason clownfish are not affected by the sting and form a close relationship with their host. It's thought that they can move about the tentacles because of a substance on their body that protects them from the sting. Their life around the anemones means that predators can't get too close to the clownfish because they'll get stung. The ones that do get close can be poisoned and eaten by the anemone. Therefore both the clownfish and the anemone benefit from this arrangement.

Clownfish are very social and live in complex hierarchies. They use clicks and popping sounds to communicate with one another. They are all born as males but can change gender if the need arises. Only the dominant male and the dominant female will mate and produce offspring. If the dominant female dies her mate, the alpha male, will become female and mate with the new dominant male. The new breeding male is likely to be the largest of the group of males.

A male guards the eggs, not surprisingly, because there is only one female and a lot of males. The female may help out guarding on occasion. Once a male becomes female there's no going back – she remains female from then on.

PATERNITY ENSURED

Caring for tiny vulnerable creatures has an energy cost for the parent. Some animal dads want to be absolutely sure they are indeed the daddy if they're going to do the work of bringing up baby. As opposed to the brush-turkey, who thinks it's all swings and roundabouts, the male giant water bug, *Abedus herberti*, takes a different approach. He incubates the eggs on his back and can't fly during this time, making him more vulnerable to predators. If he's going to risk this, he wants to be sure that these babies are his.

The female can lay a lot of eggs at any one time but to make sure he's the fertiliser of those eggs he mates with her repeatedly. The female can store sperm from previous encounters, but by flooding the market, so to speak, he makes sure there's a lot of his sperm

Stable dual-parent families offer good outcomes for children growing up in same-sex households. The way the family unit operates is more important than the gender of the parents. Australian Black Swans prove this point.

around to make it less likely another male's stored sperm is going to fertilise the eggs. After each mating, the female lays a few eggs on his back and he incubates them. This mating and egg laying is then repeated time and time again until the female has laid all the eggs she's got available. This can take a few hours.

The eggs are stuck to the male's back and he protects them from predators, including other females who destroy the eggs of the competition so there's more 'back space' for her own brood. He cares for the eggs in a most interesting way: by doing underwater push-ups! These push-ups, allow fresh water to flow around the eggs, keeping them well oxygenated.

Although he sacrifices a lot for his brood, this water bug is not going to sacrifice everything. If food is scarce, he'll eat his eggs rather than starve.

HOME-BUILDER SINGLE DADS

Three-spined Sticklebacks (*Gasterosteus aculeatus*) are little fish with attitude and style. During the breeding season, each male defends a territory and builds an elaborate nest. This starts as a shallow pit which he fills with plant material. Interestingly he constructs a spherical nest with a tunnel through to the centre and glues the whole thing together with something called *spiggin* – a gluey substance secreted from the kidneys. This proves once again that when it comes to growing babies, evolution is much more varied than you'd first imagine.

Building is difficult without hands, arms, feet or a bill but this fishy dad makes a tunnel in his nest by brute force. He simply swims through it time and time again until a tunnel is formed. He's now ready to court and does so by performing a zigzag dance for any passing female who looks like she's got eggs. If she follows him back to the nest, he may get lucky, in which case she will deposit her eggs in the nest for him to fertilise. Once the deed is done he chases her away, only to court more gravid females passing his tunnel.

This DIY dad looks after the eggs and fans them by doing a swim-on-the-spot dance at the entrance of the tunnel. The ripples he creates inside the chamber bring lovely, oxygenated water to the eggs. He fans his eggs day and night until they hatch. Once his young hatch, he tries to keep them at home a little longer by rounding them up when they stray too far. He uses his mouth to suck up any that wander off and spits them back into the nest. Not long after, the young go their own way and their dad prepares for a new batch.

THE WISDOM OF THE ELDERS

The harem system creates a lot of 'spare males' and so do matriarchies in some cases. Matriarchal elephant herds make teenage boys leave home before they become sexually mature. The adults in the herds are strictly segregated on a gender basis. The youngsters have a long way to go and a lot to learn before they will be accepted by any female as a potential sire. Young male elephants do not grow up with an adult male influence in their daily lives and once they leave their natal group they are drawn to other males to hang out with in bachelor groups. For many years it was thought that bull elephants were always aggressive, hormone-fuelled killers. Yes, they can be that

Raising kids is tough and even harder when you're doing it on your own. Some animal dads do all the hard work of raising the next generation, a commitment exemplified by some special single dads like the Emperor Penguin. Outstanding single dads are found amongst insects, fishes, amphibians, birds and humans.

when the male is in musth, a time when older bulls are flooded with almost ten times the testosterone they normally have. But what's becoming clear, as more field studies observe male elephants in the wild, is that these senior bulls form friendships and can be leaders and teachers to younger bulls. Young males are frequently seen tagging along with older males. The role these bulls play to the young males is perhaps equivalent to that of a father figure or a mentor. As with their female counterparts, the mature male may lead the group by taking the position at the front of the line. The elders are likely to fulfil a protective role as well as a mentoring role for their juvenile companions. More recent observations illustrate exactly how much of the behaviour of young males may be moderated by mature bulls.

A park in South Africa released some young, orphaned male elephants into its grounds. They immediately behaved like teenage delinquents and killed several White Rhinos. This destructive behaviour changed once six older males were added to the mix. It would seem that the wisdom of the elders allowed the young males to develop a cultural understanding of what is acceptable behaviour, how to act and to whom to defer. The older bulls in these bachelor groups may perform the role of teacher in the finishing school for male elephants, so when commercial hunters target the older bulls as trophies for their rich clients this does not only shrink the elephant population, it also removes the protectors and teachers of the younger male generation.

SINGLE DADS - WHY DO THEY DO IT?

All parenting styles evolve as a reproductive strategy to maximise the desired outcome, namely the continuation of the parents' unique genetic package into the future. Fertilisation, conception, growing the embryo, birth or hatching and care of the offspring has to suit the environment and lifestyle of each species. The contribution individuals can make to the future of the species is carefully balanced between the physical costs to each parent and the amount of support they are able to offer the young ones growing up.

The parental investment each parent makes is related to how much either gender needs to do to have surviving offspring. There's a great variation in the amount of effort some animals can or are willing to give their offspring. If there's a lot of predation in their environment, one or the other parent needs to guard the youngsters until they can fend for themselves. Parasites or disease may be a limiting factor, as is competition for food. Some species will produce a huge number of eggs in the hope that only some will make it without being eaten by another animal. Other species put all their eggs in one basket and produce a single offspring, lavishing them with tender loving care. Although, some are more successful than others, each of these strategies work for a particular species.

Solo parenting, like all other reproductive strategies, is a tactic that a species adopts because it gives them the best possible chance to pass their genes to the next generation. In the case of single dads, most often the females have put all their energy into the production of eggs. The kind of eggs these mothers produce takes it out of them. In the case of the Emu, with their extra thick shells, or kiwi, with one enormous egg, the female is totally spent energetically and nutritionally once she's popped these huge things out. If the male did *not* take over at this stage the successful hatching of the egg would be unlikely. In many instances, the father too is at the end of his nutritional limit by the time the young hatch or leave home. This means that only animals who start the breeding season in a fit and healthy state are going to be successful.

Chapter 11

DANGEROUS LIAISONS

*'You know that look that women get when
they want to have sex? Me neither.'*

STEVE MARTIN

The natural world is stunningly beautiful and intriguing. So are
the multitude of species with whom we share the planet. Some
of the animals we've met are amazing, wonderful examples of
dedication and sacrifice. Unfortunately, not all of them play fair,
just as we humans don't always play fair. Some sacrifice themselves
and are willing to die for love, whereas others prefer to sacrifice
the competition or their mates ahead of themselves. This chapter
highlights the types of sexual relationships that can lead to death or
injury in the natural world, and looks additionally at the issues that
arise when sexual intentions are misunderstood.

KILLING FOR SEX

Animals kill other animals most commonly for food. Fighting for
dominance or territory usually intends to wound, not kill. Mostly
the aggressor stops short of killing the opponent. Killing one's
own species does happen though. Despite it being a delicate topic,

infanticide has been described in a large range of animals as well as in humans. In many species, a familiar reproductive strategy is killing the offspring produced by another male so that the mother becomes sexually available more quickly. When animals kill infants, the killers and their victims are nearly always unrelated. Maternal and paternal infanticide is exceedingly rare in nature, while infanticide has been observed throughout the animal kingdom in insects, fish, amphibians, birds and mammals.

Nature and evolution have of course come up with a few solutions to this problem. Confusion over paternity is one strategy. As males usually do not kill their own offspring, making the question of paternity murky protects youngsters from being killed. A female who mates with many males can lead to all of them thinking that they are the father of her offspring. Hanuman Langurs (*Semnopithecus entellus*) evolved to have a variable ovulation which also helps to conceal the paternity of any offspring. These monkeys do not make it obvious that they are in oestrus but somehow the males work it out, most likely through the soliciting behaviour of the female. She shows she's 'in the mood' by shuddering her head and presenting her behind to potential mates. As gestation is some 200 days, by the time the offspring is born any male who mated with the mother probably thinks her kid could be his, so he won't risk hurting it.

Killing babies to have sex with their mother can, sadly, be quite a common occurrence. Infanticide in many species takes the form of a male outsider overthrowing the resident harem master and killing any youngsters who are still suckling in order to get the females cycling quickly. This happens in gorilla troops and lion prides, for example.

THE MAJESTIC LION?

The African Lion (*Panthera leo*) who fathers the youngsters in the pride gets high accolades for being a kind and tolerant father. Not so the challenger who arrives to take over control of the harem. Male lions are a well-known example of a species that commits infanticide. The killing of infants by a couple of male lions was first seen by the general public in a nature documentary called *Queen of the Beasts*, made in 1988 by a British film team in the Serengeti National Park in Tanzania. The film crew was able to document how a couple of males ousted the former male residents and then immediately searched for suckling infants to kill them.

The lion pride consists of one, two or sometimes even three males, a number of females and their young. To his own cubs, the lion is a lovely dad, allowing them to tug his tail or crawl all over him with their sharp claws. Young males are expelled from the pride before they reach sexual maturity. The mating system means that a lot of male lions out there in the veld have no mate while others command a whole harem. This inevitably leads to trouble. The young males roam around getting fit and strong until one day a male or often a few brothers challenge an older harem chief. If a challenging male is successful at ousting the father, the winner of the contest almost immediately kills any suckling cubs. This killing of the previous male's cubs is called a 'routine reproductive strategy' by biologists and is consistent among all male lions. There are no nice lions and bad lions – all males do the same thing in the same circumstances with the objective of bringing the females quickly back into oestrus, so they can mate with her and father their own cubs. In biological terms, there's little point in raising the young of another male when male lions have such a short time to sire their own offspring before themselves being replaced.

What does a male lion contribute to his pride and what makes him earn his keep? Females are polyestrous, meaning they cycle throughout the year and heat lasts for about four days. The male's main job is to make babies. As the strongest, healthiest male around, his genes are worth propagating. Important too is his role as the protector of the group, shielding the lionesses and their offspring from any danger, particularly the advances of rival males where takeovers would result in the death of their cubs. It has been observed that lionesses, on occasion, will support the alpha male in helping to attack the challenging male. The females are seriously invested in their cubs' survival. If a new male does succeed in taking over the leadership of the pride, the juveniles and adolescents are also expelled from the family unit. Although the adolescents escape infanticide, life outside an established pride is tough and starvation is a significant risk.

Trophy hunting indirectly contributes to the number of cubs killed by males taking over a pride. The largest adult males with the biggest manes are targeted as hunting trophies and they are likely to be the alpha male in a pride. With the removal of that male, a new male, or a coalition of new males, will take control, killing all the cubs in favour of making their own babies. Cubs take two years to become independent. If the frequency of leadership change increases through hunting, the pride can't sustain itself. Although trophy hunting claims it has a positive impact in some areas, contributing funds for conservation efforts in Africa, it appears to have contributed to the decline of lion numbers in Botswana, Namibia, Tanzania,

Lions tend to make excellent fathers to their cubs. The African Lion's main job in the pride is to make babies. The harem master, as the strongest, healthiest male around, has genes worth propagating. Important too is his role as the protector of the group, shielding the pride from any danger.

Zimbabwe, Cameroon and Zambia. Conservationists call for the better regulation of trophy hunting to ensure sustainability.

BABY-FACED KILLERS

Little do most people know that Bottlenose Dolphins (*Tursiops truncatus*), with their seemingly friendly faces, are in fact baby killers too. Males seem to remember which females they have mated with and therefore which calves they have sired. When the male encounters an unfamiliar female with a calf, he will try to separate the pair and may severely injure or kill the youngster so he can have his wicked way with the mother.

If the calf dies, the mother will be able to conceive again in a few months. The killer may then father her next calf. Without killing the infant, she won't be receptive for another three to four years. That's a long time for a male dolphin.

BULLY-BOY ELEPHANT SEALS

The Southern Elephant Seal (*Mirounga leonina*) is a bully and gets its name from the male's enormous size and trunk-like nasal appendage. This 'trunk' is used extensively during the breeding season to produce loud roars. The bull is six to seven times heavier than the largest living land carnivores, the Polar Bear (*Ursus maritimus*) and Kodiak Bear (*Ursus arctos middendorfii*), so they are big boys indeed. This seal shows extreme sexual dimorphism in size, with the males typically five to six times heavier than the females. Males use this size to exert control over the females. Elephant seals gather each year at the same time along the coastlines of the Subantarctic islands. The males arrive first and fight with other males to claim their favourite spot. As soon as the females are ready to join the waiting males, they look for a 'beachmaster' with the best territory.

Some males are able to attract quite a few females. Nearly all the landing females are about to give birth and do so not long after arriving on the beach. Some evidence suggests that females choose the harem they want to be in. Females who select a larger harem have better offspring survival rates. Perhaps this is because the more females a male has in his territory, the more he has to do and the less time he has to endanger any pups. Only days after she's given birth, a female is ready to mate again with the beachmaster she's chosen with the best habitat for her pup. The mating can be a brutal affair. This amorous male is twice the size of an average car and up to 4,000 kilograms (8,800 pounds) of macho muscle – he crushes many a newborn pup in his eagerness to get to their mother. The male's not too worried about bulldozing a few pups as they are unlikely to be his. The mother feeds her young on an extra-rich milk which allows them to be weaned at 24 days old, by which time they weigh in at 120 kilograms (265 pounds) and are less likely to be crushed. However, the first weeks of the pup's life are the most dangerous and its survival is severely threatened by its bully of a stepfather.

INFANTICIDE IN GREAT APES

Of all the great apes, humans, gorillas, Chimpanzees, orangutans and Bonobo, only the last two have no documented cases of infanticide. Gorillas, however, are more like lions and an incoming male who wants to bring the females back into oestrus quickly will kill her young from another silverback. In zoos we do not introduce a new male to a group of females until the youngest infant is three or four years old and fully weaned. If the mother is sexually available the stepdad does not kill his stepchild. In Chimpanzees it's frequently young males rising through the ranks who kill infants, potentially so they can impregnate the mother sooner rather than later. It is also postulated that unfortunate infants, who happen to be in the wrong place at the wrong time during a male's testosterone-fueled displays, are killed accidentally rather than for sexual access to the mother.

All great apes avoid killing their own babies. If they've mated with a female they will not kill her baby, perhaps calculating it is theirs. In Chimpanzees it's hypothesised that promiscuity may be a clever female strategy to confuse paternity and it certainly seems to work among Bonobos. Bonobos are masters at resolving social issues and have found a way around the unpleasantness of infanticide by happily mating with everyone in their troop, so the males aren't able to identify which kids are theirs and which aren't. They are the only African great ape that has not one documented case of infanticide. In addition, the female Bonobos who run the show have low tolerance for bad behaviour in their troop. Any male who commits a transgression against a youngster will be severely punished by a posse of angry females.

Having family to protect you and your baby is another safeguard against infanticide. In Chimpanzee society close family ties can act as a defence. Richard Buzas, Senior Primate Keeper at Taronga Zoo, witnessed the following events:

'On the 27th of February 2008 I was just about to do the chimp talk at Taronga Zoo when I saw Shiba, a heavily pregnant female, sitting on a log over the waterfall. This in itself wasn't unusual, except that when she started to urinate she was in obvious discomfort. This isn't normal for a simple urination and in fact her waters had just broken and she'd gone into labour. She moved over to the base of a rock ledge on the ground where no one could come up behind her and she could see everything in front of her. This was noticed by her two sons, Samaki aged 11 and his older brother Shabani aged 17, who moved to the ledge above her, quite clearly to stand guard. The group was relatively quiet at the time but any other chimps who moved in that direction were not allowed near. Shiba's face showed the clear signs of contractions, although unlike humans she did not vocalise. In the wild, too, Chimpanzee births are silent to avoid drawing attention to the mother when she is in such a vulnerable position.

Shiba's labour took 49 minutes from when I first saw her waters break to the arrival of a female, now named Sembe. The two males protected her throughout the birth, chasing away anyone who came too close. Their body language made it clear they meant business. Mum was able to give birth in peace whilst being guarded by her older offspring. Shiba's maternal instinct kicked in immediately after the birth as she cleaned her baby, cleared the nose and mouth to make sure it was breathing and then held it close to her chest. To satisfy their curiosity, her two protectors were allowed a peak at their new sibling, a little closer than anybody else would have been permitted. Samaki and Shabani were undoubtedly looking out for their family during this time.'

Chimpanzee males love their mums and they can be mummy's boys until well into their adulthood, running to her for a hug when they are upset or protecting her when she's vulnerable, like Shabani and Samaki did. Additionally, there may be an evolutionary advantage as by protecting their newborn sibling there will be more of their genes in the gene pool.

Infanticide can occur in humans as well, despite being considered just about the worst thing anyone could do. Infanticide in the Western world is less common now than it once was. Child sacrifices to the gods are certainly no longer a major cause of death in infancy. Where infanticide continues to occur, it seems to be driven by extreme poverty and overpopulation. Even now in some countries, sex-selective infanticide makes girl babies vulnerable. Where overpopulation and poverty are not an issue infanticide is more likely to be committed by a man who is not the father – a situation not unlike that which occurs with Chimpanzees or gorillas, arising when a new partner comes into the life of the infant's mother. A study by Yampolskaya and others in 2009 found that non-biological parents were 17 times more likely to commit a fatal assault on a child than biological parents.

Throughout evolution, females have evolved specific traits to prevent males from killing their offspring. In all species where this is the reproductive strategy, monogamy seems to protect against infanticide. This supports the theory that the development of monogamy in humans may have evolved as a means of preventing infanticide and because of the need for the mothers to have the father's help with protection and food supply. An evolutionary approach we humans have taken involves a similar yet slightly different strategy to protect against infanticide. Whereas other primates show visual signs of ovulation, such as swollen labia, human females give no graphic external indication of ovulation. Babies are born nearly nine months later, which is a long time after conception. This helps to keep the paternity of any progeny murky and can lead to father's assuming any offspring is theirs. The bonding between human sexual partners is also hypothesised as a way of avoiding infanticide. This long-term monogamous pairing protects infants from the probability of being killed by another male.

EXTREME FATHERHOOD

The cases above highlight sex-crazed males with only one thing on their mind, even if it means killing an infant. Such examples can be counterbalanced by those males of species who are also driven by sex but are prepared to risk their own death to get it, even if they only get laid once.

To answer the call of nature and pass on your genes, a male has to strike when the iron is hot, so to speak. The commitment of some males to this task is truly remarkable. The Brown Antechinus (*Antechinus stuartii*), a previously mentioned cute Australian carnivorous marsupial, is renowned for its sex drive and subsequent immediate demise. All males of this species die a few days after their brief and frantic mating season. Over a two-week period, a male antechinus copulates for hours and hours at a time with one or more females. At the end of this he dies from the stress. Searching for females, fighting with rivals and shagging for hours on end all lead to the marsupial's demise from stress hormones that are thought to reduce the effectiveness of his immune system. This cautionary tale about the antechinus should count as a warning to over-enthusiastic human Casanovas.

Some species literally lose their heads for sex. The male Australian Redback Spider (*Latrodectus hasselti*), also known as the Australian black widow spider (for reasons that will soon become obvious), is the ultimate dinner date. He does not produce a web himself but hangs out on the edge of a female's web during the mating season. Mr Redback is so keen to mate that he's willing to risk his life or even commit suicide for a bit of naughty time. He only gets to mate once in his lifetime and has even evolved a sort of somersault during copulation to place his abdomen directly on the fangs of the female in an act of self-sacrifice. Being eaten actually increases his chance of siring the spiderlings. The male redback is one of only two animals known where the male actively encourages the female to eat him in this way. To find out if the female is ready to mate, he stands on his head, proffering his abdomen to her mouthparts. If she's not ready, this strategy can be fatal as she squirts digestive juices on his tummy whilst he tries to insert his first palp – the organ with which he transfers sperm. If he's still going strong, he will withdraw palp one and insert palp two while she is digesting his belly. Most redback males do not survive this process. This strategy is known as reproductive cannibalism or sexual cannibalism. Sexual cannibalism is the redback's unique strategy and she will consume her suitor entirely, or if he's still alive he will die of his injuries soon after. The male is so seriously keen because his chance of ever finding a female in his lifetime is only about 20 per cent. He's willing to risk it all for the opportunity to pass on his genes.

A rather similar fate befalls the male praying mantis (family Mandidae). The lover-boy tracks down a female by following her pheromones. When he finds her he may notice that he's substantially smaller, making it easier for her to eat him. He prefers well-fed females for understandable reasons. On the whole, as a family male praying mantises have not yet worked out a way of pacifying the females with whom they copulate. Once they get on with what he came for, she may bite off his head first, which makes him thrust more and calm him down somewhat after all the excitement of finding a mate. The removal of his head instigates the mating moves he has to perform to release his sperm. It is his headless body that fertilises his female posthumously. Cannibalism only happens in a quarter of sexual encounters when a female decides to avail herself of the nutrition she needs to provide for their offspring. The male thereby provides for his future offspring by feeding their mother even after his demise.

Some male spiders risk death as they copulate but some fight back. One strategy is to try placating the female by gently stroking her, while other males come on more strongly and try to tie down the female with their silky spider ropes.

David Laux, an invertebrate specialist from Wellington Zoo in New Zealand, has seen sexual cannibalism close up many times and considers it the most altruistic act a father can make:

'In both mantis and widow spiders not only do the females eat the males but males actually sacrifice themselves to the female in order to ensure that she's had a large nutritious meal to give his seed optimal chance of success. These fathers will nourish the body of the mother to ensure their young survive and prosper. Male widow spiders will even flip themselves up on end against the jaws of a female to make sure she consumes him and gets that calorific hit – the ultimate fatherly sacrifice.'

In bees, sexual self-sacrifice is also how a male passes on his genes. Drones are the male bees in a hive and their purpose is to procreate. They live to mate and die for the same reason. They are looked after by the worker bees and they are a costly form of insurance policy. They are maintained simply as potential sperm donors in case the old queen dies and the new queen needs mates. When a virgin queen takes a nuptial flight, the drones can spot her from a long way off. The drones who get to mate with her literally lose their sex organ. Their *endophallus* is barbed like the stinger on a worker bee. The drone's ejaculation is explosive and so powerful that it ruptures the *endophallus*, tearing the drone's organ away and making him fall to his death.

Luckily, most animals on the planet have worked out less self-sacrificial ways to make babies. The idea of losing your life for sex is too much to bear for some species. David Laux, also shares his story of how some animals have evolved a compromise:

'The argonaut – a creature similar in appearance to the now-extinct ammonite – is a type of octopus that has some intriguing mating habits. Mating is extremely dangerous for the males of the species, as they are commonly consumed by the females. As such, they have evolved a novel way to avoid being eaten. Their solution is to physically remove their penis, literally ripping off their sex organ and tossing it across to the female. She then picks it up and will use it to inseminate her eggs. The male has now performed his duty of passing on his genetic material without risking his head. He is able to regrow and regenerate his penis so he can do it all over again, multiple times, hopefully breeding with multiple females with his future member.'

Talk about being dismembered.

In most cases, rather than dying for the cause, species evolve a strategy to create new life without losing their own. To make reproduction a safer option, it helps for a bond of some sort to be developed between the two parties, at least for the time it takes to copulate. Aggression has to be appeased during the sex act and in some species that bond has to endure for the time it takes the young to mature enough to fend for themselves.

WHAT TO DO ABOUT AGGRESSION?

Sex and aggression are often linked. Competition for sex can be the cause of aggression. Behaviours in all creatures, great and small, are often hardwired but many are cultural rather than innate. Birds know when to migrate, how to build a nest and incubate eggs. Ducklings take to water like, well, ducks. Spider parents don't have web-weaving classes and frogs are born knowing how to croak. Animal and human behaviour is a dance between our genes and our environment. In primates, including humans, a lot of behaviour is learned.

The amount of aggression tolerated can vary between cultures and communities. The primate blueprint of behaviour can be volatile and many primates are aggressive. It does not take much for a Chimpanzee to fly off the handle. The most famous exception, the Bonobos, have found another way to control aggression. They resolve conflict with sex and food sharing rather than fighting. Chimpanzees, by contrast, resolve all conflict with violence, bluff, threatened or actual. Chimps do demonstrate that they are particularly good at making up after an altercation though. All disputes are followed by a hug, grooming and even a big smacking kiss on the lips of the opponent. In Chimpanzee societies where aggression is common, peacemaking is essential to maintain a semblance of harmony in the group. Individuals who fight now may have to band together tomorrow to defend the territory.

We may assume that the amount of aggression in a species is more or less fixed, but cultural changes can significantly alter the behaviour of groups. An interesting example of substantial cultural change in primates is given by Robert Sapolsky and his colleague and wife, Lisa Share.

Sapolsky, a primatologist, studied baboons (*Papio* species) from the late 1970s until the mid-1980s, when a tuberculosis outbreak selectively killed off the most aggressive males in a group he was studying, which he called 'The Forest Troop'. Baboon society is normally quite violent. But Sapolsky wondered how much is hardwired and how much is cultural? Half of the males in the study area died from the TB outbreak and those victims were the top-ranking males – the ones who had been aggressive enough to fight the neighbouring clan for the infected meat on the garbage dump of an irresponsible tourist lodge. After losing so many of his subjects,

Sapolsky gave up his study and didn't return to the area for ten years.

When he did come back a decade later, however, he found drastic changes in the behaviour of the troop. When the most dominant, aggressive males were killed, those left behind were only low-ranking males, females and their young. This major change in demographic brought about a cultural shift towards a more peaceable society, with a more relaxed dominance hierarchy clearly evident. Males were fighting less, sat closer together and groomed one another, even though they still scrapped occasionally (they were baboons after all). Remarkably though, this observable change in aggression levels continued two decades later, despite the turnover of males during this time. The Forest Troop females must have liked the new order of things and found a way of instructing incoming males in the new moral code of the troop. These changes may have happened because the now-predominant female gender balance was able to instruct the young incoming males who had not yet learned to be overly aggressive.

The baboon example illustrates that we too are capable of changing parts of our cultural behaviour we don't like.

AN AMOROUS EMU

Another category of dangerous liaisons occurs when the courting couples misunderstand each other. Sometimes one party thinks the relationship is going in one way and the other may see it quite differently, as happened to my friend.

Once upon a time a little striped baby Emu was found abandoned on the road. He'd lost his daddy to a truck thundering down the highway they were crossing. It killed his father instantly, his feathers scattered to the wind. His siblings ran in all directions, never to be found again. Dubbo, as we called him, was taken to the zoo by a caring motorist who picked him up. As he was now an orphan, we took care of him. In the wild, a young bird without his father to protect him would fall prey to any predator, from a Wedge-tailed Eagle to Dingos, in no time at all.

Zookeepers looked after him, making sure he ate well and felt safe. Dubbo became a good-looking emu, tall with a regal bearing. He became so attached to humans though that he had trouble remembering he was an Emu. So badly did he forget his Emu identity that when he grew up and became sexually mature he seemed to be interested in people in an unusual way. This became clear to my poor zookeeper colleague (who wishes to remain anonymous for understandable reasons).

One foul, rainy day, wearing full wet-weather gear which limited her movement, my colleague was cleaning Dubbo's yard. As she hunched down to sweep up some debris with a dustpan and broom, a great force pushed her to the ground and held her down. Her raingear prevented her from getting up. Fortunately, she managed to get hold of her walky-talky to call for help. Help did arrive quickly although the other keepers weren't very useful due to the fact they were laughing so hard. They found her pinned to the ground by an amorous Emu who did not know that his great human friend was not meant to be his sexual partner.

After the helpers recovered themselves sufficiently to be able to act, Dubbo was persuaded that his advances were not appropriate. She, who will remain nameless, was helped up and suffered some bruising on her knees, but rather more damage to her pride. She later mentioned that Dubbo had been quite affectionate for a few days but she'd not expected he'd take his obsession that step further.

Finally, if the thought of this dance with danger just to procreate has put you off sex you may have an increased admiration for the self-inseminating hermaphrodite flatworm, mentioned earlier, which stabs itself in the head to self-inject sperm. The next chapter provides some alternative strategies on how to become or be a father.

EMBRYONIC CANNIBALISM

The Sand Tiger Shark (*Carcharias taurus*) is polyandrous and a female will mate with multiple males, but her babies often show genetic monogamy. How does that work?

Female sand tigers have two uterine horns. During the development of her embryos, she may have as many as 50 babies from different males. However, as the young start to grow into strong healthy baby sharks with precocious dentition, the biggest hatchling embryo in each uterus kills and feeds on its siblings. When one of her embryos gets to about 10 centimetres (4 inches) long it eats all the smaller babies until only one remains. This is sometimes called adelphophagy meaning 'eating one's brother'. This results in one strong, healthy and very well-fed hatchling. After quite a lengthy labour an independent offspring measuring 1 metre (3.3 feet) emerges from each uterus.

Chapter 12

MAYBE BABY

*'It is not flesh and blood but the heart
which makes us fathers and sons.'*

JOHANN FRIEDRICH VON SCHILLER

Fatherhood is changing in the modern world. You can be a biological father, an adoptive father, a foster father, a stepfather, a godfather or a father in a two-dad household. I'm sure even more variations will evolve over time. However, not everyone wants to be father in the traditional sense or is even suited to fatherhood. Some men are slower than others to warm to the idea of fatherhood, while others never do.

There are reasons why it may be better for our species if some people refrained from having offspring or perhaps delayed fatherhood until they themselves grow up. There are many other ways to contribute to the lives of young people and support youngsters to become good adults.

WHEN'S THE RIGHT TIME?

There are people whose genes would be better kept out of the gene pool all together. The Darwin Awards are given to humans who have met a superior standard of stupidity. The criterion for the award states: 'In the spirit of Charles Darwin, the Darwin Awards commemorate individuals who protect the gene pool by making the ultimate sacrifice of their own lives. The Darwin winners eliminate themselves in an extraordinarily idiotic manner, thereby improving our species' chances of long-term survival.'

The website for the Darwin Awards further notes that for reasons of necessity the award is usually bestowed posthumously. The annual list of notable nominees for this award is proof that not everyone should reproduce as passing on these 'stupid' genes to the next generation is not going to benefit our species.

A good deal of our stupid behaviour occurs when we are young and haven't really worked out that there are consequences for our actions. We might be too young to breed but then leave it too late and become too old to make it easy. So, when's the right time? Most animals breed as soon as they are sexually mature. In humans, emotional maturity may take a little longer to develop than sexual maturity. There are media reports of boys as young as 11 years old having fathered a child. But being sexually mature enough to produce viable sperm does not make one mentally mature enough to take on fatherhood and become a committed parent.

Given the examples of the Darwin Awards, fatherhood is probably best attempted once the male brain is fully grown. The rate of brain development is going to be different in different people but the general consensus is that the brain is fully developed by the mid-twenties in humans. Interestingly, one can be physically mature at 18 or 19 years old, whereas the brain keeps maturing for a little longer. The immature brain may not be as good at assessing consequences or planning actions to reach a goal. Severe risk-taking behaviour settles once the brain matures. A mature brain would come in handy for a new parent.

Being a young dad has its advantages though, and having more energy is definitely one advantage. However, not all dads get to decide when the time is right. Accidents do happen. Ideally a prospective sire is mature enough to be sensible but has young and healthy sperm. In the meantime, 'practicing' is recommended until the male matures.

Being an older dad can have advantages too. It often means you've gathered more wisdom and patience and maybe even resources (wealth). If there's a male biological clock, when does it start ticking? In the zoo, when managing breeding programs, the age of the male is not considered as important as the age of the female. Females have a finite number of eggs and when they're finished the reproductive potential comes to an end. Male animals are only limited by physical strength and fitness to perform. For example, an older male deer may not have the power in his hind legs to mount the female for long enough to do the deed even if his sperm is still healthy. However, there is evidence to suggest the decline of male fertility with age too. The effects of age on female fertility have been known for a long time but we now know that sperm quality generally starts to reduce at around 40 to 45 years of age in humans.

If there is a 'best' time to become a Dad it's somewhere when your brain is mature and whilst your sperm can still swim marathons.

HAVE YOUR SIBLINGS REPRODUCE

If you are reluctant about fatherhood there are alternatives to being a dad and still making sure your genes make it to the next generation. A simple, respectable and rewarding way to pass on your genes to the next generation is to make sure your siblings have children. In zoo breeding programs we equalise the genes represented by different family lines. This means that if some family members have lots of offspring, we limit the breeding in the rest of that bloodline.

It's simple maths: each parent passes 50 per cent of their genes to their offspring. This is a random 50 per cent. Each offspring gets a slightly different package of genes from each parent every time they make a new baby. You share genes with your brothers and sisters but you don't have the exact same genes. You are therefore likely to share around 25 per cent of your genes with your nieces and nephews – half of what you would have passed on if they were your children. If you have several nieces and nephews, you have more of your genes represented. It's as if you had children yourself. Even better, if you have an identical twin they could potentially do all the passing on of genes for you while you focus on the 'sex for fun' part. It's much less time-consuming and costs you a lot less energy if your family does the hard yards. You can be a brilliant uncle, remember their birthdays, take the kids to the zoo, babysit when called upon and still have the time and money for fabulous holidays!

Chimpanzees clearly show that blood is thicker than water, as frequently illustrated in the observations of the zookeepers who care for these magnificent animals. Chimps will protect their siblings from harm, as observed by Allan Schmidt, an experienced great ape keeper who makes the following comments about family loyalty:

'While chimps don't demonstrate much paternal behaviour, they certainly have an awareness of their responsibilities towards their siblings. Whilst their promiscuous society does not promote involved fatherhood, Chimpanzees have evolved other ways to enhance the chances that their genetic material is passed on to the next generation. This evolutionary concept was illustrated one day when a female called Lani gave birth to her first baby. Much to our surprise she abandoned the baby, simply putting it on the ground. Lubutu, her brother and the alpha male at the time, picked the baby up immediately. At no time was he violent or abusive to this newborn as chimps can be.

This happened on a Saturday night and I came into the Chimpanzee night house to investigate and to decide what to do. I needed to isolate Lubutu from the rest of the chimps before anyone in the group thought the infant was a plaything. Lubutu was willing to be separated from the group with the infant in his arms. Once I had him in a different part of the building, I tried to separate him from the infant when he placed it on the ground. I wanted him out and to let the mother, Lani, back in. Although Lubutu was happy to be isolated from all the other chimps, he refused to leave the newborn. Only once he saw Lani, the baby's mother, making her way to an adjacent raceway where he and the baby were, did he decide to go. He did not want to leave unless Lani was there taking back responsibility for his little newborn niece. He put the infant on the ground and made way for Lani to come in. Once he saw the mother, he seemed satisfied that the right order of things had been restored and off he went, back to the group.'

Lubutu's story is also a touching reminder of how closely related we are to Chimpanzees. This is exactly the reaction you would expect from a brother helping out his sister who has momentarily lost the plot. During scuffles, chimps regularly take sides with their family members against others in the troop. Friendships matter in chimp society as they do in ours, but family ties are also strong as demonstrated by Lubutu protecting his little relative from potential harm. Supporting family, especially the children of siblings, is a way of passing your genes to the next generation.

SPERM DONATION

Sperm donation is another alternative to consider if you are ambivalent about fatherhood but want to ensure your genes are represented in the gene pool. Here there are options to be involved in the resulting child's life or to remain in the background as a donor only. The act of sperm donation can be extremely rewarding for the donor and for the receiving mother and/or non-biological father. It can allow people who can't conceive, lesbian couples and people who carry a genetic disease to still become parents of healthy kids. A good deed indeed.

ALLOPARENTING – HELPING TO RAISE THE OFFSPRING OF OTHERS

If you don't want to breed but quite like children, perhaps alloparenting works for you? Many animal parents have helpers to raise their young, whether from among their own siblings or from a friendship group. Alloparenting has evolutionary advantages for all members of the group who share the same genes.

In biology, alloparenting, also called cooperative breeding, means that individuals within a pack, mob or troop will take on a parental role even though they are not the actual parents. They may help to feed, babysit, guard and carry the young or youngsters, delaying or sacrificing their own chance of breeding to help others in the group, often the dominant pair. This alpha pair is quite likely to be the parents, brother or sister of the helper. Alloparents are therefore genetically related to the little ones they are helping to survive. However sometimes alloparents are not related to the young. Alloparenting is most common in birds, primates and some other mammals such as the Black-backed Jackal, African Wild Dog and wolves.

Allan Schmidt has looked after breeding groups of Cotton-top Tamarins at Taronga Zoo for many years and shares the following insights about helpers and practicing fatherhood:

'Looking after infants is a learned experience in primates. As opposed to most mammals, where it's female experience that is the deciding factor in reproductive success, the experience of the male is crucial where a female may not have any experience. His experience counts importantly towards the success of rearing offspring. The more you learn in your family group, the better you are likely to be as a new parent. The international breeding programs take this into consideration and aim to set up breeding pairs of individuals who've had a bit of practice as helpers in their natal group. Helpers are vital to the success of the biological mum and dad and later the helper benefits from this involvement when they get to breed themselves. Ideally they've seen at least two litters born and raised before they get to implement their parenting skills on their own offspring.

Experience as a helper greatly increases infant survival once the animal is a breeding adult. Sometimes new breeding pairs are slow to start. Cotton-top Tamarins have a longer gestation than most other tamarin species and after the first born, which is usually a singleton, they have a 66 per cent chance of pumping out twins every six months. Once they've had the first few litters they become 'lean mean breeding machines'. They can only do so because of the assistance they get from the helpers.

The moment the female gives birth, the father takes the young, literally taking the load off the mother who has just given birth to two big babies. Older siblings helping with infant caring also helps to decrease the pressure on the mother, so all she has to do is regain her strength and lactate.'

Some animals remain helpers all their lives. Their genes are still in the population as their siblings and other relatives breed, so their DNA gets passed on to next generation by their breeding relatives.

Cooperative breeding evolves in situations where food is limited or there are a lot of predators. If the conditions are awfully difficult for the breeding pair to raise their young, it is more likely that alloparenting develops. Alloparenting has evolved in numerous species, demonstrating it's a worthwhile strategy that works well in certain situations.

A well-known alloparenting society can be found in Africa: the Meerkats. The British documentary series *Meerkat Manor*

Parental care in Cotton-top Tamarins is not instinctual but a learned skill. From a young age older siblings help to care for their parents' younger offspring, which are often twins. This learning process makes them good parents when it's their turn to breed.

popularised this species. At that time we noticed a marked difference in the interests of visitors to our zoo. Before 2005, when the series started, no visitor ever asked to be directed to the Meerkats. Once the animals had names and were in people's loungeroom on a regular basis, visitors knew much more about the species and wanted to see them up close. The reality soap opera portrayed by these animal characters in the Kalahari Desert became a hit.

Meerkats are extremely cooperative, living in groups of 5 to 40 individuals in large underground networks with multiple entrances.

Mum is in charge as their society is matriarchal, but she has a lot of helpers. The alpha female pairs up with an alpha male and may give birth to up to four litters each year. Producing this many young is physically exhausting and she needs to recover from pregnancy and parturition each time before she's ready to do it all again. Three to seven pups may be born each time. Most Meerkats within the same mob are siblings and offspring of the dominant pair. There's a strong hierarchy in Meerkat society and only the alpha male and alpha female get to breed.

All members of the Meerkat mob take responsibility and babysit the young in the group. The father of the litter will stand guard to protect the youngsters but the helpers take on a huge share of the rearing, feeding the pups and huddling with them to keep them warm. Babysitters stay back at the den when others go feeding and care for the alpha pair's young whilst the dominant female forages with the rest of the group. The alpha mum needs to feed a lot because she's the milk factory. Helpers will protect the young from any threat, endangering their own lives to do so. On warning of a danger, the babysitter will take the young underground to safety or collect all young together and lie on top of them when retreating underground is not possible. Whilst the alphas are busy producing the next generation, the rest of the Meerkat team makes sure that safety from predators is a top priority. It takes a village to raise a Meerkat!

Alloparenting happens in lots of birds but also in carnivores such as the Dwarf Mongoose (*Helogale parvula*), African Wild Dog (*Lycaon pictus*) and Ethiopian Wolf (*Canis simensis*), in primates such as the Common Marmoset (*Callithrix jacchus*) and Cotton-top Tamarin (*Saguinus oedipus*), *in rodents like the* Naked Mole-rat (*Heterocephalus glaber*), and in many more species. It's common in many carnivorous creatures to allow the youngsters to feed first after a hunt. African Wild Dogs live in complex hierarchies where only the dominant pair breeds but all pack members chip in to feed any puppies in the group. Pack members regurgitate food for the young and any adult will allow youngsters to eat their fill before eating themselves. This altruistic behaviour towards infants is common except in the case of the male Lion, who is a bit of a greedy guts when it comes to food and will always eat first. Lactating mothers, cubs and other lionesses have to wait until he's had his fill. This big male takes the lion's share of any kill.

The fact alloparenting has arisen in so many different types of animals from a variety of environments shows it's a good solution to the problem of keeping offspring alive. Alloparenting, sperm donation or getting your siblings to reproduce are all strategies that can be explored by reluctant prospective fathers. The alloparenting idea can also serve like a 'try before you buy' option.

KIDNAP THE HELPERS

An Australian bird, the White-winged Chough (*Corcorax melanorhamphos*), takes a long time to grow up. They are four years old before they are ready to breed and they stay with their parents until that time. Meanwhile they get to practice being parents themselves as they help with building large mud nests, incubating eggs and feeding chicks. If there's no mud they make do with cow poo or emu dung.

The raising of young choughs is a big job and although the young from previous years help raise the latest clutch, the family will recruit more helpers whenever the opportunity presents itself. They do this by kidnapping their neighbours' offspring to get enough labour to raise their own progeny. As their neighbours also utilise this strategy, I'm not quite sure how exactly this all works out, but whatever helpers they do get assist in defending the nest against nest-robbers like currawongs and other predators.

The helpers are not beyond deceit, though, which might be understandable if they are the neighbour's kidnapped kids. As they arrive at the nest to feed the nestlings, helpers have been known to quickly swallow morsels of food themselves if nobody is looking. You can't blame them really, can you? Young take some six to seven months to reach independence – a long time in a bird's life. If they are not kidnapped by the neighbours before the next breeding season, they repay their parents by helping to raise next year's nestlings. The larger the group of choughs looking after the nest, the greater the chance the youngsters have of surviving.

Barbary Macaques (*Macaca sylvanus*) seem to know that babies can change the mood of an adult for the better. When they've had a fight with another male they must apologise to the victor of the brawl. To make sure the apology is well received, they 'borrow' a baby from a nearby female to present to the winner of the argument. Neither male will harm the infant and the mother is nearby keeping an eye out. The males soon return the infant to her once the hostilities have been resolved to the satisfaction of those involved.

Kidnapping is not recommended if you want babies or young people in your life, but most offers of babysitting are gratefully received.

FOSTER OR ADOPT

Although there's no biological inheritance, adoption offers a way of being represented in future generations through the positive influence one can have on the young person being raised. Adoption is an excellent way to make a difference in the life of a child and yet again nature provides examples. In biology there are firm views on parental investment. Often the discussion is about the minimal parental investment that any species can get away with in order to pass on their genes. Yet, I've seen such kindness in so many species that had nothing to do with passing on genes and more to do with empathy and altruism.

There are numerous reports of spontaneous adoptions of orphans by primates. An infant whose mother has died or disappeared may be adopted by another member of the group, sometimes even a male. Tiny babies are sometimes adopted by lactating females, older orphans by teenagers or adult males. If the youngsters are weaned, they have a reasonable chance of survival. Wild animal research provides positive adoption stories of male or male pairs successfully bringing up baby primates.

As a zookeeper I raised a lot of orphaned critters brought to us by members of the public when the parents were killed by a car or a cat. I hand-reared or fostered many orphaned birds, mammals and reptiles. Where possible I released these orphans back into the wild, but this can be tricky as many species will not tolerate a stranger arriving in their territory. Baby animals need to learn from their elders if they are social species and facilitating that for the orphan was always a dilemma.

Growing animals need sunshine to grow strong bones and I once put the baby kookaburra I was raising inside a cage in my garden to get some filtered rays of sunshine. The local Laughing Kookaburras (*Dacelo novaeguineae*), a very territorial species, were outraged, loudly complaining and every now and then swooping to attack the cage containing the youngster. That aggressive behaviour waned over a few days. Not only did they become less aggressive, they started to try and feed it through the bars! Somehow, I assume, the adults started to feel protective of the youngster. Could their maternal and paternal instincts have been triggered by the begging calls of the young kookaburra? I will never know exactly what happened but I took advantage of the adults' instinctive parenting. I worried that perhaps they were already feeding their own brood elsewhere in the territory, so I put food on top of the young kookaburra's cage so that the foster parents did not have to work too hard to feed their 'foundling'. The youngster grew quickly and I moved him to a larger flight aviary to start exercising his wings in readiness for flight. The adults continued to feed him through the wire of the aviary. Eventually, I released the new fledgling by opening the door of the aviary when the foster parents were around. He was greeted with much enthusiasm. I'm sure they thought I'd kidnapped their baby and now I was giving him back. Before opening the aviary door, I put a band on the orphan's leg with a unique registration number. This allowed me to recognise him from a distance and if he ever got into trouble the contact details were on the ring. My study had only a sample size of one – not a big research project, I'll admit – but still an indication that perhaps the begging call from an orphan can push the empathy buttons in an adult of that same or even a different species. Perhaps an innate response is triggered in adults who hear a juvenile begging for food again and again.

Adoption of infants or juveniles has been reported in many mammal and bird species and may be more common in nature than we realise. Adult male Japanese Macaques have been reported to carry youngsters about, inviting them to cling to their bellies or ride on their backs. Interestingly, this was not seen in all macaque groups and researcher B. Alexander commented that this behaviour might have been cultural rather than biological. That's an interesting thought and may be what's happening in human society as well. Culturally, our norms are changing too and it's more and more commonplace for a man, single or paired up, to look after children.

There are reportedly 64,000 foster children in California alone, with many waiting to be reunited with their family. Of those living with foster families, 500 are not able to go back to their own family and are waiting to find a forever home. This pattern of children waiting for a forever home is repeated around the world – certainly it's a consideration for those who have love, protection and guidance to give.

PARTHENOGENESIS AND A BET EACH WAY

If all this sexual activity in the previous chapters starts to sound a little tiresome there is always another option – many animals have evolved to go it alone. Parthenogenesis, where sex with the opposite gender is not a prerequisite for reproduction. While humans haven't evolved to such a degree, not every animal needs a partner to multiply and can reproduce asexually. Sponges and corals for instance can reproduce both sexually and asexually. Asexually, new clonal polyps 'bud' off from the parent to grow and start a new colony. Aphids and stick insects hatch from unfertilised eggs. Asexual reproduction is a special kind of growth resulting in the division of cells. In this process, a cell's genetic material is doubled, then splits again and so on. New individuals developed via this process are an exact genetic copy of the originating parent. Parthenogenesis is common in some aquatic creatures called rotifers (microscopic aquatic animals), some crustaceans and insects such as aphids and ants. None of these know the thrill of the chase, of the courtship and the 'love' that can be found when one finds their soulmate.

OLDEST DADS

Despite age-related declining fertility there are some fertile older men out there. Ramjit Raghav from India claims to have sired a healthy baby boy at the ripe old age of 96. He broke his own baby-making record after making the headlines in 2010 when he became a first-time father at 94. His wife Shakuntala Devi adds that he can make love like a 25-year-old man. Ramjit was a bachelor for nearly 90 years and credits his healthy diet and abstinence from alcohol for his long life.

A famous older father is Charlie Chaplin, who had eleven children with three wives. He married his last wife, Oona O'Neil, when she was just 18 and he was 54 years old. They had eight children together, with youngest son Christopher James born in 1962 when Charlie was 73 years old.

Female Komodo Dragons are capable of conceiving without ever having any contact with a male. Their lifestyle is rather solitary and they do not always come across a potential mate – proof that virgin births do exist after all! In the absence of a father, all the female's brood will be male. This means that later on she could mate with her sons, although obviously inbreeding is not a great long-term solution in evolutionary terms.

If, despite all the trials and tribulations in the sex lives of animals and humans, you're still keen to be a biological father, the next chapter is for you.

Chapter 13

THE BEST DAD YOU CAN BE

'I believe that what we become depends on what our fathers teach us at odd moments, when they aren't trying to teach us. We are formed by little scraps of wisdom.'

UMBERTO ECO, *FOUCAULT'S PENDULUM*

PREPARING FOR FATHERHOOD

How do animals prepare themselves for the responsibilities of fatherhood? We humans have a great capacity to learn from other species, so I feel it's only right that we look at nature every once in a while to compare ourselves with other creatures on the planet. How 'they' do the stuff we do is always interesting. Perhaps these insights can help us understand the role of fatherhood in a broader context across many different species. What can human dads-to-be learn from our wild cousins?

What is it that men can do to prepare for fatherhood? We've done the courtship, we've been through mate selection, we assume that by now there's a need to practice being dad before going in cold turkey. There is a popular misconception that many primates are uninvolved dads but there's more and more evidence to support the notion of loving, caring primate dads. Perhaps some primates can give a few pointers on how to prepare.

Squirrel monkey (*Saimiri* species) males 'fatten up' before the breeding season, as it seems that the females find this quite appealing and it provides some competition with other males. The main reason however is to prepare themselves for carrying the baby, so that they are fit and ready for the extra demands on their body by the time the infant is born.

Many primates adore babies and marmosets in particular are real suckers for little ones. Even before the babies are born, dad is getting physically ready. His hormones change, connections in his brain adapt and he starts to put on weight. Basically, he's

Squirrel monkey males 'fatten up' to prepare themselves for carrying the baby. They are fit and ready for the extra demands on their body by the time their infant is born.

preparing for all the heavy lifting he will soon be doing caring for his new-born twins, which will total 20 per cent of his body weight. Daddy marmoset carries these twins from birth until they reach independence. He will climb through the trees whilst they hold on to the thermal pads between his shoulder blades. Even if they are still breastfeeding from mum, he has to fetch them and pick them up if he hears them crying.

Marmoset males really do love their babies and find them irresistible, it seems. Harmony Neale has looked after primates in Wellington Zoo, New Zealand, for 17 years and shares her memory of a remarkable foster dad:

'Pygmy Marmoset males (and tamarin males) are the ones that do most of the parenting work to start with and then, as the family grows, brothers and sisters start to help out. Some years ago, we had a difficult situation when the partner of a heavily pregnant Pygmy Marmoset became ill and died. Pygmy Marmoset gestation is around 141 days. They were a newly matched breeding pair and had no helpers yet. The male's role is essential in these circumstances. We knew we had to try and get her someone else to help with caring for the baby.

We decided to move one of our young males in with her as he had been a big helper with his brothers and sisters and always wanted to be with the babies. Wicket gave birth seven days after we introduced Cuzco to her. From the first day he sat by her and wanted to hold the baby. He would have known this was not his baby as she did not come into season during the time they were together as she was heavily pregnant when they were introduced.

However, they bonded quickly and by the time the baby was three days old mum Wicket felt comfortable enough to let Cuzco take the baby and look after it together with her from then on.

The story ended well with the pair going on to have nine more babies, including a few pairs of twins. Pygmy Marmosets have remarkable paternal instincts and the fact that Cuzco had been a helper in his family group made him an excellent choice under these challenging circumstances. He stepped up and filled the vacancy with great skill.'

Cuzco's training in baby care in his natal group made him an excellent choice as a foster dad and a helpmate to the pregnant female. Experience in caring for infants is crucial in primates and practicing on siblings makes good sense.

Male birds of some species almost experience pregnancy symptoms if they brood the eggs. This has been known to happen in expecting human fathers too, and is known as Couvade syndrome – a 'compassion pregnancy' or phantom pregnancy. The future dad can put on weight and experience hormone changes, sleep disturbance, labour pains and even post-partum depression. Male morning sickness is more common than we think. Sympathy pregnancies can also happen in different human cultures and across socioeconomic classes.

FIRST-TIME FATHERS

Mental preparation is important for soon-to-be fathers, but there are also practical things that need to be organised before a dad can welcome his first offspring. This preparation may include building a nest or claiming a territory, incubating the egg or the foetus, keeping it warm and protected from predators and feeding and protecting mum while she gives birth. Once the young have arrived, many fathers need to find food for their offspring until they're independent or weaned and in some cases they need to continue teaching and guiding their offspring long after they can feed themselves (which is definitely the case with human kids). Wild animal fathers get involved in these aspects of parenting in widely varying forms and degrees.

The amount of effort parents put into their babies seriously impacts the survival rate of offspring. But to what degree is this parenting instinctive and what is learned? We may not always know the answers to these questions, but by looking at animals we can deduce a lot about ourselves too. Having cared for wild creatures for decades, I've witnessed countless animals with their young. One thing that struck me time and time again was how often wild parents don't know what to do with their first clutch, litter or single newborn. Sometimes the mother is puzzled and baffled by what's just happened and has no idea what to do with a wriggling neonate. Some mothers work it out, while others just get on with life as if nothing had happened. Neglect of the first-born litter or first hatchings is frequently seen.

Parenting undoubtedly must be learned. The animal parents usually get better at rearing their offspring each time they have a go. This is the case with humans as well. Often new parents are confused and bewildered by their newborns and are not particularly good at caring for them, looking to other parents for guidance. By the time a second child arrives, they may feel more confident and in control. The offspring of first-time animal parents may suffer from some neglect as the newbies work out how much energy they need to put into raising their young. In the past, if zookeepers noticed that a young primate was not thriving, they would remove it to hand-rear the baby. Over time, carers noticed that this would lead to the next baby or litter being neglected too. As hard as it is, it's a necessary learning process new animal parents must go through.

First-born humans are nearly always their parents' experimental baby these days. In the Western world we are having fewer and fewer children and rightly so for the sake of the environment. But this also means that valuable training opportunities for parenting are being lost for humans. In previous generations, families were bigger and older children looked after their parents' younger children. Later, the youngest children became helpers with the offspring of their older siblings and so on. These training opportunities rarely exist in the immediate family nowadays. It is not uncommon for new parents to have to attend parenting classes to learn how to care for babies and toddlers. All the more reason to look at our wilder cousins to see how some of their child-rearing techniques may apply to us.

Rearing offspring can come at a great cost to parents, one being the sacrifice of the parents' own fitness. The kiwi, the iconic bird of New Zealand, lays an egg that takes about 20 per cent of the mother's body weight. By comparison, a human baby at full term may weigh about 5 per cent of mum's body weight. The kiwi mother is so depleted after laying such a big egg that the male has to take over. He incubates the egg, living off his fat reserves until it hatches. Like the mother, he too needs to build-up his condition again afterwards. In evolutionary terms, the health and fitness of the parent is a trade-off against raising one or more progeny. This means there's only so much any parent can do before they undermine their own fitness for the sake of their offspring. The amount of energy – both physically and nutritionally – that a parent can dedicate to a young or a clutch has to be balanced against their own needs for survival. Unless you're a male spider and your species practices sexual cannibalism.

In his book, *The Evolution of Parental Care*, Tim Clutton-Brock states: 'Offspring will commonly attempt to extract higher levels of investment than it is in the parents interests to provide, lowering the parents' fitness where they are successful. Parents may respond by setting fixed limits to the level of investment.' This conflict of interest is common in wild parents and we can assume it is the case in humans too. Perhaps in our society, with its accusations of 'helicopter parenting' among some classes, parents need to set limits to the amount of nurturing they can and should provide for a juvenile, sub-adult or even an adult child.

The biparental system, used by humans in mostly monogamous relationships, can be extremely gratifying. It rewards parents with offspring who are more likely to survive and encourages enduring love between parent and child, as well between the bonded pair during their long lives. The workload for a human raising a kid is greater than for any other species. Mothers patently go through a lot of trouble with pregnancy, birthing and breastfeeding for a couple of years, but fathers are usually there for the long-haul also to nurture, protect and love. Other animals may take to parenthood with as much commitment and passion as humans do, but in our species nearly two decades are dedicated to raising our progeny, whilst at the same time we have the shortest interval between births of any related primate species. No wonder we need involved fathers for our little humans more than most other creatures on earth.

PROTECTIVE MAGPIE FATHERS

The Australian Magpie (*Cracticus tibicen*) is a very protective father. For six weeks of the year he's fiercely defensive of his chicks. It's his job to scare off intruders. They have exceptionally long memories and sometimes swoop because a person reminds them of someone who's previously caused a threat to their babies. They have excellent memories and can remember a face for years, knowing if that person was trustworthy or not. They identify previous or potential enemies and keep them away from the family. Females don't swoop at all as they are busy sitting on eggs. Only 12 per cent of magpie males do ever swoop and befriending your local magpies outside the breeding season makes it less likely that they will swoop you. If you are nice to them, they will remember you for that too. There are many anecdotes about magpies coming to show off their new babies to people with whom they have built a good rapport.

MAKING THE KIDS LEAVE HOME

Nature gives us examples of splendid fathers. How can we sum up the qualities and characteristics of perfect animal dads and what we can learn from them? An exemplary wild father is protective, backs up his children, is tolerant and teaches them what they need to

Male Australian Magpies are dedicated fathers and it's their job to protect their offspring from potential harm.

know. Animal fathers who are involved in the lives of their offspring during infancy through to the teenage years hope that they have prepared the kids as best they can for adult life. The young one then usually departs to live an independent life. However, humans never stop being a parent and never lose interest in the lives of their children, often finding it difficult to see them go after such a long time caring for them. We have so few offspring and invest a lot of our lives in each one. Species which are similar to us in terms of this investment of time and effort are the Emperor Penguin and the Wandering Albatross. Both these species concentrate on raising the one special offspring like humans do and go to extraordinary lengths to rear them. But when it's time to go, it's time to go. Many

Penguin chicks leave home to fend for themselves once they realise their parents are not coming back to feed them.

animal parents just stop feeding their young when they reach a certain age or level of independence. Unless they are needed to help raise next year's brood, the youngest generation will be encouraged to leave and start their own lives. Some animal parents literally push their young out of the territory, while others depart on their annual migration, leaving the young behind to fatten up before they begin their first migration journey on their own.

I researched Little Penguins on an island near Sydney for some years. The penguin parents stopped feeding the youngsters around eight weeks after hatching. When the chicks realised they were not coming back they would eventually leave the burrow to go to sea and catch some fish.

Animal parents of species that usually leave the family upon puberty or sexual maturity have set times for this to happen. However, humans, once parents, never stop being parents. We are a species that keeps feeding its young long after they are able to feed themselves. Independence is achieved in animal terms once the offspring feeds itself, becomes sexually mature or leaves the territory. But this marker has become increasingly blurred in contemporary human society. In indigenous populations there are initiations to mark the progression into adulthood and independence, but what do we have as equivalent? Going to university, perhaps? Backpacking around the world? Getting married?

In the past humans had set times for children to leave home. Previous generations sent children off to work as young as 12 or 14 or married off girls as soon as they menstruated. Now the dependence of juveniles on their parents can be extended well into adulthood, with children not leaving home until they are well into their twenties or even thirties.

The natural world provides good examples of when kids should leave the family. If they are needed to run the household or look after siblings, it makes sense for them to stay, as in the case of marmosets, tamarins and meerkats. However, if they are likely to cause problems with inbreeding once they are sexually mature, either the males or the females must go, subject to the reproductive behaviour of the group. Chimpanzee and Bonobo females leave the group as they reach sexual maturity, while baboon males do the leaving, searching out a new troop to join. In gorillas, however, both males and females leave the troop once they reach sexual maturity.

If you don't need them to care for younger siblings, they are sexually mature and they can feed themselves (even if that means takeaway food), then maybe it's time for them to go. But how well have you prepared them?

HOW TO BE A GOOD MALE

The loyal, committed fathers out there don't get mentioned enough for all that they do. Fathers like the wolf, the marmoset, the seahorse and the emu all broaden our perspectives of what it is to be a dad. They look after their brood with utter dedication until they reach the time they can look after themselves. A good gorilla father passes on more than his genes to the next generation – he brings up his sons and daughters by example.

They will have observed their father for years and seen the strategies he uses to keep the peace in the group and fend off predators or intruders. Just as young gorilla females learn about rearing babies from their mothers and aunts, the males learn how to be a good, strong but gentle leader by watching their father carefully. A gorilla female learns what to expect from a silverback so that she is prepared when she matures and moves to a new group.

Even male elephants, although they do not usually have a lot to do with their young, will get involved and be a role model for their offspring or other young bulls in the right circumstances.

Lucy Melo, a senior elephant keeper at Taronga Zoo in Sydney, tells this story:

'In late 2006, Taronga Zoo imported five Asian Elephants from Thailand, in order to participate in a global breeding and conservation program for this endangered species. The herd consisted of four females – Porntip (14 years old), Pak Boon (13 years old), Thong Dee (8 years old) and Tang Mo (7 years old) – and one male – Gung (6 years old). The elephants were sourced from various elephant camps throughout Thailand and were unrelated to each other. When the elephants arrived in Sydney, Gung was still young enough to be considered a juvenile and in need of protection and guidance from the older females, especially Porntip and Pak Boon. He was treated as the 'baby' of the herd and the females doted and fussed over him. However less than a year later, Gung went from 'baby' to 'baby-maker' when he successfully mounted and impregnated Thong Dee. Siring a calf at seven years of age would be highly unusual in the wild. However, given that Gung had no other males to compete with, or to hormonally suppress him, he became sexually mature rather early on in his development. That, coupled with Thong Dee's small stature and patient nature, gave Gung the edge he needed to secure his place as one of the youngest known naturally breeding bulls of his time. Roughly 18 months later, Gung cemented his status as a breeding bull by successfully impregnating the much older and taller Pak Boon. He only managed to do so by positioning Pak Boon downhill and standing on the tips of his toes!

Gung was quite pleased with himself, having proven to himself and to the females that he had made the transition from playful calf to randy bull. Gung was also in the stage of his life where he would be gravitating towards other young bulls to spar, play-fight and learn the skills necessary to be a competitive mature bull elephant. In the absence of any other males to roughhouse with in his herd,

Gung looked to the older females. He relentlessly prodded them in the rear with his tusks or squared off with them, engaging in face-to-face combat.

What Gung did not anticipate, was that the females did not welcome his change of status in the herd, nor did they appreciate his rough and rowdy attention. Pak Boon and Porntip quickly teamed up and put Gung in his place. They did not tolerate his incessant aggressive horseplay and they made it their mission to displace Gung from the matriarchal herd. In the wild, adolescent males are forced to leave their natal herd and usually form bachelor groups with other ousted young bulls. In these bachelor groups, males practice their sparring skills and learn from the older bulls, preparing them for adulthood. Sexually mature adult male elephants are usually solitary, but still maintain loose associations with other bulls or non-natal female herds. As we had already planned for this rite of passage faced by Gung, a completely separate and purpose-built bull facility had been prepared ready for when this time came. Less than three years after he arrived at Taronga Zoo, Gung was moved to his own bachelor pad, which was located approximately 400 metres (1,300 feet) from where the female elephants were housed. Gung settled into his new digs very quickly and wasted no time establishing his territory.

He charged and threatened any large work vehicles driving past his enclosure, as if they were competing bulls. He was less interested in playing and more interested in moving massive logs around the enclosure in a show of strength. A couple of months later, we brought Porntip and Pak Boon over to visit Gung in his new facility. Thong Dee, being heavily pregnant, stayed with Tang

Mo at the female facility to focus and prepare for her upcoming delivery. The last time Porntip and Pak Boon had seen Gung, they considered him to be a young punk bull who had overstayed his welcome. However, this time they recognised that Gung had truly come into his own and treated him accordingly with deference and respect. They ate side by side, swam and mud-wallowed together. The days of constant conflict were gone, replaced by a more mature and peaceful relationship amongst them. Gung enjoyed the regular but brief visits from the females but was equally happy to have his own space.

Three months after Gung moved into his new bull facility, the female elephants welcomed the addition of another bull when Thong Dee gave birth to a male calf, Luk Chai. Eight months later, Porntip gave birth to a male calf, Pathi Harn, conceived through artificial insemination with a bull from Melbourne Zoo. Luk Chai and Pathi Harn enjoyed rough and tumble pay with one another, practicing the sparring skills they would need to compete with adult bulls in the future. However, we knew that Luk Chai could benefit tremendously by learning the ropes from a proper mature bull. There was no better role model that we could think of than his dad, Gung. Shortly after Luk Chai's first birthday, we brought Thong Dee, Luk Chai and Tang Mo over to visit Gung. We knew that Gung now had a gentle nature with the females but were not sure how he would react to a boisterous young bull. Gung initially treated Luk Chai with mild curiosity and investigated him with his trunk, touching him all over. There was absolutely no aggression or antagonistic behaviour on Gung's part. Luk Chai was completely awestruck and in wonder of Gung. He just stood there, letting

Gung touch him. Then Gung let Luk Chai reciprocate and caress his tusks, touching him at will. Gung even laid down to get to Luk Chai's level, so that his son could continue to investigate and touch him everywhere.

Before long, Luk Chai was climbing all over Gung. Gung not only tolerated it, he seemed to encourage it. We watched on in amazement as father and son continued to play. Luk Chai would charge and push on Gung and Gung would behave as if Luk Chai had bested him and throw himself on the ground. It was as if Gung was helping Luk Chai to understand his own strength, to promote the self-confidence tactics that Luk Chai would need as an older bull. We continued these valuable visits on a regular basis and even gave Luk Chai the opportunity to be present to observe his father in action when Gung was mounting and breeding the females. Luk Chai witnessed first-hand how Gung successfully courted and won over the females and then mounted them with little resistance. With any luck, Luk Chai learned these best practices from his dad and will one day be a respected breeding bull himself.'

Fathers have a big role to play as youngsters mature. Gung and Luk Chai's relationship potentially influences the kind of bull elephant Luk Chai will become and the father he might turn out to be himself. In zoos, we look after the animals in our care with much love but there are things we can't teach the young. The essence of what it is to be a bull elephant comes from a patient elephant mentor. Gung showed Luk Chai how to treat the females, how to be kind and gentle, how to have a playful side. Children equally benefit from close bonds with adults who show them how to act as a grown up.

The older elephant bulls in bachelor groups perform the role of teacher in the finishing school for younger males. When commercial hunters target the older bulls as trophies for their rich clients this does not only shrink the elephant population, it also removes the protectors and teachers of the younger male generation.

FATHERS IN THE MODERN WORLD

The 1960s brought fast and dramatic changes in the Western world. The role of women was revolutionised with the availability of the contraceptive pill and workplaces were opening up more to women. In Australia, the ban on married women in the Commonwealth Public Service was finally lifted in 1966. These changes brought about an improved capacity for women to choose their participation in the workforce, which in turn led to fathers becoming more actively involved in the daily care of children for all sorts of practical reasons.

Human fathers too have evolved to look after their children and feed and protect the family unit. How much of that human fathers do is not as prescribed as it is in other species. It varies on the basis of culture, beliefs and the practicalities of domestic circumstances. Human fathers seem to be the only species that can decide how involved they get with their kids. In all other animals, the amount of involvement is more or less the same across all the individuals of that species. If the 'book' on marmoset biology spells out that the father helps to carry his young then that's exactly what he does. There may be some mild variation in their dedication but all male marmosets follow their instinctive 'textbook'. Not so in humans.

Involved fatherhood is the successful reproductive strategy that has evolved in humans to help a male's genes survive to the next generation. However, in reality, paternal involvement ranges from completely absent to being the primary carer. Some fathers care for their children all day every day for years, while others see their children only briefly when they come home at the end of a long day. Some fathers have access to their children only on occasional visits once a month or even once a year; others have no access at all. Only in humans do we see this huge range of fatherly involvement.

Who actually does the fathering is also more flexible in humans than in any other species and children can find themselves being raised by single dads, two-dad households, stepdads, foster dads, adoptive dads, biological dads, godfathers, grandfathers or any other kind of fatherly men. Most human fathers, however involved they are on a daily basis, love their child passionately. We are not the only species to have evolved to love their offspring and be willing to protect them even if it risks life and limb.

HOW TO BE A GOOD DAD - WHAT HAVE WILD ANIMALS TAUGHT US ABOUT BEING A DAD?

It's fascinating to think that love for one's offspring or empathy for an orphan can be so universal. When people disparagingly say of some violent criminal 'they're an animal' I'm sure they are not thinking of the Emperor Penguin keeping his chick warm on his feet, the pregnant male seahorse or the marmoset carrying his babies everywhere. Humans spend a lot of effort trying to stress how different we are from animals, whereas I see more similarities than difference. We've evolved from a shared evolutionary ancestor and so many of our innate emotional responses are shared with animals. We see this in the way humans and animals care for their offspring.

Advice on ways to pass on your genes, courtship enhancements and other matters are given elsewhere in this book, but in the following list, I've summarised in no particular order of priority what excellent animal dads do:

- Good wild fathers, like tamarins, look after their kids' mum. Being a father also means looking after your mate by giving her or him what they need and supporting them to do the job of child-rearing.
- Bull elephants show young bulls how to be an adult. Role model how to be a good man. Show don't tell.
- Gorilla silverbacks care and protect the females in their family. Show your girls how a good man cares for and respects his partner so she will choose the father of her own children well.
- African Wild Dogs teach 'adulting' on the job, supporting their young whilst they learn the ropes. Listen to the ideas of

your young ones, validate their opinions.
- Being a 'good provider', like a wolf or an Emperor Penguin, extends to providing unconditional love and care even in extreme and dangerous circumstances.
- All wild parents play with the young ones to teach adult skills.
- Alloparenting other people's kids before you have your own may provide some useful parenting skills.

Wild animal fathers demonstrate their dedication by raising their young to be independent and self-sufficient in adulthood. We've seen how some run themselves ragged trying to feed them, often willing to give their own life to protect them. Yet, most animal dads never see their offspring again once they have left the nest or dispersed to find a territory of their own. Animal parents have followed the same baby-raising 'textbook' their species has had for millennia. But their world has changed too. The silverback gorilla may now have to teach his children how to avoid the poacher's snare. Does the Emperor Penguin know the ocean temperatures are rising? Animals may be aware of the changing world they are sending their babies into – a world of over-fishing, pollution, climate change, poaching, trophy hunting and humans everywhere.

We have no idea what the world will look like when the current generation of children are grown up. Much of what children learn today may not be relevant at all in 2050. Even if we don't know what's coming we can still teach them common sense, resilience and love, hoping they'll happily muddle through like we did.

There's one huge advantage human fathers have over their animal counterparts: storytelling. People have been telling yarns to young ones as lessons for life since we first developed language. Preparing a child for life as an adult in this often-cruel world is challenging. Injustice, unkindness, environmental vandalism and other inhumanities are things every father would like to spare their child. All the more reason to teach children resilience and optimism. Fathers can role model how to live a joyful life with respect for the natural world. They can share their own mistakes, showing children that life isn't about not making errors but learning from them. By living a life of kindness, compassion and caring for other humans and the creatures we share this beautiful planet with, fathers can

Children can find themselves being raised by single dads, two-dad households, stepdads, foster dads, adoptive dads, biological dads, godfathers, grandfathers or any other kind of fatherly men.

become the change they'd like to see in the world by modelling it to their children.

OLD TIME DADS

In the olden days fathers were often expected to be the disciplinarians. 'Wait till your father gets home!' The enforcer of good behaviour. Whilst good behaviour plainly needs to be instilled, there are kind and gentle ways to reinforce this. In zoos, we train the animals we care for with positive reinforcement only. Punishment is to be avoided wherever possible. Sometimes that means you spend a whole day in the bushes observing the animal in order to catch the good behaviour you want to see, so that you can reward it. Ideally, apart from loving a child unconditionally with all your heart, the animal world shows us that being the example they need to become will go a long way. A father may feel compelled to prepare his beloved child for the hard, cruel world outside the warm family home, hoping to protect them from the realities of life by hardening them up in advance. Perhaps nothing will prepare them better for life in the wild world than understanding empathy and compassion for their fellow beings, human and animal. Be the example your children need to see, a kind and compassioned man who cares about the planet and all the creatures on it.

ACKNOWLEDGEMENTS

Taronga Zoo gave me the opportunity to work with the most wonderful animals and allowed me to stay for decades. Working closely with other zoo staff in Taronga and around the world – people who are truly dedicated to caring for these precious charges – has been a privilege I treasure. I learned so much from all of you. Ideas for this book are the result of conversations during many morning teas, lunches and drinks after work, or at conferences with these passionate humans. These are the times when yarns about animals' intimate lives are divulged.

Many people gave their time to tell me stories about the animals they work with and gave permission to share these with you the reader. I am grateful for their willingness to impart their tales. My sincere thanks to Anna Bennett, Richard Buzas, Libby Kartzoff, David Laux, Michelle Lloyd, Lucy Melo, Harmony Neale, Allan Schmidt and Jo Walker. Thanks also to Pascale Benoit who originally told me the story of Nicolai the Przewalski's Horse.

Several lovely people provided comments and suggestions on some selected chapters – thank you Libby Kartzoff and Cathy Saunders. Kevin Evans kindly reviewed a section of text for 'tone' and accuracy. Anna Bennett made a great contribution to some of the more subtle intricacies of hyena amorous behaviours and checked hyena penis photos for me. Now you can't ask too many people for a favour like that!

Keith and Anita Cook sent me a book with a wonderful title, *Hung Like An Argentine Duck*, thus ensuring that this legendarily proportioned waterfowl gained the additional recognition it obviously deserves.

Thanks also to the members of the Bellingen Writers on Writing group who reviewed some extracts of the early manuscript and helped me find my 'voice' for this potentially salacious topic. To Sara Brice, thank you for helping me find some historic information on a couple of tigers. Thanks to Karen Fifield for putting me in touch with the Wellington Zoo staff who had some great stories to share.

My husband Rob ploughed through some very rough text early on and gave me some solid feedback, made lots of cups of tea and tolerated my writing obsession with good grace. The topics in this book made for great chats on our morning walks.

Joanne Riccioni's eye for detail and ability to shape a manuscript into one that's ready for publication, combined with her understanding of the publishing world, significantly improved my writing. I am grateful for her invaluable encouragement and feedback with respect to scope, structure and style.

I'm thankful for many fun times spend with my dear friend Paul Andrew who sadly died last year. We had many heated and interesting discussions on many topics including those covered in this book. I'll miss his counsel on my next writing adventures.

Many helpful comments were made by primate authority and former colleague, the very well-read and knowledgeable Allan Schmidt. He reviewed the entire manuscript and made some very valuable observations. His critical appraisal saved me from some potentially embarrassing mistakes.

I owe each of these primates a debt of gratitude. Any omissions or mistakes are obviously entirely mine.

Thank you to all at New Holland, in particular publisher and editor Simon Papps for liking my stories and believing in me, and designer Yolanda La Gorce.

Last but not least, my utmost gratitude to all the animals that have intrigued and inspired me throughout my life. I hope in some way that by telling their stories in this book it helps to give them the respect and protection they deserve.

SOURCES – FURTHER READING

This book is intended for a general readership and those interested in how to become and be a father. I have therefore not quoted references directly in the text. Interested readers can find the books, articles and papers that provided information and inspiration listed below.

1. Becoming a Dad: Passing on Your Genes

Andersson, G. (1999). 'Childbearing trends in Sweden 1961–1997.' *Eur. J. Popul.* 15: 1–24. pmid: 12158988

Buchan, J., Alberts, S.C., Silk, J.B. and Altmann, J. (2003). 'True paternal care in a multi-male primate society'. *Nature* 425: 179–181.

Berg, V. and Rotkirch A. (2014). 'Faster transition to the second child in late 20th century Finland: A study of birth intervals.' *Finnish Yearb Popul Res.* 49: 73–86.

Copen, C.E., Thoma, M.E. and Kirmeyer, S. (2015). 'Interpregnancy intervals in the United States: Data from the birth certificate and the national Survey of Family Growth.' *Natl Vital Stat Reports.* 64.

Hamilton, A. (1981). *Nature and Nurture: Aboriginal Child Rearing in North-Central Arnhem Land.* Canberra: Australian Institute of Aboriginal Studies.

Janofsky, M. (2002). 'Mormon Leader is Survived by 33 Sons and a Void.' *The New York Times.*

Laderman, C. (1983). *Wives and Midwives: Childbirth and Nutrition in Rural Malaysia.* University of California Press, Berkeley.

Lueders, I., Niemuller, C., Rich, P., Gray, C., Hermes, R., Goeritz, F. and Hildebrandt, T.B. (2012). 'Gestating for 22 months: luteal development and pregnancy maintenance in elephants.' *Proceedings of the Royal Society B: Biological Sciences.* DOI. org/10.1098/rspb.2012.1038

Meigs, A. (1984). *Food, Sex, and Pollution: A New Guinea Religion.* Rutgers University Press, New Brunswick.

van Noordwijk, M.A., Atmoko, S.S.U., Knott, C.D., Kuze, N., Morrogh-Bernard, H.C., Oram, F., Schuppli, C., van Schaik, C.P. and Willems, E.P. (2018). 'The slow ape: High infant survival and long interbirth intervals in wild orangutans.' *Journal of*

Human Evolution. Volume 125. DOI. org/10.1016/j.jhevol.2018.09.004

Novak, R.M. (1999). *Walker's Mammals of the World*. 6th edition. Johns Hopkins University Press.

Ott, S. (1979). 'Aristotle among the Basques: The 'Cheese Analogy' of Conception.' *Man* 14: 699–711.

Sapolsky, R. (2017). *Behave: The Biology of Humans at Our Best and Worst*. Penguin Random House.

Weiner, A.B. (1988). *The Trobrianders of Papua New Guinea*. Holt, Rinehart, and Winston, New York.

Zerjal, T., Xue, Y., Bertorelle, G., Wells, R.S., Bao, W., Zhu, S., Qamar, R., Ayub, Q., Mohyuddin, A., Fu, S., Li, P., Yuldasheva, N., Ruzibakiev, R., Xu, J., Shu, Q., Du, R., Yang, H., Hurles, M.E., Robinson, E., Gerelsaikhan, T., Dashnyam, B., Mehdi, S.Q., Tyler-Smith, C. *et. al.* (2003). 'The genetic legacy of the Mongols.' *American Journal of Human Genetics 72*(3): 717–21.

Websites

Quote: 'If you watch animals objectively for any length of time, you're driven to the conclusion that their main aim in life is to pass on their genes to the next generation.' David Attenborough *https://www. brainyquote.com/quotes/david_ attenborough_454694* Downloaded 21.6.2020

Dutch fertility doctor inseminates women with his own sperm. https://www.bbc.com/news/world-europe-47907847 Downloaded 9.9.2020

https://www.abc.net.au/news/2018-04-06/woman-sues-fertility-doctor-for-using-his-sperm-to-father-her/9625400 Downloaded 12.10.2020

https://www.telegraph.co.uk/news/9193014/British-man-fathered-600-children-at-own-fertility-clinic.html Downloaded 18.4.2020

https://slate.com/technology/2013/01/when-did-humans-realize-sex-makes-babies-evolution-of-reproductive-consciousness-of-the-cause-of-pregnancy.html Downloaded 20.6.2020

http://www.bbc.com/earth/story/20160704-the-real-reasons-why-we-have-sex Downloaded 11.8.2020

https://www.theguardian.com/society/2012/nov/02/worlds-biggest-sperm-bank-denmark Downloaded 13.11.2020

https://www.scientificamerican.com/article/male-panda-sex-drive/ Downloaded 3.9.2020

https://www.thevintagenews.

com/2018/06/09/genghis-khan
Downloaded 24.11.2020

2. Sexual Rivalry and Our Wilder Cousins

Arnocky S. and Carré J.M. (2016). 'Intrasexual Rivalry Among Men'. In: Weekes-Shackelford, T. and Weekes-Shackelford, V. (eds) *Encyclopedia of Evolutionary Psychological Science*. Springer. Cham. https://DOI.org/10.1007/978-3-319-16999-6_874-1

Clutton-Brock, T.H. (1991). *The Evolution of Parental Care*. Princeton University Press.

Diamond, J. (1992). *The Rise and Fall of the Third Chimpanzee*. Vintage Arrow.

Goodall, J. (1971). *In the Shadow of Man*. Dell Publishing Co.

Greene, L.K., Grogan, K.E., Smyth, K.N., Adams, C.A., Klager, S.A. and Drea, C.M. (2016). 'Mix it and fix it: functions of composite olfactory signals in ring-tailed lemurs.' *Royal Society Open Science*. https://royalsocietypublishing.org/DOI/10.1098/rsos.160076

Morris, D. (2017). *The Naked Ape* (50th Anniversary Edition). Vintage Penguin Books.

Novak, R.M. (1999). *Walker's Mammals of the World*. 6th edition. Johns Hopkins University Press.

In brief, (2002). 'Top pandas hit the high spots.' *New Scientist*. 2 March 2002.

Tan, J. and Hare, B. (2013). 'Bonobos Share with Strangers.' *PLOS ONE*, 2013; 8 (1): e51922 DOI:10.1371/journal.pone.0051922

De Waal, F. (2007). *Chimpanzee politics: power and sex among the apes* (25th Anniversary Edition). John Hopkins University Press.

Wrangham, R. and Peterson, D. (1997). *Demonic males – Apes and the Origins of Human Violence*. Bloomsbury.

Websites

Quote: 'In love there are no friends, everywhere there is a pretty woman hostility is open.' Victor Hugo. https://www.goodreads.com/quotes/636287-in-love-there-are-no-friends-everywhere-where-there-Downloaded 17.4.2020

https://www.scientificamerican.com/article/the-weapons-of-sexual-rivalry1/ Downloaded 29.9.2020

https://theconversation.com/what-are-the-chances-that-your-dad-isnt-your-father-24802 Downloaded 29.9.2020

https://www.smh.com.au/national/
anu-ape-skull-study-links-sagittal-
crest-size-and-social-behaviour-
20170503-gvy9ie.html
Downloaded 30.9.2020

How marriage changed over the
centuries. https://theweek.com/
articles/475141/how-marriage-
changed-over-centuries
Downloaded 2.11.2020

Ethics Guide: Honour Crimes. BBC.
http://www.bbc.co.uk/ethics/
honourcrimes/crimesofhonour_
1.shtml
Downloaded 2.11.2020

Naranjo, R. 'Marriage in
Ancient Mesopotamia and
Babylonia'. eHistory.osu.edu. Ohio
State University. https://ehistory.
osu.edu/articles/marriage-ancient-
mesopotamia-and-babylonia
Downloaded 2.11.2020

https://www.nationalgeographic.com/
animals/mammals/r/ring-tailed-
lemur/
Downloaded 7.11.2020

3. Wild Courtship

Baker, R. (1996). Sperm Wars:
Infidelity, Sexual Conflict, and other
Bedroom Battles. Basic Books,
New York.

Bondar, C. (2015). The Nature of Sex:
The Ins and Outs of Mating in the
Animal Kingdom. Weidenfeld &
Nicholson.

Borgia, G. (1985). 'Bower destruction
and sexual competition in the
satin bowerbird (Ptilonorhynchus
violaceus).' Behavioral Ecology
and Sociobiology. 18 (2): 91–100.
DOI:10.1007/BF00299037

Darwin, C. (1876). 'Sexual Selection in
Relation to Monkeys.'
Nature 15: 18–19.

Darwin, C. (1871). The Descent of Man,
and Selection in Relation to Sex.
John Murray, London.

East, M. L., Burke, T., Wilhelm, K.,
Greig, C. and Hofer, H. (2003).
'Sexual conflicts in spotted hyenas:
male and female mating tactics
and their reproductive outcome
with respect to age, social status
and tenure.' Proceedings Biological
Sciences 270 (1521): 1247–54.

Eguchi, K. Katsuno, Y. And Noske,
R.A. (2019). 'The Relationship
between Bower Orientation,
Platform Choice and Mating
Success in the Great Bowerbird
Chlamydera nuchalis.' Ornithological
Science 18 (1): 59. DOI:10.2326/
osj.18.59

Kaplan, G. (2019). Bird Bonds:
sex, mate-choice and cognition
in Australian native birds. Pan
Macmillan, Sydney.

Novak, R. M. (1999). Walker's
Mammals of the World. 6th edition.
Johns Hopkins University Press.

Payne, R. (2000). Quoted in: S. Millius. 'Music without borders.' *Science News*. Vol. 157.

Trather, P.N., Forcada, J., Atkinson, R., Downie, R.H. and Shears, J.R. (2008). 'Population assessments of gentoo penguins (*Pygoscelis papua*) breeding at an important Antarctic tourist site, Goudier Island, Port Lockroy, Palmer Archipelago, Antarctica.' *Biological Conservation* 141 (12): 3019–3028. DOI:10.1016/j.biocon.2008.09.006.

van Noordwijk, M.A., Atmoko, S.S.U., Knott, C.D., Kuze, N., Morrogh-Bernard, H.C., Oram, F., Schuppli, C., van Schaik, C.P. and Willems, E.P. (2018). 'The slow ape: High infant survival and long interbirth intervals in wild orangutans.' *Journal of Human Evolution*. Vol. 125. https://DOI.org/10.1016/j.jhevol.2018.09.004

Warburton, N.M. Philip W. Bateman, P.W. and Fleming, P.A. (2013). 'Sexual selection on forelimbs of western grey kangaroos (Skippy was clearly a female).' *Biological Journal of the Linnean Society*, Volume 109, Issue 4, Pages 923–931. https://DOI.org/10.1111/bij.12090

Wedekind, C., *et al*. (1995). 'MHC-dependent preferences in humans.' *Proceedings of the Royal Society of London*. 260 (1359): 245–49. DOI:10.1098/rspb.1995.0087. PMID 7630893

Wright, A.J. and Walsh, A (2010). 'Mind the gap: why neurological plasticity may explain seasonal interruption in humpback whale song.' *Journal of the Marine Biological Association of the United Kingdom*. 90 (8): 1489–1491. DOI:10.1017/s0025315410000913.

Websites
Quote: 'No case interested and perplexed me so much as the brightly coloured hinder ends and adjoining parts of certain monkeys.' Charles Darwin.
https://infidels.org/library/historical/charles_darwin/descent_of_man/supplement.html
Downloaded 26.12.2019

Morgan, T. (2005). Bronze Age Perfume discovered. BBC News Nicosia
http://news.bbc.co.uk/2/hi/europe/4364469.stm
Downloaded 4.3.2019.

https://www.statista.com/statistics/289686/market-value-of-fragrances-in-great-britain/
Downloaded 4.3.2019

https://blog.nationalgeographic.org/2013/02/14/wild-romance-weird-animal-courtship-and-mating-rituals/
Downloaded 6.10.2020

https://www.newscientist.com/article/2139105-birds-play-sick-

jungle-beat-with-drumsticks-they-make-themselves/
Downloaded 10.10.2020

https://www.msn.com/en-au/news/australia/biofluorescent Australian mammals and marsupials take scientists by surprise in accidental discovery
Downloaded 2.1.2021

4. Sexual Selection – Choosing a Mate

Bateson, P.P.G. (1985). 'Mate Choice.' Cambridge University Press.

Choudhury, A., Lahiri Choudhury, D.K., Desai, A., Duckworth, J.W., Easa, P.S., Johnsingh, A.J.T., Fernando, P., Hedges, S., Gunawardena, M., Kurt, F., Karanth, U., Lister, A., Menon, V., Riddle, H., Rübel, A. and Wikramanayake, E. (IUCN SSC Asian Elephant Specialist Group). (2008) *Elephas maximus*. The IUCN Red List of Threatened Species 2008: e.T7140A12828813. http://dx.DOI.org/10.2305/IUCN.UK.2008.RLTS.T7140A12828813.en.

Dakin, R and Montgomerie, R. (2013). 'Eye for an eyespot: How iridescent plumage ocelli influence peacock mating success.' *Behavioral Ecology*. 24 (5): 1048–1057. DOI: 10.1093/beheco/art045

Darwin, C. (1859). *On the Origin of Species by Means of Natural Selection, or the Preservation of Favoured Races in the Struggle for Life.* John Murray, London.

Darwin, C. (1871). *The Descent of Man, and Selection in Relation to Sex.* John Murray, London.

Eberhard, W.G. (1996). *Female Control: Sexual Selection by Cryptic Female Choice.* Princeton University Press.

Fiske, P. Rintamaki, P.T. and Karvonen, E. (1998). 'Mating success in lekking males: a meta-analysis.' *Behavioral Ecology* 9 (4): 328–338. DOI:10.1093/beheco/9.4.328

Miller, G. (2001). *The Mating Mind: How Sexual Choice Shaped the Evolution of Human Nature*. Vintage Books.

Novak, R.M. (1999). *Walker's Mammals of the World.* 6th edition. Johns Hopkins University Press.

O'Connell-Rodwell, C. (2010). 'How Male Elephants Bond.' *Smithsonian Magazine*, November 2010. Downloaded 23.10.2020

West, P.M. and Packer, C. (2002). 'Sexual selection, temperature and the lion's mane.' *Science* 297: 1339–1343.

Websites

Quote: 'Sex is a part of nature. I go along with nature.' Marilyn Monroe
https://stylecaster.com/sex-quotes/
Downloaded 8.8.2020

https://nationalzoo.si.edu/animals/
news/gorilla-group-social-structure
Downloaded 23.10.2020.

The evolution of mutual mate choice.
https://www.journals.uchicago.edu/
DOI/pdf/10.1086/688658
Downloaded 30.6.2020

http://www.bbc.co.uk/earth/
story/20150303-peacocks-make-
din-you-cant-hear#:
Downloaded 1.10.20

https://www.newscientist.com/article/
dn28668-pandas-dont-lack-sex-
drive-they-just-need-to-fancy-each
other
Downloaded 7.5.2020

5. Wild Sex – Mating Systems
Black, M.P. and Grober, M.S. (2003).
'Group sex, sex change, and
parasitic males: Sexual strategies
among the fishes and their
neurobiological correlates.' *Annual
Review of Sex Research* 14: 160–84.

Díaz-Muñoz, S.L. (2011). 'Paternity
and relatedness in a polyandrous
nonhuman primate: testing
adaptive hypotheses of male
reproductive cooperation.' *Animal
Behaviour* 82 (3): 563–571.
DOI:10.1016/j.
anbehav.2011.06.013. S2CID 53188748

Firman, R.C.; Simmons, L.W.
(2008). 'Polyandry, sperm
competition, and reproductive
success in mice.' *Behavioral
Ecology* 19 (4): 695–702. DOI:
10.1093/beheco/arm158
Goldizen, A.W. (1987). 'Facultative
polyandry and the role of
infant-carrying in wild saddle-
back tamarins (Saguinus
fuscicollis).' (PDF). *Behavioral
Ecology and Sociobiology* 20 (2):
99–109.
DOI:10.1007/BF00572631. hdl:
2027.42/46876. S2CID 206782867.

Hrdy, S.B. (2000). 'The optimal
number of fathers: Evolution,
demography, and history in
the shaping of female mate
preferences.' *Annals of the New York
Academy of Sciences* 907: 75–96.

Kaplan, G. (2019). *Bird Bonds: Sex,
mate choice and recognition
in Australian native birds*. Pan
Macmillan, Sydney.

Klemme, I. and Ylönen, H.
(2010). 'Polyandry enhances
offspring survival in an infanticidal
species.' *Biology Letters* 6 (1):
24–6. DOI:10.1098/
rsbl.2009.0500. PMC 2817239. PMID
19675002

Murdock, G.P. (1967). *Ethnographic
Atlas*. University of Pittsburgh Press.

Murray, C.M., Stanton, M.A., Lonsdorf,
E.V., Wroblewski, E.E. and Pusey, A.E.
(2016). Chimpanzee fathers bias their
behaviour towards their offspring.
Royal Society open science 3 (11),
160441. DOI:10.1098/rsos.160441

Novak, R.M. (1999). *Walker's Mammals of the World.* 6th edition. Johns Hopkins University Press.

Rylands, A.B. and Mittermeier, R.A., (2008). 'Saguinus imperator.' *The IUCN Red List of Threatened Species.* 2008: e.T39948A10295512.

de Waal, F. (1995). 'Bonobo, Sex and Society.' *Scientific American,* March 1995.

de Waal, F. (2005). *Our Inner Ape: The Best and Worst of Human Nature.* Granta Books, London.

Websites

Quote: 'Everything in the world is about sex except sex. Sex is about power.' Oscar Wilde https://quoteinvestigator.com/2018/06/05/sex-power/ Downloaded 12.12.2019

https://www.washingtonpost.com/world/asia_pacific/two-husband-strategy-may-be-a-remedy-for-chinas-one-child-policy-professor-posits/2020/06/10/56e6eff8-aac0-11ea-a43b-be9f6494a87d_story.html Downloaded 23.9.2020

https://www.pinknews.co.uk/2019/04/12/trans-gender-bending-animals-change-sex/ Downloaded 1.12.2020

6. Monogamy – Just You and Me, Babe

Angier, N. (2010). 'Paternal bonds, Special and Strange. Science.' *The New York Times,* 14 June 2010.

Bondar, C. (2015). *The Nature of Sex: The Ins and Outs of Mating in the Animal Kingdom.* Weidenfeld & Nicholson.

Darwin, C. (1871). *The Descent of Man, and Selection in Relation to Sex.* John Murray, London.

Dunbar, R. (2004). *The Human Story: A New History of Mankind's Evolution.* Faber and Faber, London.

Dunbar, R. (1998). *Grooming, Gossip and the Evolutionary Language.* Faber and Faber, London.

Gardner, M., Bull, C. and Cooper, S. (2002). 'High levels of genetic monogamy in the social Australian lizard *Egernia stokesii.' Molecular Ecology* 11: 1787–1794. 10.1046/j.1365-294X.2002.01552.x.

Hrdy, S. (2009). *Mothers and Others.* Harvard University Press.

Kaplan, G. (2019). *Bird Bonds: sex, mate-choice and cognition in Australian native birds.* Pan Macmillan, Sydney.

Morris, D. (2017). *The Naked Ape* (50th Anniversary Edition). Vintage Penguin Books.

Novak, R.M. (1999). *Walker's Mammals of the World.* 6th edition. Johns Hopkins University Press.

Rutherford, A. (2018). *The Book of Humans: The Story of How We Became Us*. Weidenfeld & Nicholson.

Ryan, C. and Jetha, C. (2011). *Sex at Dawn: How We Mate, Why We Stray and What It Means For Relationships*. Harper Perennial.

Sapolsky, R. (2017). *Behave: The Biology of Humans at Our Best and Worst*. Penguin Random House.

Scheele, D., Wille, A., Kendrick, K.M., Stoffel-Wagner, B., Becker, B., Güntürkün, O., Maier, W. and Hurlemann, R. (2013). 'Oxytocin enhances brain reward system responses in men viewing the face of their female partner.' *Proceedings of the National Academy of Sciences*, Dec 2013, 110 (50): 20308–20313; DOI: 10.1073/pnas.1314190110

Schneiderman, I., Zagoory-Sharon, O., Leckman, J.F., and Feldman, R. (2012). 'Oxytocin during the initial stages of romantic attachment: relations to couples' interactive reciprocity.' *Psychoneuroendocrinology* 37 (8): 1277–1285. https://DOI.org/10.1016/j.psyneuen.2011.12.021

Sockol, M.D., Raichlen, D.A. and Pontzer, H. (2007). 'Chimpanzee locomotor energetics and the origin of human bipedalism.' *Proceedings*

National Academy of Sciences 104 (30): 12265–12269.

Snowdon, C.T. and Ziegler, T.E. (2007). 'Growing up cooperatively: family processes and infant care in marmosets and tamarins.' *Journal of Developmental Processes*, 2007, 2: 40– 66.

de Waal, F.B.M. and Gavrilets, S. (2013). 'Monogamy with a purpose.' *Proceedings of the National Academy of Science* 110 (38): 15167–15168. DOI:10.1073/pnas.1315839110

Wang, H., Duclot, F., Liu, Y., Wang, Z., and Kabbaj, M. (2013). 'Histone deacetylase inhibitors facilitate partner preference formation in female prairie voles.' *Nature Neuroscience* 16: 919–924. http://dx.DOI.org/10.1038/nn.3420

Weimerskirch, H., Barbraud, C., and Lys, P. (2000). 'Sex Differences in Parental Investment and Chick Growth in Wandering Albatrosses: Fitness Consequences.' *Ecology* 81 (2), 309–318. DOI:10.2307/177428

Websites

Quote: 'I reject monogamy as an affront to evolution.' Dan Brown. *https://danbrown.com/originexcerpt* Downloaded 14.8.2020

https://cbs.umn.edu/sites/cbs.umn.edu/files/public/downloads/The_lions_mane-West_2005.pdf Downloaded 17.11.2020

New plastic surgery statistics reveal trends toward body enhancement. EurekAlert! Science News. Downloaded 2.1.2021

https://australianmuseum.net.au/learn/animals/spiders/redback-spider/ Downloaded 2.9.2020

https://www.the-scientist.com/news-opinion/self-fertilizing-worms-stab-their-own-heads-35201 Downloaded 20.5.2020

https://macmillanreport.yale.edu/videos/eduardo-fernandez-duque-talks-about-monogamy-monkeys Downloaded 18.5.2020

https://www.psychologytoday.com/us/basics/oxytocin Downloaded 4.6.2020

https://iytmed.com/morning-sickness-feeling-nauseous-men/#10-couvade-syndrome Downloaded 23.5.2020

https://www.birdlife.org/worldwide/news/world-first-rhinoceros-hornbills-give-artificial-nest-box-seal-approval Downloaded 18.9.2020

https://www.livescience.com/44791-monkeys-monogamy Downloaded 7.10.2020

https://www.backyardbuddies.org.au/backyard-buddies/shingleback Downloaded 9.10.2020

https://www.reptilesmagazine.com/the-iconic-australian-shingleback-skink-in-the-wild-and-in-captivity/ Downloaded 16.10.2020

https://www.Legend of Storks, Storks.com Downloaded 12.10.2020

7. Tools for the Job

Ellis, R. (2005). *Tiger Bone and Rhino Horn: The Destruction of Wildlife for Traditional Chinese Medicine*. Island Press.

Fasel, N.J., Mamba, M.L. and Monadjem, A. (2020). 'Penis morphology facilitates identification of cryptic African bat species.' *Journal of Mammalogy*. https://DOI.org/10.1093/jmammal/gyaa073

Jobling, J. A. (2010). *The Helm Dictionary of Scientific Bird Names*. London: Christopher Helm.

Johnston, S., Smith, B., Pyne, M., Stenzel, D. and Holt, W. (2007). 'One-Sided Ejaculation of Echidna Sperm Bundles'. *The American Naturalist* 170 (6): E162-E164. DOI:10.1086/522847

Kantsler, V., Dunkel, J., Blayney, M. and Goldstein, R.E. (2014). 'Rheotaxis facilitates upstream navigation of mammalian sperm cells.' *eLife*. DOI: 10.7554/eLife.02403

Larsen, C. S. *(2003)*. 'Equality for the sexes in human evolution? Early hominid sexual dimorphism and implications for mating systems and social behavior.' *PNAS* 100 (6): 9103–9104.

Rutherford, A. (2018). *The Book of Humans: The Story of How We Became Us*. Weidenfeld & Nicholson.

Long, J. (2011). *Hung like an Argentine Duck: A Journey Back in Time to the Origins of Sexual Intimacy*. HarperCollins.

Novak, R.M. (1999). *Walker's Mammals of the World*. 6th edition. Johns Hopkins University Press.

Rodriguez, K.M., Kohn, T.P., Davis, A.B., and Hakky, T.S. (2017). 'Penile implants: a look into the future.' *Translational Andrology and Urology* 6 (Suppl 5): S860–S866.

Ryan, C. and Jetha, C. (2011). *Sex at Dawn: How We Mate, Why We Stray and What It Means For Relationships*. Harper Perennial.

Sharma, V., Lehmann, T., Stuckas, H. Funke, L. and Hiller, M. (2018). 'Loss of *RXFP2* and *INSL3* genes in Afrotheria shows that testicular descent is the ancestral condition in placental mammals.' *PLoS Biol*

16(6): e2005293. https://DOI.org/10.1371/journal.pbio.2005293

Van Valkenburgh, B and Sacco, T. (2002). Sexual Dimorphism, Social Behaviour and Intrasexual Competition in Large Pleistocene Carnivores.' *Journal of Vertebrate Paleontology* 22(1): 164–169.

Zang, Z. (2013). 'Better father have smaller testicles.' *Nature*. DOI:10.1038/nature.2013.13701

Websites

Quote: 'Sometimes a cigar is just a cigar.' Sigmund Freud. *https://quoteinvestigator.com/2011/08/12/just-a-cigar/*
Downloaded 16.11.2020

https://museumsvictoria.com.au/website/melbournemuseum/discoverycentre/wild/biogeographic-regions/palaearctic/lady-amhersts-pheasant/index.html
Downloaded 1.10.2020

Origin of word lek: https://www.merriam-webster.com/dictionary/lek
Downloaded 5.5.2020

Salleh, A. (2001) Found! The longest bird penis ever. *ABC OnLine*. http://www.abc.net.au/science/articles/2001/09/14/366856.htm
Downloaded 16.11.2020

Yong, E. (2016) A little Australian mammal has so much sex that it dies. *National Geographic*.

https://www.nationalgeographic.com.au/animals/why-a-little-australian-mammal-has-so-much-sex-that-it-dies.aspx
Downloaded 16.11.2020

https://carta.anthropogeny.org/moca/topics/penis-size-and-morphology
Downloaded 29.10.2020

https://io9.gizmodo.com/why-do-snakes-have-a-hemipenis-1711449227
Downloaded 9.11.2020

https://www.nytimes.com/2017/08/30/health/fathers-united-states-age.html
Downloaded 5.5.2020

www.webmd.com/men/news/20170725/sperm-counts-continue-to-fall-in-wester...
Downloaded 1.10.2020

8. Sexual Trickery on Both Sides
Albo, M.J., Bilde, T. and Uhl, G. (2013). 'Sperm storage mediated by cryptic female choice for nuptial gifts.' *Proceedings of the Royal Society B: Biological Sciences* 280 (1772): 20131735.

Baker, R. (1996). *Sperm Wars: Infidelity, Sexual Conflict, and other Bedroom Battles*. Basic Books, New York.

Buss, D.M. (2016). *The evolution of desire: Strategies of human mating*. Basic Books, New York.

Cappa, C., *et al.* (2013). *Female Genital Mutilation/Cutting: A Statistical Overview and Exploration of the Dynamics of Change*. United Nations Children's Fund, New York.

Davies, N. (2011). 'Cuckoo adaptations: trickery and tuning.' *Journal of Zoology* 284: 1–14. DOI: 10.1111/j.1469-7998.2011.00810.x

East, M.L., Burke, T., Wilhelm, K., Greig, C. and Hofer, H. (2003). 'Sexual conflicts in Spotted Hyena; male and female mating tactics and their reproductive outcome with respect to age, social status and tenure.' *Proceedings of the Royal Society of London B* 270: 1247–1254.

Fatouros, N.E., Broekgaarden, C., Bukovinszkine Kiss, G., van Loon, J.J.A., Mumm, R., Huigens, M.E., Dicke, M., and Hilker, M. (2008). 'Male-derived butterfly anti-aphrodisiac mediates induced indirect plant defense.' *Proceedings of the National Academy of Sciences of the United States of America* 105 (29), 10033–10038. DOI.org/10.1073/pnas.0707809105

Fitzpatrick. J., Willis, C., Devigili, A., Young, A., Carroll, M., Hunter, H.R. and Brison, D.R. (2020). 'Chemical signals from eggs facilitate female cryptic choice in humans.'

Proceedings of the Royal Society B. DOI.org/10.1098/rspb.2020.0805

Holekamp, K.E., Sakai, S.T. and Lundrigan, B.L. (2007). 'Social intelligence in the Spotted Hyena (*Crocuta crocuta*).' *Philosophical Transactions of the Royal Society B.* 362 (1480); 523-538.

Holekamp, K.E., Sakai, S.T. and Lundrigan, B.L. (2007). 'The Spotted Hyena (*Crocuta crocuta*) as a Model System for the Study of the Evolution of Intelligence.' *Journal of Mammology* 88 (3). DOI. org/10.1644/06-MAMM-S-361R1.1

Holmes, M. and Gunton, M. (2009). *Life: Extraordinary Animals, Extreme Behaviour.* BBC Books.

Norman, M.D., Finn, J. and Tregenza, T. (1999). 'Female impersonation as an alternative reproductive strategy in giant cuttlefish'. *Proceedings of the Royal Society B.* 266 (1426): 1347–1349. DOI: 10.1098/ rspb.1999.0786. PMC 1690068

Novak, R. M. (1999). *Walker's Mammals of the World.* 6th edition. Johns Hopkins University Press.

Russell, T., *et al.* (2019). 'Multiple paternity and precocial breeding in wild Tasmanian devils, *Sarcophilus harrisii* (Marsupialia: Dasyuridae).' *Biological Journal of the Linnean Society.* DOI: 10.1093/biolinnean/blz072

Sapolsky, R. (2017). *Behave: The Biology of Humans at Our Best and Worst.* Penguin Random House.

Toma, C.L., Hancock, J.T. and Ellison, N.B. (2008). 'Separating fact from fiction: An examination of deceptive self-presentation in online dating profiles.' *Personality and Social Psychology Bulletin* 34: 1023–1036.

Websites

Quote: *'Anything worth having is a thing worth cheating for.'* W.C. Fields.
https://www.goodreads.com/ quotes/106276-a-thing-worth- having-is-a-thing-worth-cheating- for
Downloaded 6.12.2019

https://allthatsinteresting.com/ chastity-belt
Downloaded 21.9.2020

https://www.birdlife.org/worldwide/ news/world-first-rhinoceros- hornbills-give-artificial-nest-box- seal-approval
Downloaded 26.9.2020

Adams, S. (2009-01-04). 'Cuckoo chicks dupe foster parents from the moment they hatch'. *The Daily Telegraph*, London.
Downloaded 16.10.2020.

Parker, M.R. and Mason, R.T. (2012). How to make a sexy snake: estrogen activation of female sex pheromone in male red-sided garter snakes.

Journal of Experimental Biology, 2012; 215 (5): 723. DOI: 10.1242/jeb.064923 Downloaded 1.12.2020

9. Award-winning Wild Dads
Busch, R. (1995). *The Wolf Almanac.* Lions & Burford.

Fernandez-Duque, E., Valeggia, C. and Mendoza, S. (2009). 'The Biology of Paternal Care in Human and Nonhuman Primates.' *Annual Review of Anthropology* 38: 115–130. 10.1146/annurev-anthro-091908-164334.

Digby, L.J. (1995). 'Social organization in a wild population of Callithrix jacchus: II, Intragroup social behavior.' *Primates* 36 (3): 361–75. DOI: 10.1007/bf02382859. S2CID 2144576

Dixon, R.B. (1916). *Australia-Oceanic Mythology.* Bibliobazaar.

Dunbar, R. (1995). 'The mating system of callitrichid primates: II. The impact of helpers.' *Animal Behaviour* 50: 1071–1089.

Foster S.J and Vincent C.J. (2004). 'Life history and ecology of seahorses: implications for conservation and management'. *Journal of Fish Biology* 65: 1–61. DOI: 10.1111/j.0022-1112.2004.00429.x

Goldizen, A.W. (1989). 'Social relationships in a cooperative polyandrous group of tamarins (*Saguinus fuscicollis*).' *Behavioral Ecology and Sociobiology* 24: 79–89.

Goldizen, A.W. (1987). 'Facultative polyandry and the role of infant-carrying in wild saddle-back tamarins (Saguinus fuscicollis).' *Behavioral Ecology and Sociobiology* 20 (2): 99–109. DOI: 10.1007/BF00572631. hdl: 2027.42/46876. S2CID 206782867.

Huchard, E., Canale, C.I., Le Gros, C., Perret, M., Henry, P.Y. and Kappeler, P.M. (2012). 'Convenience polyandry or convenience polygyny? Costly sex under female control in a promiscuous primate.' *Proceedings: Biological Sciences* 279 (1732): 1371–1379.

Kaplan, G. (2019). *Bird Bonds: sex, mate-choice and cognition in Australian native birds.* Pan Macmillan, Sydney.

Mazzoni, C. (2010). *She-Wolf: The Story of a Roman Icon.* Cambridge University Press.

Mech, L.D. (1970). *The Wolf: The Ecology and Behavior of an Endangered Species.* University of Minnesota Press.

Mech, L.D. and Boitani, L. (Eds) (2003). *Wolves: Behavior, Ecology and Conservation.* The University of Chicago Press.

Milius, S. (2000). 'Pregnant: And Still Macho.' *Science News* 157 (11): 168-170. DOI: 10.2307/4012130. JSTOR 4012130

Monsanto (1987). 'Long term observation of the wandering albatross: conclusions on migration, habitat, and breeding.' *Journal of Ornithology* 12 (28): 110-126.

Novak, R.M. (1999). *Walker's Mammals of the World*. 6th edition. Johns Hopkins University Press.

Terborgh, J. and Goldizen, A.W. (1985). 'On the mating system of the cooperatively breeding saddle-backed tamarin (Saguinus fuscicollis).' *Behavioral Ecology and Sociobiology* 16 (4): 293-299. DOI: 10.1007/BF00295541. hdl: 2027.42/46874. S2CID 32094448

Vincent, A.C.J. and Sadler, L.M. (1995). 'Faithful pair bonds in wild seahorses, *Hippocampus whitei*.' *Animal Behaviour* 50 (6): 1557-1569. DOI: 10.1016/0003-3472(95)80011-5. ISSN 0003-3472.

Vincent, A.C.J. (1990). 'A seahorse father makes a good mother.' *Natural History* 12: 34-43.

Williams, T.D., (1995). *The Penguins*. Oxford University Press.

Websites
Quote: Your children are not your children. They are the sons and daughters of life's longing for itself. Kahlil Gibran. https://www.brainyquote.com/topics/father Downloaded 8.10.2020

Wandering Albatross, *BirdLife International* (2012). *'Diomedea exulans'*. IUCN Red List of Threatened Species. 2012. DOI: 10.2305/IUCN.UK.2012-1.RLTS.T22698305A38939569.en Downloaded 13.10.2020

http://www-personal.umich.edu/~phyl/anthro/polyandry.html Downloaded 12.10.2020

https://nationalzoo.si.edu/animals/emperor-tamarin Downloaded 12.10.2020

10. Remarkable Single Dads
Bagemihl, B. (2000). *Biological Exuberance – Animal Homosexuality and Natural Diversity*. St Martin's Press.

Birks, S.M. (1997). 'Paternity in the Australian brush-turkey, *Alectura lathami*, a megapode bird with uniparental male care'. *Behavioral Ecology* 8 (5): 560-568. DOI:org/10.1093/beheco/8.5.560

Braithwaite, L.W. (1981). 'Ecological studies of the Black Swan III – Behaviour and social organization.' *Australian Wildlife Research* 8: 134-146.

Coddington, C.L., Cockburn, A. (1995). 'The mating system of free-living emus'. *Australian Journal of Zoology* 43 (4): 365–372. DOI: 10.1071/ZO9950365

Crouch, S.R., McNair, R. and Waters, E. (2016). 'Impact of family structure and socio-demographic characteristics on child health and wellbeing in same-sex parent families: A cross-sectional survey'. *Journal of Paediatrics and Child Health* 52 (5). DOI: org/10.1111/jpc.13171

Darwin, C. (1871). *The Descent of Man, and Selection in Relation to Sex.* John Murray, London.

Kaplan, G. (2019). *Bird Bonds: sex, mate-choice and cognition in Australian native birds.* Pan Macmillan, Sydney.

Kunz, T. and Hosken, D. (2009). 'Male lactation: why, why not and is it care?' *Trends in Ecology & Evolution* 24 (2): 80–85. DOI: 10.1016/j.tree.2008.09.009.

Novak, R.M. (1999). *Walker's Mammals of the World.* 6th edition. Johns Hopkins University Press.

Raxworthy, C.J. (1990). 'Non-random mating by size in the midwife toad *Alytes obstetricans*: Bigger males carry more eggs.' *Amphibia-Reptilia* 11 (3): 247. DOI: 10.1163/156853890X00168

Taylor, E.L., Blache, D., Groth, D., Wetherall, J.D. and Martin, G.B. (2000). 'Genetic evidence for mixed parentage in nests of the emu (*Dromaius novaehollandiae*)'. *Behavioral Ecology and Sociobiology* 47.

Tinbergen, N. (1951). *The study of instinct.* Clarendon Press, Oxford.

Varricchio, D.J., Moore, J.R., Erickson, G.M., Norell, M.A., Jackson, F.D. and Borkowski, J.J. (2008). 'Avian Paternal Care Had Dinosaur Origin.' *Science* 19: 1826-1828. DOI: 10.1126/science.1163245

Veloso, A., Charrier, A., Valenzuela, A., *et al.* (2018). '*Rhinoderma darwinii*'. *IUCN Red List of Threatened Species.* DOI: 10.2305/IUCN.UK.2018-1.RLTS.T19513A79809372.en

Wells, K. (1978). 'Courtship and parental behavior in a Panamanian poison-arrow frog (*Dendrobates auratus*)'. *Herpetologica* 34 (2): 148-155.

Websites

Quote: 'Your children are not your children. They are the sons and daughters of life's longing for itself.' Kahlil Gibran
https://poets.org/poem/children-1
Downloaded 8.11.2020

https://australian.museum/learn/
animals/birds/emu/
Downloaded 17.10.2020

Homosexual Animals Out of
the Closet. November 16,
2006. LiveScience.
Downloaded 22.10.2020

https://thedragonflywoman.
com/2011/11/07/giant-water-bug-
mating/
Downloaded 27.10.2020

https://environment.des.qld.gov.
au/wildlife/animals/living-with/
brushturkey
Downloaded 3.10.2020

www.bbc.com/earth/story/20141101-
male-elephants-have-a-sweet-side
Downloaded 27.10.2020

https://www.barrierreef.org/the-reef/
animals/clownfish
Downloaded 1.12.2020

11. Dangerous Liaisons
Andrade, M.C.B. and Banta, E.M.
(2002). 'Value of Male Remating
and Functional Sterility in Redback
Spiders.' *Animal Behaviour*. 63 (5):
857–70. DOI: 10.1006/
anbe.2002.2003. S2CID 5998731

Barry K.L. (2015). 'Sexual deception
in a cannibalistic mating system?
Testing the Femme Fatale
hypothesis.' *Proceedings Biological
Sciences* 282 (1800), 20141428.

DOI.org/10.1098/rspb.2014.1428
Bauer, H., Packer, C., Funston, P.F.,
Henschel, P. and Nowell, K. (2016).
'*Panthera leo* (errata version
published in 2017).' The IUCN
Red List of Threatened Species
2016: e.T15951A115130419. DOI.
org/10.2305/IUCN.UK.2016-3.RLTS.
T15951A107265605.en.

Diaz Lopez, B., Lopez, A. Methion, S.
and Covelo, P. (2018). 'Infanticide
attacks and associated epimeletic
behaviours in free-ranging common
bottlenose dolphins (*Tursiops
truncatus*).' *Journal of the Marine
Biology Association of the United
Kingdom* 98 (5).

Forster, L.M. (1992). 'The
Stereotyped Behavior of Sexual
Cannibalism in Latrodectus-
Hasselti Thorell (Araneae,
Theridiidae), the Australian
Redback Spider.' *Australian Journal
of Zoology* 40: 1. DOI: 10.1071/
ZO9920001.

Herman-Giddens, M.E.; Smith, J.B.,
Mittal, M. Carlson, M. and Butts, J.D.
(2003). 'Newborns Killed or Left to
Die by a Parent A Population-Based
Study.' *JAMA* 289(11): 1425–1429.
DOI:10.1001/jama.289.11.1425.

Hrdy, S. (1979). 'Infanticide among
animals: A review, classification,
and examination of the implications
for the reproductive strategies
of females.' *Evolution & Human
Behavior* 1: 13–40.

DOI: 10.1016/0162-3095(79)90004-9

Hurd, L.E.; Eisenberg, R.M.; Fagan, W.F.; Tilmon, K.J.; Snyder, W.E.; Vandersall, K.S.; Datz, S.G.; Welch, J.D. (1994). 'Cannibalism reverses male-biased sex ratio in adult mantids: female strategy against food limitation?' Oikos 69 (2): 193–198. DOI: 10.2307/3546137.

Lawrence, S.E. (1992). 'Sexual cannibalism in the praying mantid, Mantis religiosa: a field study.' Animal Behaviour 43 (4): 569–583. DOI: 10.1016/S0003-3472(05)81017-6.

Lowe, A.E., Hobaiter, C. and Newton-Fisher, N.E. (2019). 'Countering infanticide: Chimpanzee mothers are sensitive to the relative risks posed by males on differing rank trajectories.' American Journal of Physical Anthropology 168 (1). DOI: org/10.1002/ajpa.23723

Maxwell, M.R. (1998). 'Lifetime mating opportunities and male mating behaviour in sexually cannibalistic praying mantids.' Animal Behaviour 55 (4): 1011–1028. DOI: 10.1006/anbe.1997.0671.

McMahon, C. and Bradshaw, C. (2004). 'Harem choice and breeding experience of female southern elephant seals influence offspring survival.' Behavioral Ecology and Sociobiology 55. DOI: 10.1007/s00265-003-0721-1.

Novak, R.M. (1999). Walker's Mammals of the World. 6th edition. Johns Hopkins University Press.

Putkonen, H., Amon, S., Almiron, M.P., Cederwall, J.Y., Eronen, M., Klier, C., Kjelsberg, E. and Weizmann-Henelius, G. (2009). 'Filicide in Austria and Finland – A register-based study on all filicide cases in Austria and Finland 1995–2005.' BMC Psychiatry 9: 74. DOI:10.1186/1471-244x-9-74.

Sapolsky, R.M. and Share, L.J. (2004). 'A pacific culture among wild baboons: its emergence and transmission.' PLoS Biology 2(4): E106. DOI.org/10.1371/journal.pbio.0020106

Sapolsky, R. (2017). Behave: The Biology of Humans at Our Best and Worst. Penguin Random House.

Wrangham, R. and Peterson, D. (1997). Demonic Males: Apes and the Origins of Human Violence. Bloomsbury.

Yampolskaya, S., Greenbaum, P. and Berson, I. (2009). 'Profiles of child maltreatment perpetrators and risk for fatal assault: A latent class analysis.' Journal of Family Violence 24 (5), 337-348.

Websites
Quote: 'You know that look that women get when they want to have sex? Me neither.' Steve Martin

https://stylecaster.com/sex-quotes/
Downloaded 19.11.2020

'Gendercide Watch: Female
Infanticide.' Gendercide.org
https://web.archive.org/
web/20080421141103/http://www.
gendercide.org/case_infanticide.
html
Downloaded 26.10.2020

'The war on baby girls: Gendercide.'
The Economist. 4 March 2010.
https://www.economist.com/
leaders/2010/03/04/gendercide
Downloaded 24.9.2020

https://www.perfectbee.com/learn-
about-bees/the-science-of-bees/
honey-bees-reproduce
Downloaded 28.10.2020

https://www.sezarc.org/sand-tiger-
shark-reproductionhttps
Downloaded 7/1/2021

12. Maybe baby
Alexander, B.K. (1970). 'Parental
behavior of adult male Japanese
monkeys.' Behaviour 36: 270–285.
Clutton-Brock, T. (1991). The Evolution
of Parental Care. Princeton
University Press.

Clutton-Brock, T. (2008). Meerkat
Manor: Flower of the Kalahari.
Phoenix.

Boland, C.R.J., Heinsohn, R. and
Cockburn, A. (1997). 'Deception
by helpers in cooperatively
breeding white-winged
choughs and its experimental
manipulation.' Behavioral Ecology
and Sociobiology 41 (4): 251–
56. DOI: 10.1007/s002650050386.

Hamilton III, W.J., Busse, C. and Smith,
K.S. (1982). 'Adoption of infant
orphan chacma baboons.' Anim.
Behav. 30: 29–34.

Itani, J. (1959). 'Paternal care in the
wild Japanese monkey, Macaca
fuscata fuscata.' Primates 2: 61–93.

Kaplan, G. (2019). Bird Bonds: sex,
mate choice and recognition
in Australian native birds. Pan
Macmillan, Sydney.

Macdonald, D.W. (2014). 'Suricata
suricatta Meerkat (Suricate).' In
Kingdon, J.; Happold, D., Hoffmann,
M.; Butynski, T., Happold, M. and
Kalina, J. (eds.). Mammals of Africa.
V – Carnivores, Pangolins, Equids
and Rhinoceroses. Bloomsbury.
pp. 347–352.

Novak, R.M. (1999). Walker's
Mammals of the World. 6th edition.
Johns Hopkins University Press.

Riedman, M.L. (1982). 'The evolution
of alloparental care and adoption in
mammals and birds.' Q. Rev. Biol. 57:
405–435.

Thierry, B. and Anderson, J.R.
(1986). 'Adoption in Anthropoid
primates.' *Int J Primatol* 7, 191–216.
DOI.org/10.1007/BF02692318

de Waal, F. (2019). *The Age of
Empathy: Nature's Lessons for a
Kinder Society.* Profile Books Ltd.

Websites
Quote: 'It is not flesh and blood but
the heart, which makes us fathers
and sons.' Johann Friedrich Von
Schiller
https://parenting.firstcry.com/articles/
magazine-50-beautiful-father-son-
quotes

Gadd, David (June 15, 2013). '11-year-
old Auckland boy fathers
child.' *Stuff.co.nz*
Downloaded 12.9.2020

https://www.all4kids.org/news/blog/
the-benefits-of-foster-care/
Downloaded 19.10.2020

https://www.barnardos.org.au/get-
involved/become-a-carer/types-of-
foster-care/#Respite
Downloaded 19.10.2020

https://en.wikipedia.org/wiki/Darwin_
Awards
Downloaded 19.10.2020

https://mentalhealthdaily.
com/2015/02/18/at-what-age-is-
the-brain-fully-developed/
Downloaded 19.10.2020

https://www.betterhealth.vic.gov.au/
health/conditionsandtreatments/
age-and-fertility
Downloaded 20.10.2020

https://genetics.thetech.org/ask-
a-geneticist/range-shared-dna-
between-relatives
Downloaded 19.10.2020

https://www.spermdonorsaustralia.
com.au/why-donate/top-10-
reasons-to-donate/
Downloaded 20.10.2020

https://metro.co.uk/2012/10/18/
World's oldest dad, 96, fathers
second baby in two years
Downloaded 1.12.2020

13. Be the Best Dad You Can Be
Kaplan, G. (2019). *Australian
Magpie: Biology and Behaviour
of an Unusual Songbird.* CSIRO
Publishing.

Kaplan, G. (2019). *Bird Bonds:
sex, mate-choice and cognition
in Australian native birds.* Pan
Macmillan, Sydney.

Novak, R.M. (1999). *Walker's
Mammals of the World.* 6th edition.
Johns Hopkins University Press.

Skakkebaek, N.E., Rajpert-De Meyts,
E., Buck Louis, G.M., Toppari,
J., Andersson, A.M., Eisenberg,
M.L., Jensen, T.K., Jørgensen, N.,
Swan, S.H., Sapra, K.J., Ziebe, S.,
Priskorn, L., and Juul, A. (2016).

'Male Reproductive Disorders and Fertility Trends: Influences of Environment and Genetic Susceptibility.' *Physiological Reviews* 96 (1), 55–97. DOI. org/10.1152/physrev.00017.2015

Websites
Quote: '*I believe that what we become depends on what our fathers teach us at odd moments, when they aren't trying to teach us. We are formed by little scraps of wisdom.*' Umberto Eco
https://www.goodreads.com/quotes/178037-i-believe-that-what-we-become...
Downloaded 2.1.2021

https://www.scientificamerican.com/article/sperm-count-dropping-in-western-world/
Downloaded 4.10.2020

https://www.nytimes.com/2017/08/30/health/fathers-united-states-age.html
Downloaded 4.10.2020

https://metro.co.uk/2012/10/18/worlds-oldest-dad-ramajit-raghav-96-fathers-second-baby-in-two-years
Downloaded 4.10.2020

https://news.amomama.com/212554-charlie-chaplin-shared-11-kids-3-differe.html
Downloaded 4.10.2020

https://www.backyardbuddies.org.au/backyard-buddies/magpies
Downloaded 16.10.2020

https://www.backyardbuddies.org.au/backyard-buddies/magpies
Downloaded 16.10.2020

Other Natural History titles by Reed New Holland include:

**Wild Leadership:
What Wild Animals Teach Us About
Leadership**

Erna Walraven

ISBN 978 1 92554 635 4

**Insects of the World:
A fully illustrated guide
to the planet's most populous
group of animals**

Paul Zborowski

ISBN 978 1 92554 609 5

**A Field Guide to Butterflies of
Australia: Their Life Histories and
Larval Host Plants**

Garry Sankowsky and Geoff Walker

ISBN 978 1 92151 788 4

**A Complete Guide to
Native Orchids of Australia**

(Third Edition)

David L. Jones

ISBN 978 1 92151 770 9

**A Complete Guide to Reptiles
of Australia**

(Sixth Edition)

Steve Wilson and Gerry Swan

ISBN 978 1 92554 671 2

**A Tribute to the Reptiles
and Amphibians of Australia and
New Zealand**

Australian Herpetological Society

Edited by Chris Williams and
Chelsea Maier

ISBN 978 1 92554 659 0

**Field Guide to New Zealand
Seabirds**

(Third Edition)

Brian Parkinson

ISBN 978 1 86966 547 0

**A First Book of Unique Australian
Bird Songs**

(book with built-in speaker)

Fred van Gessel

ISBN 978 1 92554 640 8

**A First Book of Unique New Zealand
Bird Songs**

(book with built-in speaker)

Fred van Gessel

ISBN 978 1 92554 641 5

**The Slater Field Guide to Australian
Birds**

(Second Edition)

Peter Slater, Pat Slater
and Raoul Slater

ISBN 978 1 87706 963 5

For details of these books and hundreds of other Natural History titles see
newhollandpublishers.com and follow Reed New Holland on Instagram and Facebook

First published in 2021 by Reed New Holland Publishers Pty Ltd
Sydney • Auckland

Level 1, 178 Fox Valley Road, Wahroonga, NSW 2076, Australia
5/39 Woodside Avenue, Northcote, Auckland 0627, New Zealand

www.newhollandpublishers.com

A record of this book is held at the National Library of Australia and New Zealand.

ISBN 978 1 92554 672 9

Managing Director: Fiona Schultz
Publisher and Project Editor: Simon Papps
Designer: Yolanda La Gorcé
Production Director: Arlene Gippert

Printed at SOS Print & Media Group Australia

10 9 8 7 6 5 4 3 2 1

Keep up with Reed New Holland and New Holland Publishers on Facebook
www.facebook.com/ReedNewHolland
www.facebook.com/NewHollandPublishers

US $19.99